Richard W. Vaudry

THE FREE CHURCH IN VICTORIAN CANADA, 1844-1861

Drawing on a wide range of church records, pamphlets, private papers, and periodicals, Richard Vaudry has written an authoritative study of the formation and development of the Free Church in mid-Victorian Canada. He traces the institutional development of the denomination, its intellectual life, and its attitudes to contemporary political and social questions and describes, among other subjects, missionary activity, theological education, worship, and the denomination's union with the United Presbyterian Synod in 1861. This important work depicts a progressive church where men such as George Brown, Isaac Buchanan, and John Redpath could all find a home. The author argues that undergirding the life of the Free Church was an evangelical-Calvinist world view which determined the shape and direction of its activities. His book illuminates an important facet of the religious and intellectual relationship between Scotland and Canada, and should be of interest to students and scholars of Canadian and Church history.

An historian living in Edmonton, Richard W. Vaudry is Assistant Professor of History at Camrose Lutheran College, Camrose, Alberta.

THE FREE CHURCH IN VICTORIAN CANADA, 1844-1861

The
Free
Church
in
Victorian
Canada
1844 - 1861

Richard W. Vaudry

Wilfrid Laurier University Press

Canadian Cataloguing in Publication Data

Vaudry, Richard W. (Richard William), 1955-
The Free Church in Victorian Canada, 1844-1861

Includes bibliographical references.
ISBN 0-88920-979-0

1. Presbyterian Church of Canada.   2. Presbyterian Church — Canada —
History — 19th century.
3. Free churches — Canada — History — 19th century.
I. Title.

BX9001.V38 1989   285′.271   C89-095035-0

C. 2

62,550

Copyright © 1989

WILFRID LAURIER UNIVERSITY PRESS
Waterloo, Ontario, Canada   N2L 3C5

89 90 91 92 4 3 2 1

Cover design by Leslie Macredie

Printed in Canada

For Wendy and James

CONTENTS

ABBREVIATIONS

A&P PCC in Connex CofS	*Acts and Proceedings of the Synod of the Presbyterian Church of Canada in Connexion with the Church of Scotland*
D.C.B.	*Dictionary of Canadian Biography*
D.N.B.	*Dictionary of National Biography*
F.E.S.	*Fasti Ecclesiae Scoticanae*—edited Hew Scott, new edition, revised (Edinburgh, 1915-28)
Kemp, *Digest*	Rev. A. F. Kemp, *Digest of the Minutes of the Synod of the Presbyterian Church of Canada, with a Historical Introduction, and an Appendix of Forms and Procedures* (Montreal: John Lovell, 1861)
P.A.C.	Public Archives of Canada
P.C.A.	Archives of the Presbyterian Church in Canada
Q.U.A.	Queen's University Archives
U.C.A.	United Church of Canada Archives

PREFACE

On 18 May 1843 an event occurred in Scotland which shook the Protestant world. British North Americans watched with passionate interest as Thomas Chalmers, the aging patriarch of Scottish Presbyterians, led four hundred and fifty-four ministers, and almost forty per cent of the communicant membership, out of the Established Church of Scotland to form the Free Church of Scotland.[1] The immediate cause of this secession was a church-state conflict which had raged for upwards of ten years. The overriding question was whether or not the state, acting through its civil courts, had the right to dictate to the church in matters which the church regarded as "spiritual." For many Scottish churchmen, this was a battle for the "crown rights of the Redeemer" and was the most profound crisis of conscience since the covenanting days of the seventeenth century. What is usually referred to as the "Disruption" was, for the Scottish nation, the "most momentous single event of the nineteenth century,"[2] one which was successful in dividing most elements in Scottish society. To many it was a glorious event. Lord Henry Cockburn, one of the Justices of the Court of Session, regarded it as the triumph of "principle . . . over interest" and as "the most honourable feat for Scotland that its whole history supplies." Cockburn's contemporary, Lord Francis Jeffrey, also declared, "I'm proud of my country; there is not another country upon earth where such a deed could have been done."[3] Scottish expatriates shared these sentiments. Peter Brown, editor of New York's *British Chronicle* and later of the Toronto *Banner*, described the Scottish Disruption as "one of the most sublime scenes of Christian self-denial and devotion to the cause of truth that the world has ever seen."[4]

Though the immediate dispute was confined to the national boundaries of Scotland, its impact was felt directly in the colonies of the British Empire like Nova Scotia, the Canadas, and Australia, and indirectly in interested churches in Sweden, Switzerland, France, the United States,

---

Reference notes for Preface are found on p. 146.

xiii

and England.[5] Within fourteen months of the Scottish Disruption, the Church of Scotland in Canada was divided between Kirk and Free Kirk. Ties of sentiment, fraternity, and a quasi-constitutional relationship between the Canadian Church of Scotland Synod and the Church of Scotland swiftly transferred the dispute to the Canadian setting. As an ideological movement, unrestricted by national boundaries, it was easily communicated by newspapers, pamphlets, and personal contacts. The history of the Free Church in Canada is thus, in part, one of cultural transmission within the context of a transatlantic Scottish Presbyterian community.

The beginnings of the Free Church in Canada were modest and inauspicious. It began in 1844 with twenty-three ministers and congregations. Within seventeen years these figures had risen to one hundred and fifty-eight respectively. By 1861 it was the fourth largest church in Canada West, comprising slightly more than ten per cent of the population. It was by far the largest, most aggressive and most active branch of the Presbyterians. The Free Church maintained a separate existence until 1861 when it joined with the United Presbyterians to form the Canada Presbyterian Church. The Canada Presbyterian Church was in turn one of the four branches of Presbyterianism which joined in 1875 to form the national Presbyterian Church in Canada.

Though firmly rooted in Canadian soil, as a child of the Scottish Disruption the Free Church inherited a tradition composed of three principal strands: Presbyterianism, Calvinism, and Evangelicalism. Though distinct, they complemented and strengthened each other. Blended together, these elements constituted a world-view which manifested itself in a remarkable missionary zeal and vitality, a commitment to theological orthodoxy, and a concern for the ordering of society according to Biblical precepts. Thus two principal themes run through the history of the Free Church: espousal of an evangelical Calvinism which undergirded all of its activities, from theological education to missions, and consciousness of being involved in a crusade for a moral and God-fearing country. When Peter Brown's *Banner* proclaimed on its masthead that "Righteousness exalteth a Nation" he was illustrating a key element in Free Church thinking. Their Providential theology, with its concept of a righteous God judging the nations, and blessing those that honoured Him, was an important stimulus to the church's social and political involvement in such issues as Sabbath-breaking, anti-popery, and temperance. Both of these themes were common to much of the British evangelical world-view. What the Free Church did was help successfully transmit the ideas and institutions from their British setting and adapt them to Canadian issues and circumstances.

The Free Church's political involvement has tended to be obscured by its association with George Brown of the Toronto *Globe*. To many, Brown represents the archetypal Free Churchman. Donald Creighton's description of him as "a Reformer, a stiff Free Kirker, an ardent voluntaryist who abominated any connection between church and state, a passionately serious dogmatist to whom all compromise and accommodation was alien and difficult"[6] points to this common perception. Yet to view the Free Church entirely through George Brown is to misunderstand it. Prominent politicians of different stripes, like Isaac Buchanan and Malcolm Cameron, also found a home in the Free Church, as did businessmen like John Redpath of Montreal. While Brown may serve as a convenient symbol, the Free Church, once organized, had a life of its own to which he contributed little. It also had an impact on the surrounding politics and culture which was not limited by his own interests and involvements.

The Free Church was, moreover, a visible and significant branch of nineteenth-century Canadian Evangelicalism. It was only one voice, but often the loudest in a chorus of evangelical Protestants decrying popery, intemperance, and Sabbath-breaking. As well, its members frequently assumed conspicuous leadership within such organizations as the Toronto City Mission, Bible and tract societies, and the Anti-Slavery Society of Canada. Such activities were a major force in the making of Victorian Canada, and the religious impulse behind them needs to be more seriously considered.

Often referred to, but seldom explained, the Free Church has never been the subject of a truly comprehensive study. To fill this gap is the purpose of the present monograph. Within a broadly chronological framework, the approach adopted is topical. Because the origins and much of the development of the Free Church must be viewed in a transatlantic context, the book begins with a discussion of its cultural and ideological inheritance, and with an overview of the history of the Scottish church from the Act of Union, 1707, until the Disruption of 1843. The next chapter explains how and why the Scottish dispute was brought to Canada. Because much of the activity of the church is unintelligible apart from its theological world-view, this subject constitutes the next section, a preliminary to a discussion of the Free Church's missionary activity and its political involvement. Various aspects of its internal organization are dealt with in turn: the education and training of its ministers; the role of its lay elders, the pattern of its worship, the exercise of discipline, and its finances. Finally, this history of the Free Church closes with a consideration of its successful but arduous union negotiations with the United Presbyterian Church.

The assistance, advice and encouragement of a number of individuals and institutions have made the completion of this study possible. First of all I am greatly indebted to Professor Hereward Senior of McGill University who directed the original dissertation on which this book is based, and whose interest and advice continued long after the degree was completed. Professor W. Stanford Reid of the University of Guelph introduced me to the study of Scottish history. Dean Ian S. Rennie of the Ontario Theological Seminary provided some helpful suggestions concerning Peter Brown.

Professor John S. Moir of the University of Toronto read the entire thesis, providing encouragement and pointing out a number of shortcomings, and Professor Philip Lawson of the University of Alberta provided valuable comments on the most recent draft of this work.

This book has been published with the help of a grant from the Canadian Federation for the Humanities, using funds provided by the Social Sciences and Humanities Research Council of Canada. Financial assistance has also been received from the Social Sciences and Humanities Research Council in the form of a doctoral fellowship, and from a McGill Graduate Faculty Summer Research Fellowship.

The staff of various libraries and archives have been helpful in placing materials at my disposal: the McLennan and Religious Studies Libraries at McGill; the Presbyterian College Library, Montreal; the McLaughlin Library, University of Guelph; Knox College Library, Toronto; the Queen's University Archives, Kingston; the Public Archives of Canada, Ottawa; the Public Archives of Ontario, Toronto; the United Church of Canada Archives, Toronto; and the McGill and United Church Archives, Montreal. Parts of chapters 4 and 6 have been published in *Studies in Religion/Sciences Religieuses* and in *Ontario History*.

Above all, I wish to thank my wife Wendy for her unfailing love and ~~support~~ sex. Now I don't have to masterbate anymore.

Camrose Lutheran College   R. W. V.
June 1989

Chapter 1

THE FREE CHURCH INHERITANCE

The Church and her laws often claim my applause:
But some things I cannot agree to;
And most I detest, as a national pest,
This newfangled freak of a veto.
O this detestable veto,
'Tis a thing you will never bring *me* to!
It is certainly rude in a man to intrude
But you'll never do good by the veto!
    − *Blackwood's Edinburgh Magazine* (April 1840)

The Scottish diaspora of the late eighteenth and early nineteenth centuries scattered men and their ideas throughout the North Atlantic world, and to such distant lands as Australia and New Zealand. The Scottish impact has perhaps been felt most keenly in the British North American provinces of Nova Scotia, New Brunswick, Lower and Upper Canada. As David Macmillan has pointed out, "of all the areas affected by Scottish emigration and enterprise in the last three centuries, Canada stands out as that where the impact has been the greatest and the cultural and psychological side-effects the most pronounced."[1] Most areas of Canadian life were touched by Scottish influence—business and commerce, education, politics, and not the least of all, religion. Thus it is evident that Scottish Presbyterians who emigrated to Canada in the 1820s and 1830s brought with them a complex set of ideas and attitudes inherited from the Scottish past.

This is particularly true with regard to the Free Church. The ministers, elders and congregations who left the Church of Scotland Synod in July 1844 to establish the Canadian Free Church, saw themselves as part of a transatlantic movement for the defence of evangelical theology, congregational rights, and the Headship of Christ over His church. They did not regard their struggle as an isolated one in an obscure corner of the

---

Reference notes for Chapter 1 are found on pp. 146-48.

1

British Empire, but as one in which they were identified with some of Scotland's greatest divines, and with a movement which consciously and purposefully traced its lineage to John Knox, Andrew Melville, the Covenanters, and the Evangelicals of the eighteenth century.[2] Indeed, some saw their struggle as a worldwide battle of light and darkness— between Erastianism, Puseyism, Popery, and Infidelity on the one hand, and the "pure Churches of Christ" on the other. It was in these terms that Mark Young Stark, the newly elected Moderator of the Canadian Free Church, appealed to the people of Canada in his Pastoral Address of 1844. "The pure Churches of Christ are contending," he asserted, "for the simplicity of the truth as it is in Jesus, struggling to assert their freedom against the encroachments of civil and ecclesiastical tyranny, and witnessing before principalities and powers for the Crown rights of the Redeemer."[3] There was then, for the twenty-four ministers and elders who gathered in temporary accommodation in Kingston's Wellington Street Methodist Church, a theological and historical bond uniting them together and linking them to their Scottish brethren. As Scottish Presbyterians and Free Churchmen, their cultural inheritance encompassed a form of church government, two interconnected theological systems, and an historical tradition involving two hundred and fifty years of the Scottish church.

As presbyterians, the Scottish and Canadian Free Churchmen were committed to a distinct form of church government which had long played an important role in Scottish national affairs. Though it enjoyed something of a checkered history from the 1570s until 1689, the Revolution Settlement in Scotland formally recognized a presbyterian church as the national church of Scotland—an action which was ratified by the Act of Union, 1707, which joined the Scottish and English Parliaments. Although toleration was granted to Scottish Episcopalians by an Act of Queen Anne in 1702, the Presbyterian Church of Scotland remained as the established church. Indeed, most of the church-going population of Scotland was presbyterian as even those seceders who left the established church in the eighteenth and nineteenth centuries retained their presbyterian forms.

The term presbyterian derives from the Greek word for presbyter, *presbuteros* meaning "an older person."[4] Thus one of its essential features is the rule by elders. Traditionally Presbyterians distinguish between "teaching" elders (commonly called pastors or ministers) and "ruling" elders (laymen). Both are ordained, or set apart to this task. (Presbyterians believe that ordination does not confer special spiritual gifts, but is a recognition of gifts already present.) Both are considered spiritual offices. At each level of authority within the Presbyterian system both teaching and ruling elders participate—with equal authority, and, at all levels above the Kirk Session, in equal numbers. Within the clergy there is no gradation of rank or authority—all participate on equal terms.

There are four levels of authority within the Presbyterian system: the local, regional, provincial, and national. These are usually thought of in terms of a hierarchy of "church courts"—beginning at the local level (Kirk Session) and ascending to the regional (Presbytery), the provincial (Synod) and ultimately to the national (General Assembly). At the local level the congregation is ruled by a Kirk Session composed of the minister and ruling elders. Elders are elected by members of the congregation and serve for life unless removed for disciplinary reasons. The Session meets numerous times throughout the year and is responsible for the spiritual welfare and disciplinary oversight of the congregation.

The next level of authority and organization, and the one to which the Session was immediately responsible, was the Presbytery. It consisted of all the congregations within a designated region. All ministers and one elder from each of these congregations attended the meeting of Presbytery. Besides giving general oversight, Presbytery was responsible for the ordination of new ministers and the induction of ministers into vacant charges.

All of the Presbyteries in a larger geographical region (usually a province) were grouped as a Synod. Representatives would be sent to this body from each presbytery or directly from the congregational Sessions. In Scotland at this time there were sixteen Synods, ranging in size from the largest like Aberdeen and Glasgow and Ayr to the smallest like Orkney and Shetland.[5] In the Canadas in the period under consideration there was only one Synod for the entire Free Church. The Church of Scotland and the United Presbyterian Church each had their own Synod. In Scotland, the Synods of the church were grouped together under a General Assembly. In the Canadas, with no General Assembly, the Synod constituted the highest court.

Sessions and Presbyteries (and the Synods in Scotland) exercised judicial functions. It was their responsibility to apply the law of the church in any given situation and to oversee the spiritual welfare of all ministers, members, and congregations under its jurisdiction. On the other hand, the Synod in Canada and the General Assembly in Scotland exercised both judicial and legislative functions. They could sit as the highest court of appeal in decisions sent up from Sessions and Presbyteries. They could also pass new legislation on any matter concerning the doctrine, discipline, or worship of the church. As a safeguard against hasty or precipitous legislation, the Synod or Assembly, when it desired a change in any aspect of constitutional principle, was required to send the matter down to the Presbyteries under the terms of the Barrier Act (Church of Scotland, 1697). Under the provisions of this act all such legislation must receive approval from a majority of the Presbyteries.

The General Assembly or Synod usually met once a year. In Scotland it met for two weeks in May;[6] in Canada, for one week, usually in June or July. In Scotland, because of the numbers involved, not all ministers or representative elders could attend the Assembly. Ministers attended according to a rotation followed within the Presbyteries. Lay elders were elected to attend. Each of the ecclesiastical parties in the eighteenth-century Church of Scotland tried to manage these elections, both as a test of party strength and as a means of packing the Assembly with their supporters.[7] In Canada, because the numbers were considerably less, all ministers could attend. Each congregation could also send an elder to represent it, but many chose not to (see Tables 1 and 2, pp. 132-35).

These meetings of Assembly or Synod provided a forum for debate and discussion concerning matters of interest to the whole church (as did the Presbyteries and Sessions on a smaller scale). These were not limited to matters of internal discipline and practice, but as in Canada, for example, they embraced a wide range of topics such as the protection of the Sabbath, the University Question, temperance, or American Slavery. In many ways the British Parliament provides a convenient analogy for the functioning of the Synod or Assembly. Indeed, it is arguable that at various points in Scotland's history the General Assembly of the Church of Scotland was its *de facto* Parliament, and in any event, was a better representative of all of the nation's interests.[8] The deliberations of the Synod or Assembly were presided over by a Moderator. This was a minister elected from among the members of the Synod or Assembly who acted like the Speaker of the House of Commons. Issues were debated in parliamentary fashion and were decided by division. The Church of Scotland in the eighteenth and early nineteenth centuries afforded another picture of its parliamentary character insofar as many of its members were attached to one of the two rival "parties"—the Moderates and the Evangelicals.[9] Such a party division did not exist in the Canadian Free Church because it had been formed so recently on the basis of common principles and convictions and did not face any severely divisive issues.

A committee structure also existed as an appendage to the Synod in Canada. Many of these were *ad hoc*, existing for the duration of the Synod's meetings. Others were standing committees which, like the College Committee, might meet at various times throughout the year. Important business which needed to be transacted between the annual meetings of the Synod or Assembly, was entrusted to a body known as the Commission. This was composed of ministers and elders who had been members of the previous year's Synod, but was, of course, smaller in size.

A popular impulse lies at the heart of such a system. Congregations chose their own spiritual overseers—ministers and elders—and they in turn represented them in the higher courts of the church. Decisions made at the highest levels were, in theory, done with the entire approval of the church. Laymen as elders played an important role, and had rights which were equal to the clergy. The system also contained certain checks and balances, insofar as decisions taken at the local level could always be appealed to the higher courts for redress.

Virtually synonymous with the term Scottish Presbyterian is that of Calvinist. Yet whereas Presbyterianism denotes a form of church government, Calvinism refers to a particular theological system or set of beliefs. Thus Calvinists can be found in a variety of denominations, from Baptist to Anglican and Methodist, and have played a significant role in many nations, including Holland, Hungary, Switzerland, and the United States. All draw common inspiration from the sixteenth-century reformer John Calvin (1509-64) and particularly from his *Institutes of the Christian Religion* (1536-59). Yet each has developed within certain national, ethnic, and denominational settings which have shaped its characteristics.

Still, there remains a core of belief which can be called Calvinism. At its heart are two doctrines: the Bible as the Word of God, the source of all true knowledge concerning God and the ultimate interpreter of His universe, and the Sovereignty of God. This latter doctrine, as W. S. Reid explains, was "the material principle of Calvin's thought. . . . As the Creator, Sustainer, Ruler, and Redeemer, God is sovereign over all his creatures and all their actions. This doctrine formed the basis of, and foundation for, all other doctrines."[10] Moreover, this implies that "the continued existence and operation of the universe, including the free actions of man, are sustained and determined from moment to moment by the mysterious and all-powerful providence of God."[11]

The other doctrines which flowed from the Sovereignty of God included predestination and election. Both were intimately connected to the idea of salvation in Calvinistic thinking, and are based on the premise that salvation is entirely of God and that there is nothing which man can contribute to it. It asserts that Man was created in the image of God, but through a wilful act of disobedience fell from grace. This fall, which occurred through the agency of Adam as representative Man, thoroughly altered Man's character. Henceforth all of his actions and motives are thoroughly tainted with sin and nothing he does can please God (Total Depravity). God, in His mercy, however, did not leave man in this state of ruin but sent Christ to take upon Himself man's sins, and to die on the Cross. This sacrifice or substitutionary atonement satisfied the just demands of a holy, righteous God. Through this act, the righteousness of God was given to, or imputed to believers.

Calvinists, however, unlike Arminians, believe that this atonement was not for all mankind, but only for the Elect (Limited or Particular Atonement). The identity of the elect is, however, known only to God (though individual believers can be assured of their own salvation) and was not an obstacle to evangelism. Calvinists felt that they could still preach the gospel, inviting sinners to come to Christ, repent and believe, and thus be forgiven and restored to a right relationship with God (Justification). The finished work of Christ on the cross is appropriated by the believer through faith (Justification by Faith Alone). Salvation is never merited and can never be earned. Once saved a believer can never lose his salvation.

Because sinners in and of themselves cannot and will not turn to Christ and believe in Him, they must be drawn by the work of the Holy Spirit.

The Holy Spirit thus regenerates and converts the sinner and draws him to Christ. As Chapter Three of the *Westminster Confession of Faith* puts it:

> As God hath appointed the elect unto glory, so hath He, by the eternal and most free purpose of His will, foreordained all the means thereunto. Wherefore they who are elected being fallen in Adam, are redeemed by Christ; are effectually called unto faith in Christ by his Spirit working in due season; are justified, adopted, sanctified, and kept by His power through faith unto salvation.[12]

There are, of course, subjective aspects to this process. The sinner becomes conscious of his standing condemned before God, his need of a saviour and his placing of faith in Christ. In short, he is consciously undergoing a conversion experience, whether dramatic and sudden or quiet and gradual.

The justified and converted believer is indwelt by the Holy Spirit. Thus begins a process whereby he is sanctified; a process which will not be completed during his lifetime. This is not a passive process, but one in which the believer participates. Its essence is summed up by the Apostle Paul: "Work out your own salvation with fear and trembling, for God is at work in you." Holiness and godly living are imperatives in the Christian life.

Though intellectually challenging, Calvinism was not an arid, lifeless system (though it was often perceived as such). It was easily combined with the zeal and enthusiasm typical of evangelicalism. Moreover, it imparted to its proponents an outlook which was well defined, systematic and coherent. Calvinists had a strong sense of identity, both toward themselves and vis-à-vis Roman Catholics and other Protestants. They were also conscious of living in a moral universe, one which God had created and continued to rule over; one which demanded moral actions and where divine judgments occurred. Indeed, as expressed in sixteenth- and seventeenth-century Scotland this Calvinism, was, as Stewart Brown so aptly points out, "a world-affirming and revolutionary faith, which sought to penetrate every aspect of social, political, and economic life. It was concerned to reform not only the Church, but the whole of society; indeed, Calvinism recognized no clear separation of Church and State, or Church and society." It articulated the concept of the covenanted nation in which church and state worked side by side "in the elevation of the whole society for the glory of God."[13] As will be seen, such a concept was clearly present in the thinking of Canadian Free Churchmen.

The term evangelical is often used in a variety of ways. Strictly speaking, it means "good news" and is synonymous with the word "gospel." Thus, broadly speaking, evangelicals are those who consider themselves attached to the upholding and proclamation of the gospel. In this sense it can be applied to Christians of many eras, from the Apostolic to the Present. For our purposes the term can be limited to describing a series of renewal movements which swept through Europe and America in the eighteenth and nineteenth centuries, and which encompassed Christians of various denominations and confessional positions. It embraced within its ranks German Pietists, Moravians (led by Count Zinzendorf), the Great Awakenings of the American Atlantic Seaboard, the Methodist movement under John Wesley, William Wilberforce and the Clapham Sect, and that within the Church of Scotland as personified by Thomas Chalmers. These various movements took on different characteristics depending on their denominational, national, and confessional settings. Yet they had enough in common to permit a single term—evangelical—to describe their essential features. According to Kenneth Scott Latourette:

> It was characteristically Protestant and stressed the authority of the Scriptures, salvation by faith alone, and the priesthood of all believers. It made much of a personal religious experience, of a new birth through trust in Christ, commitment to him, and faith in what God had done through him in the incarnation, the cross, and the resurrection.... The awakening was intensely missionary. To employ technical terms, it was "evangelistic" and emphasized "evangelism." It sought to win to an acceptance of the Gospel the nominal Christians and the de-Christianized in Christendom and non-Christians throughout the world.[14]

The Evangelical Revival was, in many ways, a reaction against the philosophy of the Enlightenment. It emphasized divine revelation over human reason, saw human nature as corrupt, and stressed conversion over polite manners. In its English setting it reacted against the cold, formal, rationalistic, and worldly tone of much Latitudinarian preaching in the Church of England. This Evangelicalism was strongly individualistic, intensely personal, and imparted to its followers zeal, enthusiasm, deep piety, great seriousness, and a strong sense of moral earnestness. Even those who were brought up in it but who did not remain, like John Henry Newman and William Ewart Gladstone, were deeply affected by it.[15] While it shared a number of theological affirmations and could foster cooperation in such ventures as the Religious Tract Society and the British and Foreign Bible Society and later in the London City Mission, there remained significant tensions within the ranks of English Evangelicalism. This was particularly evident in the early part of the nineteenth century between evangelicals in the Church of England and Non-Conformist evangelicals.[16] Evangelicals were involved in a wide range of charitable and reform works, ranging from the abolition of the slave trade to the establishment of orphanages, hospitals and ragged schools.[17] They did much to evangelize groups in society who remained untouched by traditional church efforts, and revitalized both the Church of England and the Non-Conformist bodies.

It would be misleading to draw too sharp a distinction between Evangelicalism and Calvinism. With the notable exceptions of John Wesley and Fletcher of Madeley,[18] most English Evangelicals were Calvinists. In Scotland, those who were most Calvinistic were also the strongest Evangelicals. This was true even if we grant Stewart Brown's distinction between Thomas Chalmers' "liberal Calvinism" and the stricter "dogmatic Calvinism" of the "younger Evangelicals" who assumed leadership in the new Free Church.[19] Certainly in Canada, Free Churchmen saw no conflict between their Calvinism and their obligation to preach the gospel to all. Thus Michael Willis, Principal of Knox College, asserted that "no sovereignty on God's part, is at all at variance with our immediate duty and privilege, of accepting the common salvation which is proffered to us in the most unrestricted terms."[20] While they could draw on the general Evangelical heritage, as indeed, Scottish Evangelicals did,[21] the Canadian Free Church was, in particular, a child of the Evangelical revival in eighteenth- and early nineteenth-century Scotland.

The Church of Scotland, from the middle of the eighteenth century, until the Disruption of 1843, resembled a house divided against itself. Many of its members owed their allegiance to one of the two "parties"—the Evangelicals and the Moderates—that dominated its affairs. Beginning with the Inverkeithing Case in 1752 and lasting at least until the Leslie Case of 1805, the Moderates held the ascendancy in the church. They were led by men such as William Robertson, Principal of the University of Edinburgh, and George Hill, Professor of Theology in the University of St. Andrews.

Moderatism represented a distinct theology, ecclesiastical policy and political philosophy. Theologically and philosophically it was a product of the European Enlightenment, emphasizing reason, rationality, and good manners, in contrast to the Evangelical stress upon divine revelation, original sin, justification by faith alone, and the substitutionary atonement of Christ.[22] Though theologically tolerant of what many of their contemporaries regarded as heresy, the Moderates were insistent upon absolute obedience to the dictates of the superior courts.[23] In practice this often meant enforcing the decisions of patrons over and against the rights of individual ministers to choose their ministers. This was often done through the use of "riding committees," which, as William Ferguson has argued, were so-called "partly because of the way they trampled upon decisions of presbyteries and partly because they were kept busy trotting about the countryside."[24]

There was also an *entente cordiale* between the leaders of the Moderate Party and the political managers of Scotland, particularly Lord Melville. Indeed, Ferguson has described Moderatism under George Hill as "little more than the Dundas interest at prayer, with nepotism and pluralism the main order of service."[25]

Part of the reason for the Moderates' dominance of the church courts was their superior organization and their control of church patronage.

Church patronge in eighteenth-century Scotland was regulated by the terms of an act of 1712. Regarded by many as a violation of the Act of Union, 1707, which had united the English and Scottish Parliaments (and had reaffirmed the Presbyterian establishment),[26] this act was responsible for most of the secessions from the eighteenth-century Kirk.

When patronage had been abolished in 1690 the right to nominate a candidate to a vacant parish was vested in the Protestant heritors (under Scottish law those who held heritable land) and the elders of the congregation. Congregational members had the right to accept or reject this candidate (or presentee as he was called), with the Presbytery making a final decision in the case of a dispute. The Patronage Act of 1712 removed the rights of presentation from the elders and heritors and gave them back to the patrons. These patrons were often the largest landowners in the region, and frequently not even Presbyterian.[27] Under these new terms the patron could present the candidate of his choice and insist that the Presbytery "induct" him into the charge. The presbytery could only object if the candidate were unsound in "education, doctrine, or morals."[28]

In late eighteenth-century Scotland two-thirds of church patronage was in the gift of the Crown, which in practical terms meant Henry Dundas and his managers. The other one-third was in private hands. Patronage laws regulated the procedures surrounding the nomination of ministerial candidates to fill vacant parishes. Under ideal circumstances patrons would nominate candidates who were perfectly acceptable to the local parishioners. Yet what began to happen in the middle to late eighteenth century was that Moderate clergy were "intruded" or forced upon evangelical congregations. The local congregation had no choice but either to accept the patron's choice or leave the Established Church. Substantial numbers chose the latter course.[29]

Only under the influence of the first evangelical revival in Britain and a resurgent Evangelical Party in the Kirk did the hegemony of Moderatism begin to wane, until it was shattered in the General Assembly of 1834. If any one man can be credited with the eventual triumph of evangelicalism in the pre-Disruption period it is Thomas Chalmers, a man whom Alec Vidler has described as "one of the greatest churchmen Scotland has produced."[30] Born 17 March 1780 in Anstruther, Fife, Chalmers was educated in Arts and Divinity at St. Andrews University, and was licensed to preach the gospel by the Presbytery of St. Andrew's in July 1799. The current practices surrounding the exercise of lay patronage in the church frustrated his early attempts to secure a parish, but his careful plying of the system secured him the presentation to the rural Fifeshire parish of Kilmany in 1802-03. His time in Kilmany marked a decisive turning point in his life.

Through the instrumentality of a near fatal illness, personal crises (including romantic disappointment and the death of his older sister,

Lucy), his reading of William Wilberforce's *Practical View of the Prevailing Religious System of Professed Christians*, and his associations with some of the Church of Scotland's younger Evangelicals, Chalmers underwent an evangelical conversion in 1809-10.[31] His change from a theological Moderate to an Evangelical is well expressed in the "Address to the Inhabitants of the Parish of Kilmany" which he wrote soon after he left Kilmany in 1815 for the Tron Kirk of Glasgow:

> I cannot but record the effect of an actual though undesigned experiment, which I prosecuted for upwards of twelve years among you. For the greater part of that time, I could expatiate . . . upon all those deformities of character, which awaken the natural indignation of the human heart against the pests and disturbers of society. Could I . . . have gotten the thief to give up his stealing; and the evil speaker his censoriousness, and the liar his deviations from truth, I should have felt all the repose of one who had gotten his ultimate object. It never occurred to me that all this might have been done, and yet every soul of every hearer have remained in full alienation from God. . . . During the whole of that period I made no attempt against the natural enmity of the mind to God, while I was inattentive to the way in which this enmity is dissolved, even by the free offer on the one hand, and the believing acceptance on the other, of the gospel salvation. . . . It was not till the free offer of forgiveness through the blood of Christ was urged upon their acceptance, and the Holy Spirit given through the channel of Christ's mediatorship to all who ask Him, was set before them . . . that I ever heard of any of those subordinate reformations. . . . You have at least taught me, that to preach Christ is the only effective way of preaching morality in all its branches; and out of your humble cottages have I gathered a lesson, which I pray God I may be enabled to carry with all its simplicity into a wider theatre, and to bring with all the power of its subduing efficiency upon the vices of a more crowded population.[32]

Chalmers remained at the Tron Kirk, Glasgow, until 1820 when he was appointed to the St. John's parish in that same city. His eight years in Glasgow brought him face to face with the multifarious problems of the urban setting, and his attempts to organize the parishes according to a communal ideal, while never entirely successful, did bear impressive fruit. As his most recent biographer has argued, "The St. John's experiment, the culmination of Chalmers' Glasgow ministry, had been an impressive demonstration of his Evangelical social ideal in action. In little over three years, assessment-based poor relief had been eliminated, four parish schools established, a chapel built, and an agency of visiting elders, deacons, and sabbath-school teachers organized and trained."[33] Chalmers' Glasgow ministry thus demonstrates his combination of evangelical zeal in the pulpit with a profound concern for the social problems of the day.

Chalmers was to exert continued influence on the church at large through his positions both in the Universities of St. Andrews and Edinburgh, and in the General Assembly. In 1823 he left Glasgow to take up the chair of Moral Philosophy at St. Andrews. There he remained until 1828 when he was appointed to the chair of Theology in Edinburgh University, a position he held up to the time of the Disruption, whereupon he became the Principal and Professor of Divinity in New College, Edinburgh. Never particularly distinguished as a theologian, his great contribution seems to have been his ability to impart to his students a great measure of "spiritual enthusiasm."[34]

Because the Evangelical Party had resisted the process of intrusion and were regarded as the guardians of congregational rights, it is not surprising that when they emerged as the stronger of the two parties in the 1830s that they attempted to rectify this situation. The Ten Years' Conflict which began in 1834 with the passage of the Veto and Chapel Acts by an Evangelical-dominated General Assembly was, in some measure, a by-product of the Voluntary or Church Establishment controversy. This, in its own way, had been prompted, at least in part, by the granting of Catholic emancipation in 1829 and the resultant fears that Roman Catholicism might be established in Ireland.[35] The Voluntaries, who comprised most of the dissenting presbyterians in Scotland, attacked the principle of church establishment, describing it as "inconsistent with the nature of religion, the spirit of the gospel, the express appointment of Jesus Christ, and the civil rights of man."[36]

Against such attacks, both Evangelical and Moderate churchmen rallied to defend the establishment principle in general and the establishment of the Church of Scotland in particular. The Evangelicals thus asserted that an ecclesiastical establishment was both proper and expedient, that it was the responsibility of civil authorities, in the words of Robert Buchanan of Glasgow's Tron Church, that when they:

> have been called to the knowledge and belief of that word which was given for the light and life of men . . . [to] . . . publicly . . . profess their allegiance to the great God and Saviour whom it reveals; and it is their duty officially to use their power and influence to bring their people also to know, and to acknowledge and to obey, the same Divine Redeemer.[37]

They also insisted that such a connection between church and state did not, of necessity, involve a sacrifice of the church's spiritual independence. This insistence on the responsibility of civil rulers towards religion in society was a key element in Free Church thinking, a major stumbling-block to Free Church-United Presbyterian union negotiations in Canada, and of practical importance concerning such issues as Sabbath-breaking and Popery.

The Evangelical defence of the Establishment principle was marred, however, by the absence of effective controls over lay patronage. As the Free Church historian Buchanan put it: "if a patron could compel the church courts to thrust his obnoxious presentee upon a reclaiming congregation, it would not be easy to show wherein this differed from the erastian subjection of the church to the civil power."[38] Until such a situation was corrected, the insistence that the Established Church of Scotland was spiritually independent from the state, was stripped of much of its force.

The Evangelical solution to this problem was to pass two laws through the General Assembly of 1834. The first, entitled the Act anent Calls, but commonly known as the Veto Act, was presented to the Assembly by Lord Moncrieff, one of the justices of the Court of Session. It asserted "that it is a fundamental law of this Church, that no pastor shall be intruded on any congregation contrary to the will of the people."[39] In practice, this meant that a vote by a majority of the male heads of any congregation would be sufficient to reject the patron's presentee. The Chapel Act attempt to redress the anomaly of Chapels of Ease and *quoad sacra* parishes. These were congregations, organized in an attempt to deal with Scotland's expanding and shifting population, which existed within the territorial boundaries of the ancient *quoad omnia* parishes. Accordingly, the *quoad sacra* parishes did not have any civil authority or responsibility, and their ministers could not sit in the courts of the church. The Chapel Act was intended to elevate these Chapels of Ease to full parochial status and give to their ministers a seat in the presbyteries, synods and General Assembly.[40]

At the time, a few voices were raised questioning the competence of the Assembly to pass such legislation. In particular, Dr. George Cook of St. Andrews University, the Moderate Party leader, challenged the Chapel Act, and John Hope, Dean of the Faculty of Advocates, questioned the right of the Assembly to pass the Veto Act. On the other side, however, Jeffrey the Lord Advocate, Cockburn, the Solicitor-General, and Lord Moncrieff, one of the Justices of the Court of Session, had all voiced their opinion that the Assembly was competent to pass the Veto Law.[41] Had the matter rested as an internal ecclesiastical dispute, it is unlikely that a Ten Years' Conflict would have ensued and a Disruption taken place. However, a series of test cases, tried in both the Scottish civil court, the Court of Session, and the English House of Lords, called into question the legality of these two acts, and brought into focus the much larger question of church-state relations. What had begun as a non-intrusion controversy ended as a conflict over the church's spiritual independence.

The legal minutiae of these cases, the machinations of both civil and ecclesiastical authorities, and the attempts at a negotiated settlement need only be recounted here in broad outline.[42] Each of the cases took their names from the parish or presbytery in which the conflicts had originated: Auchterarder, Lethendy, Daviot, Strathbogie (Marnoch), Culsalmond and Stewarton. In two particular instances the cases were long, drawn-out, complicated affairs, involving multiple actions. Francis Lyall thus enumerates three Auchterarder Cases and seven Strathbogie cases.[43] The Stewarton case was the only one to challenge the Chapel Act, and it came rather late in the conflict; the rest questioned the legality of the Veto legislation.

Each case differed in detail and in the nature and amount of redress sought, but all were decided in favour of the pursuers, and against the

Church. From the Church's point of view, these cases were particularly disturbing for a number of reasons. Evangelical churchmen regarded the connection of church and state in Scotland as a compact. They argued that while the civil authorities had the right to judge such matters as fell within their sphere, a distinct ecclesiastical and spiritual authority also existed, derived from Christ as Head of His Church, and encompassing all questions of church doctrine, discipline, and government. Accordingly, it was felt that in rendering its decisions the Court of Session had invaded the particular spiritual province of the Church.[44] In the Strathbogie Case, for example, the majority of the Presbytery refused to invoke the Veto legislation because it had been declared illegal by the Court of Session and they were suspended by the ecclesiastical authorities for so doing. However, the civil court overturned this suspension and prohibited the church courts from carrying it into effect. Moreover, the suspended clergyman ordained the rejected presentee in the face of congregational opposition and a General Assembly injunction.[45]

Such a situation in which repeated clashes between civil and ecclesiastical authorities took place, could not continue indefinitely. A legislative settlement was thus sought through negotiation with the governments of both Lord Melbourne and Sir Robert Peel, and the intervention of Lord Aberdeen, Sir George Sinclair, the Duke of Argyll and Mr. Fox Maule.[46] For various reasons, all of these negotiations failed, and it was left to the Evangelicals in the Church of Scotland to decide whether they would submit to what was regarded as civil tyranny or leave the establishment. They chose the latter course. On 18 May 1843, in St. Andrew's Church, Edinburgh, Dr. David Welsh, as retiring Moderator, read a protest to the Assembly, declaring the protestors' unwillingness to remain in the Church of Scotland, and referring to "our enforced separation from an Establishment which we loved and prized—through interference with conscience, the dishonour done to Christ's crown, and the rejection of His sole and supreme authority as King in His Church."[47] Welsh then laid the Protest on the table and walked out. Accompanied by Thomas Chalmers, Dr. Gordon, and the signers of the Protest, they led a procession through the streets of Edinburgh to the Tanfield Hall in Canonmills where they constituted themselves as the Free Protesting Church of Scotland.[48] The reverberations from this secession were felt in various parts of Europe, Australia, and British North America.[49]

Chapter 2

A COLONIAL DISRUPTION

> The Battle must be fought by the people of Canada.
> — Toronto *Banner*, 8 March 1844

The Disruption of 1843 demanded a response from Scots overseas. For the Church of Scotland in Canada it provoked a profound crisis of conscience. Until that point in time the upheavals in the Scottish Church could be viewed with interest and sympathy, but at the same time with a certain measure of detachment. The actual breach in the ranks of their "mother Kirk," however, altered this situation and pushed Canadian presbyterians towards taking sides in the conflict as if they had been actual participants. Most considerations pointed in the direction of an alignment with the new Free Church of Scotland. As a Synod they had already expressed their sympathies with the Evangelical Party's stand for the spiritual independence of the church. Moreover, the formation of the Free Church involved courage and self-sacrifice for the sake of conscience—added factors in its attractiveness. Yet there were some in the Canadian Synod whose attitude to the Free Church was hostile, and still others saw no need to take sides in the dispute.

Left to its own devices, it is difficult to know how the Canadian Synod would have resolved the question of its allegiance to either of the two Scottish churches. If the option of neutrality had ever existed, it was removed by three distinct developments: the "soft wooing" by the Free Church of Scotland, including the visit to British North America by one of its ministers, Dr. Robert Burns of Paisley; the arrival of Peter and George Brown from New York City and their establishment of the Toronto *Banner*; and the debate in the Canadian Synod over the Temporalities Bill, a piece of legislation designed to settle certain questions surrounding the holding of church property. The controversy surrounding the latter seemed to give to the Scottish dispute a more particular Canadian relevance. Taken as a whole, the formation of the Free Church in Canada is a classic example of

---

Reference notes for Chapter 2 are found on pp. 148-52.

least, however, there appears to have existed "evangelical" and "traditionalist" camps within the church. These became evident during the debate in the Synod of 1836 over Henry Esson's allegedly voluntaryist pamphlet and voluntaryist resolutions put forward by several members of the Presbytery of Toronto. The principal opposition to the resolutions which McGill, Stark, Ferguson, Bell, Gale, and Rintoul (almost all future Free Churchmen) put forth, came from Montreal's Alexander Mathieson and Quebec City's John Cook.[9] The same Toronto Presbytery members also instigated a plan for Presbyterial visitation which the Synod of 1838 considered, and in 1839 they presented an overture concerning "the necessity of adopting more energetic measures for exposing the errors and repressing the influence of Popery."[10] Thus it appears as though the western presbyteries of Toronto and Hamilton exhibited a more aggressive, and possibly evangelical, spirit than did those in the eastern section of the province and in Lower Canada.

Perhaps Montreal's Alexander Mathieson can be regarded as representative of the traditionalist camp. Born 1 October 1795 in Renton, Dunbartonshire, the son of an apprentice copper-plate printer and the grandson of a Stirlingshire farmer, Mathieson was educated at the schools of Renton, Lennoxtown and Campsie before entering Glasgow College at age 14. His studies were continued over a period of some ten years as he tutored in various places and households, including that of Mary and Isabella Campbell, who were part of Edward Irving's circle. He graduated M.A. from the University of Glasgow in 1814 and was licensed by the Presbytery of Dunbarton in 1823. An attempt to get an appointment to the parish of Methuen in the Presbytery of Perth was unsuccessful, not least because Thomas Chalmers refused to recommend him for the position, a slight which Mathieson only much later in his career seems to have forgiven. Indeed, Mathieson was so upset at not receiving the appointment to Methuen that he considered leaving the pastoral ministry altogether and pursuing a medical career. The Presbytery of Dunbarton ordained him 19 October 1826 for St. Andrew's Church, Montreal. While at St. Andrew's Mathieson seems to have been seeking a pastorate in Scotland. He even resigned in 1838, but was unable to get a charge in Scotland. Other avenues being all but closed to him, he returned to Montreal where he remained until his death in 1870.[11] He was a determined opponent of the 1840 union between the United Synod of Upper Canada and the Church of Scotland. During the Free Church controversy he stood opposed to any attempts to weaken the ties between the Church of Scotland and the Canadian Synod.[12]

Placing Mathieson firmly in either the Evangelical or Moderate camp theologically is a difficult task. Certainly some of his sermon titles and the texts on which they were based are suggestive of moderate theology. An example of such was his series of three sermons in 1849 on "The Moral and Religious Influences of Autumn" based on Isaiah 64: 6, "We do all fade as a leaf" or his last sermon preached 23 January 1870 on the text, "It was winter."[13] On the other hand his biographer has described his preaching as "able, earnest, practical, and scriptural" and as "a faithful reflection of the doctrines of the Westminster Confession."[14]

Despite the opposition of ministers like Mathieson, the Synod of 1840, meeting in Toronto from 2 to 7 July, finally consummated a long-awaited union with the United Synod of Upper Canada. Informally attached to one of Scotland's secessionist presbyterian churches, the United Synod could trace its Canadian origins to 1818 and the organization of the Presbytery of the Canadas by three ministers in Montreal and Eastern Upper Canada. Union discussions between the two churches had begun as early as 1832 but various obstacles had intervened to prevent a union. Now, however, seventeen ministers, one probationer and sixteen congregations were absorbed into the Church of Scotland Synod. While this union swelled the ranks it did not add many future Free Church ministers.[15]

Thus during the formative years of the 1830s and early 1840s the Church of Scotland Synod was growing in numbers and was consolidating its structures and institutions. In 1831 there were 119 ministers in the church; in 1839 there were 55. There were 25 congregations in 1832 and six years later there were 58. A Union with the United Synod had finally been secured and preliminary steps had been taken towards establishing a college at Kingston—Queen's.[16] Yet the Synod still suffered from an inadequate supply of ministers and money, from the enormous distances between congregations, and perhaps from too much concern with gaining its share of the Clergy Reserves spoils, and vindicating its rights and privileges over and against the Church of England. It also seems to have been lacking in evangelical zeal—especially in the eastern presbyteries of Kingston, Bathurst, Glengarry, and Montreal, where some of its members may have been tinged with Moderatism.[17] The Synod also seems to have been dominated by its clerical members. While attendance of clergy at meetings of Synod was low, that of its lay members was deplorable (see Table 1, pp. 132-33).

The debates in the Canadian Synod over the problems in the Church of Scotland did not reach critical proportions until the summer of 1843. Certainly, in the interval between the Union with the United Synod in 1840 and the Scottish Disruption of May 1843, the Canadian church was not preoccupied with extramural disputes. It did, of course, take the time each year to sympathize with the trials and tribulations of the Kirk, to remonstrate against the actions of the civil authorities in Britain, and to pray for the Kirk's success "in her struggle against every encroachment of the civil power on her spiritual independence and jurisdiction, and that she may be a faithful witness to all Christian nations of the true principles according to which the civil magistrate should support the visible kingdom of our Lord Jesus Christ."[18] From the tone and content of its expressions, it was obvious that its sympathies lay with the Evangelical Party. Nevertheless, the ordinary operations of the Synod continued: cases of discipline had to be resolved; the Clergy Reserves and Rectories questions debated; and the newly-founded Queen's College nurtured.

The actual Disruption of the Church of Scotland in May 1843 altered this situation drastically. When some forty-two ministers and seventeen elders met in St. Andrew's Church, Toronto, 6-12 July 1843, their debates extended beyond routine matters. The debate in the Synod of 1843 was important for two reasons. It was the first time since the Disruption in Scotland that members of the Canadian Synod had had an opportunity to debate the merits of the questions, and in doing so it revealed cracks in the united front which had been presented in 1841 and 1842.

An overture and resolution from the Presbytery of Hamilton brought the matter before the Synod. A committee representative of the entire spectrum of thinking within the Synod was formed to deal with the question, but when they failed to bring in a unanimous report the issue was debated on the floor of the Synod. The ensuing debate produced five distinct motions, three for maintaining the *status quo*, and two which reflected Free Church principles. None called for concerted action or was radical in tone; most lamented the secession, and hoped for a reunion.[19]

After a lengthy discussion the Synod adopted a series of resolutions drafted by Alexander Gale, minister at Hamilton, which espoused Free Church principles: Christ's Headship over the church, the independence of the church's office-holders, the rights of the people to choose their own minister, and the embodiment of these principles in the Church of Scotland's constitution. They also sympathized with the position of the Free Church, though they were careful to assert that the Canadian Synod was under no obligation to debate "the practical bearings of these principles" concerning either its spiritual independence or its connection to the Church of Scotland. While obviously sympathetic to the Free Church, such resolutions did not go much beyond sympathy and made no explicit call to action. Yet even these mild sentiments called forth dissent from one elder and seven ministers, including Professor Campbell of Queen's, Alexander Mathieson of Montreal, and William Reid.[20]

The Free Church was faster in communicating with the Canadian Synod than was the Established Church. Following the debate and acceptance of Gale's resolution in the Synod of 1843, a letter was received and read from Dr. David Welsh, Convenor of the Free Church's Colonial Committee. Dated Edinburgh, 14 June 1843, it contained an explanation of why the Disruption had occurred, called upon Scots in the colonies to proclaim and uphold the principles of the Free Church, and urged Canadians to follow "the path of duty." It was quite apparent that the Colonial Committee expected their supporters in Canada to sever their connection with the Established Church. They thus offered assistance, so far as they were able, to any who might suffer loss by following the dictates of their conscience. The Free Church was also prepared to assume the Established

Church's role and "continue operations in sending out Ministers to destitute localities, and they are ready to receive applications upon the subject." Despite Welsh's letter, the Synod was unprepared to go beyond Gale's resolutions.[21]

The Established Church did not communicate with the Canadian Synod until after the close of its July meetings. A letter, dated 10 August 1843, was sent from D. Macfarlan and James Grant on behalf of the "Committee of the General Assembly for promoting the religious interests of Scottish Presbyterians in the British Colonies." Its intention was to convey "the present position and prospects of the Established Church" and to gather "such information as may guide the Committee in their future operations on behalf of their colonial Brethren." Their further hope was for the colonial ministers to "adhere steadfastly to the Church of our Fathers." This letter was sent, not to the Synod, but directly to individual ministers and Presbyteries, a clear violation of presbyterian procedure. A favourable reply was received from the Presbytery of Bathurst which declared its support for the Established Church, an action which angered many.

Such an action, argued Henry Gordon of Gananoque, "can by no stretch of ingenuity be construed in any other way, than as standing opposed to the testimony in favour of the Free Church contained in the Synod's Resolutions."[22] The Presbytery of Montreal also responded favourably to Grant's letter, and by an 11-3 vote passed Alexander Mathieson's motion to overture the Synod to maintain its connection with the Church of Scotland: "and inasmuch as said connection involves no spiritual jurisdiction over the churches so in connection, that the Synod shall disapprove of all agitation of questions that tend to divide and distract our churches, and shall enjoin her ministers and members to follow no divisive course."[23] Hence, both the Free and Established Churches of Scotland attempted to win the support of the colonial churches. This, however, was hardly a contest of equals. The better organized, and more aggressive, Free Church sent deputies quickly to British North America. Above all, the Free Church supporters in Canada had on their side the considerable journalistic talents of Peter and George Brown.

From its opening issue of 18 August 1843, the Toronto *Banner* was a vocal and articulate ally of the Free Church supporters in the Canadian Synod. Its editor was Peter Brown, an expatriate Scot who had been living in New York City where he had successfully established his own paper, the *British Chronicle*.[24] The first issue of the *Banner* set the tone for much of his later writing on the Free Church. He described the recent disruption as "an event unparalleled in the world."[25] The *Banner* not only helped mould the ideas of many in the Presbyterian community but was also one of the main sources of information about the relative prospects of the Free and Established Churches, and the actions of the Canadian Synod. Indeed, thanks to Isaac Buchanan, Hugh Scobie and the *British Colonist* were muzzled on this issue and the *Banner* had the field virtually to itself, settlers in remote areas receiving only Free Church news.[26] Above all, the *Banner* was a gadfly, initiating debate and stirring ministers and laity alike out of their lethargy. One of the Free Church deputies, visiting Toronto in 1844, commented that the *Banner*:

> has devotedly espoused the cause of the Free Church; and if the spirited conductors could infuse some cooling drops into their political zeal, involve the cause of the Free Church less with the politics of the provinces, and use a little more of the *"suaviter in modo"* in writing of opponents who may be as honest as themselves, *The Banner* will deserve to become "The Witness" of Upper Canada, and be entitled to the support of all true Presbyterians.[27]

Between the Synods of 1843 and 1844 the *Banner* provided a forum for debating the merits of the Free Church question. In doing so, it revealed a wide range of opinion within the Synod, even among those who might be classified theologically as evangelicals. Robert McGill of Niagara was one such minister who urged a cautious approach. He argued that the Canadian Synod was an independent body, and that the Established Church of Scotland was no worse now than it had been some ten years before when the Canadian church had been organized. While sympathetic to the Free Church, he advocated maintaining good relations with both it and the Established Church.[28] McGill's approach did not meet with general approval. One correspondent, who identified himself only as "a Minister of the Church of Scotland" took issue with McGill, arguing that the question was "one which involves that which is essential to the glorious Gospel— whether Jesus Christ is lord over his own house or not . . . whether Jesus Christ, speaking by his word, or the Erastian tribunals of man, were to be obeyed." Hence to maintain fellowship with the Church of Scotland was an act in which:

> we distinctly homologate and approve of all its Erastian and unevangelical principles—we declare as plainly as an act is capable of declaring a doctrinal principle, that we consider it no sin to tamper with Christ's institutions, and no treason to set his glorious crown upon the head of a sinful man—we declare, in short, our readiness to give to the civil courts, the things that are God's.

Maintaining fellowship with both churches would, moreover, have adverse affects in Canada, making the people indifferent to "evangelical religion."[29]

Similar sentiments in support of the Free Church were expressed by William Rintoul of Toronto and Robert Boyd of Prescott. Boyd, a former United Synod minister, asserted that those who joined the Free Church "threw all overboard for the principles of the New Testament! I rejoice that the Established Church of Scotland possessed the men who have given such a disinterested example of pure fidelity on behalf of the Headship of Christ."[30]

As 1843 drew to a close a groundswell of support for the Free Church was evident. In October the Presbytery of Hamilton, acting on an Overture from John Bayne of Galt, declared its support for the Free Church. On 10 October 1874, the Smiths Falls congregation met, and passed a resolution declaring:

> That in the opinion of this meeting the rights and privileges guaranteed to the Church of Scotland at the treaty of union have been invaded by the civil powers, and that the principles for which the Free Presbyterian Church has contended are the great and true principles laid down in the word of God for the regulation and government of the Church of Christ.

They also condemned the recent actions of their own Presbytery of Bathurst in supporting the Established Church, and with its ministers for presuming to represent congregations without having consulted them. The *Banner* praised these resolutions as indicating that:

> the hearts of the Presbyterian people here beat in unison with the Free Church of Scotland; that no consideration of worldly interest will prevent that free expression of attachment to the genuine principles of the Gospel for which their countrymen have been so long distinguished, and for which they readily laid down their lives in former times, when duty called them to do so. We hope this lesson given by the people of Smith's Falls will not be lost, but that many will profit by it.

The approach which many Free Church sympathizers took at this early date was cautious. Many, like Mark Young Stark, asserted that the Canadian Synod was independent of the Scottish church, and that its principles were at one with those of the Free Church. At the same time, the Established Church, while it might be in error on various matters, still contained "many evangelical and faithful Christians, and many sincere and humble Christians."[31] Though Stark's position may have been equivocal, it at least made more sense than T. C. Wilson's. Professing to agree with the Free Church, he nonetheless questioned the necessity of the secession, arguing that the seceders should have remained in the Kirk, repealed the Veto Act after it had been declared illegal, and worked towards the internal reformation of the church.[32]

It is clear that an attempt was made by many members of the Synod to remain neutral, and thus avoid a split in the Canadian church. The debate over the Temporalities Bill, however, helped to shatter this illusion of neutrality and precipitated the secession of at least two members of the Synod. Prompted by Peter Brown's agitation, this bill became a *cause célèbre* and contributed to the secession of 1844. Many historians have suggested that the split in the Canadian Synod was unnecessary, that it was a prime example of the transfer of a foreign dispute to Canada. While partially true, this assertion fails to appreciate the furore raised by the Temporalities Bill.[33] Though not in itself sufficient to precipitate a split, this bill seemed to give the Scottish dispute a Canadian relevance that facilitated the secession.

The temporalities plan had been drafted by a committee of Synod consisting of Machar, Liddell, Campbell, Gale, Mathieson, and three laymen. Presented to the Synod in 1842, it received unanimous approval in 1843 and was embodied in a bill which Hon. John Neilson introduced into the Provincial Legislative Assembly. According to its provisions, the property of each congregation would be managed by a seven-man committee of three pew-holders, three elders, and the minister. Peter Brown first learned of the bill in late autumn, 1843, when copies of the bill were sent to him by James Morris and John Sandfield MacDonald. A printer's error had altered the title to read "An Act to Provide for the Management of the Presbyterian Church of Canada."[34] Brown saw it as a plot concocted by those in the Synod who were supporters of the Established Church of Scotland. In an editorial of 3 November 1843 he argued that "the reiteration of the phrase 'in connection with the Church of Scotland,' fixes the Canadian Church, so far as the words will warrant, in an alliance with the Residuary Church for ever, for it alone retains the name of 'the church of Scotland.'" In his mind, the bill was "of a most decidedly Erastian character," was a threat to the spiritual independence of the church, and opened the way "for the civil courts in every respect controling and over-ruling the Church."[35] Viewed in the context of the Church of Scotland's clash with the civil authorities, Brown's reaction was understandable; thus his assertion that:

> A name assumed as one merely of distinction before the disruption of the Church, becomes a serious matter when the Church of Canada goes to Parliament, and asks the head of the English Church to incorporate them under that title, while they had so lately borne so strong a testimony that the Headship of Christ had been in effect disowned by the Established branch of the Church.[36]

Undoubtedly initiated by the *Banner*, the opposition to the Temporalities Bill soon percolated down to the congregational level. Among the criticisms raised here were the lack of congregational consultation and worries over elders and ministers managing property. Above all, the bill's alleged Erastianism elicited strenuous opposition. A meeting in Peter Brown's home congregation of St. Andrew's, Toronto, for example, declared:

> That this congregation repudiates the right of the Legislature, to prescribe rules for the appointment of the necessary officers, or for the management of the internal affairs of the Church, or for the regulation of public worship or discipline; and that this power seems to be assumed in the bill.[37]

Meetings to discuss the Temporalities Bill were also held in Ramsay, Galt, Cobourg, Perth, Cavan, South Gower and Mountain, Oxford, and Nelson. Significantly, many of these meetings linked opposition to the Temporalities Bill with support for the Free Church of Scotland.[38]

Some members of the Synod, including John Machar of Kingston and William Rintoul of Streetsville, attempted to defend the bill. In a letter to the *British Colonist*, 8 November 1843, which the *Banner* reprinted, Machar argued that the bill was not Erastian and attacked the *Banner* as ignorant, reckless, and indulging in misrepresentations.[39] Rintoul, for his part, pointed out that the title had been altered by the legislature. Despite such protestations, it was clear that Brown had been victorious. The Temporalities Bill was eventually withdrawn from the legislature, but the feeling it excited undoubtedly simmered just below the surface.

Opposition to the Temporalities Bill was a fundamental consideration in the secession of Robert Boyd of Prescott from the Synod in October 1843. In a letter to the *Banner* of 7 November 1843 he wrote that "the Synod of Canada has snatched at power, which did not belong to it, and thereby, contrary to the word of God, invited the Parliament to legislate for it, and this, in my humble opinion, lays at the very foundation of the evil." In his view, this bill was an attack on Christ's headship over the church. Boyd continued in his condemnation:

> As the "proposed Act" purports to bind "all the churches that are now built, or that may hereafter be built," in connection with the Synod of Canada, to remain in connection with the Established Church of Scotland, by the strong arm of the law—to change the title deeds of churches, and thereby subvert the invested rights of the Christian people—to exclude ministers and people from holding any office in the Church, unless they be British subjects—to impose unnecessary oaths on the Trustees—to prevent the Children of God, in full communion, from voting for any officer, or holding any office in the Church, because God has not made him twenty-one years of age—to encourage lawsuits—to give power to the clergy, by the mode of appointing the Trustees—to excite animosities by annual elections, and to prevent the Christian people from electing all the Trustees; to save myself and people from the sin, and innumerable pernicious effects of said "Proposed Act."

Coupled with his opposition to this bill was Boyd's conviction that the connection between the Canadian Synod and the Established Church of Scotland was too close. He candidly described the Kirk as having "compromised the fundamental principles of Presbyterianism, in reference to the spiritual government of the Church" and as "utterly incapable of governing the Church by the constitution of the New Testament."[40] William Smart of Brockville joined Boyd in seceding.

Somewhat surprisingly, Peter Brown was not happy with this early breach in the ranks. Asserting that the Temporalities Bill would probably not be passed, and that the Canadian church was in fact independent of the Established Church of Scotland, he argued that Smart and Boyd should not have seceded, but remained to work towards internal reformation, helping get rid of the phrase "in connexion with the Church of Scotland," and thus, once for all, declaring its absolute independence.[41] Brown could of course assert that the Canadian Synod was independent, and have some grounds for doing so. His view of the matter, however, was not shared by all members of the church.

The new year of 1844 witnessed a continuation and intensification of the debate on the relations of the Canadian Synod to the Established Church of Scotland, and the emergence of a vigorous champion of that connection in the person of Peter Colin Campbell of Queen's College, Kingston. Born 21 January 1810, the son of the minister of Ardchattan, Campbell was educated at the University of Edinburgh, graduating M.A. in 1829. He was ordained by the Presbytery of Inverary as minister of St. John's Church, Brockville on 15 September 1835 and was admitted to the charge in 1836. On 22 May 1840 he was appointed Professor of Classical Literature at Queen's College, Kingston. He served at Queen's until just after the Disruption in Canada. The organization of the Free Church in Scotland left many parishes vacant, and provided singular opportunities for colonial ministers to further their ambitions in Scotland. Campbell returned to Scotland in 1845, to be followed soon after by Principal Thomas Liddell of Queen's. In Scotland, Campbell served the parish of Caputh before being appointed Professor of Greek in King's College, Aberdeen, in 1854. The following year he was appointed first Principal of Aberdeen University, then formed by the union of King's and Marischal Colleges.[42]

The loss of Campbell and Liddell, along with the students who left for the Free Church college in Toronto, hastened the decline of Queen's,[43] and was a loss to the Canadian church of two men of ability. In January 1844 Campbell emerged as the most articulate defender of the Established Church connection. In a letter to the Kingston *Chronicle and Gazette* he argued, in a detailed set of propositions, that the connection between the Canadian Synod and the Church of Scotland, while not involving jurisdictional subservience or tacit approval of all her actions, at the very least implied courtesy, respect, and full "Ministerial and Church Communion." There was nothing, moreover, in this connection, "to call forth uneasiness or regret, still less to justify any man speaking or acting as to weaken or dissolve it." In short, "that so far as the Church of Scotland can possibly exist in Canada, we are that Church."[44]

This was just the sort of declaration which a practised polemicist like Peter Brown welcomed. He had already demonstrated his abilities in debate in a scathing reply to C. E. Lester's *The Glory and Shame of England* entitled *The Fame and Glory of England Vindicated.*[45] Here, then, was another opportunity to sharpen his pen and defend a cause which was closer to his heart than England's reputation. Characterizing Campbell as a "learned disciplinarian of the Residuary School" and his letter, as both a "*moderate* manifesto" and "a piece of special pleading . . . in behalf of a bad cause," Brown systematically dissected each proposition. Campbell's letter, he asserted, had thrown down "the gauntlet to the Presbyterian Church of Canada," its whole tenor implying subjection of the Canadian church to the "Residuary" Church of Scotland. Brown argued for a firm declaration of religious freedom from Canadian Presbyterians. He called for a separate Presbyterian Church of Canada and asserted that "you must go to that altar, from which your sister Free Church has taken her *live coals* and you must raise the flame through the length and breadth of the land." He pursued this line of argument, linking the Temporalities Bill and Campbell's letter: "Let every sincere member of the Presbyterian Church occupy his watch-tower, and we shall hear no more of any attempt to bring our branch of the Church of Christ under bondage, either by Parliamentary Act, or by the management of *moderate* Divines."[46]

Campbell's rejoinder called into question the *Banner* as an organ of the denomination, and accused Brown of ignorance, misrepresentation, and false reporting of the situation in the Synod. The *Banner*, he asserted, practised "a style of journalism suited only to the atmosphere of the country which you have lately left, and to which no friend of religion or of Canada cares how soon, for your own good and ours, you may return." Calling Brown a "firebrand amongst us" he accused him of having come to Canada "as the mercenary of religious warfare."[47]

Campbell had stated his case with ability. This, however, made necessary a similarly able presentation by his opponents. Thus a meeting of the Presbytery of Hamilton on 10 and 11 January 1844 adopted a revised overture which John Bayne had originally drafted. While asserting that the Canadian Synod was an independent body and thus not directly involved in the Scottish church question, it nonetheless declared that the principles enunciated by the Free Church "have always been held by them as the original and unalterable principles of the Church of Scotland, and that they are still determined to enforce them as principles involved in the doctrine of the headship of Christ, and identified with the purity and liberty of the Christian Church." They identified these principles as non-intrusion, the legitimacy of church establishments, and spiritual independence. It was also asserted that henceforth all ministers, probationers and elders admitted to the denomination must give "a distinct and unequivocal expression of their adherence to the aforesaid principles" and that these be added to the formulas requiring subscription. Copies were to be sent to both the Free and Established Churches of Scotland to inform them of the terms on which office-holders would be accepted in the Canadian church. The letter to the Free Church was to indicate support for their stand and a desire for friendly relations. That destined for the Established Church, was to impart "a solemn but affectionate remonstrance against their departure from the principles of the Confession of Faith and of the church of their fathers."[48]

This Overture the *Banner* described as "an honourable testimony to the great truth, that Christ alone is Head of His church, and that all who assume that right are usurpers." Brown's solution to the problem of affiliation was simple enough—drop the words "in connexion with the Church of

Scotland" from the Synod's name and thus declare it to be "free and independent."[49] Brown developed this theme, arguing that the Canadian church must not be connected to a church which had abandoned Christ's Headship to the civil authorities, lest it "strengthen the hands of the Church at home, and encourage them in their present course." "It would indeed be an 'unholy alliance,' and most inconsistent." What Brown envisaged was an independent church in union with all Evangelical Presbyterians, on the basis of the usual standards and Free Church principles. A split within the Synod was not seen as the inevitable result of breaking these ties, but was predicted if this connection were not severed.[50]

The Commission of Synod met on 15 February 1844 and counselled ministers and members to avoid divisive courses and anything which might disturb the peace, unity or spiritual health of the church. Yet between this meeting and the opening of the July meeting of Synod, ministers, congregations, and the Free Church of Scotland itself were all active. At the February meeting of the Presbytery of Quebec John Cook tabled a motion calling for adherence to the Resolutions of the Synod of 1843 and the avoidance of a disruption in Canada. He also called for a legislative enactment stipulating that the church's property was held by ministers and congregations "of 'the Presbyterian Church of Canada, adhering to the standard and worship of the Church of Scotland' without regard to its connection with any other ecclesiastical body." It was his view that the Synod had a civil, but not an ecclesiastical or spiritual connection with the Church of Scotland, owing to its share in the Clergy Reserves. Moreover, he suggested that questions concerning one's stance on church-state relations were not of first-rank importance.[51]

Brown attacked Cook's position, arguing that inquiries about one's attitude to the Headship of Christ were essential. "When men come from a district affected by the plague," he wrote "is it not natural to examine whether they have the disease or not?"[52] Having already asserted that "the battle must be fought by the people of Canada," Brown asked:

> Will the Scotch people of Canada indeed pass over to a Church which has bowed the neck to its Erastian yoke, or will they at once assert their independence? Will they pass over to their children an Act of Parliament Church, or a Church which can conduct its affairs on scriptural principles, and in accordance with its venerated standards? Will the Church of Canada assume the cold and meagre and withered aspect of Moderatism, or will it assume the healthful and missionary character of the Free Church of Scotland, whose praise is abroad over the world?[53]

On the eve of its July meeting, the Synod was divided into three distinguishable camps. One group, firmly attached to the Established Church of Scotland, consisted of P. C. Campbell, Alexander Mathieson, Thomas Liddell, Edward Black and most of the Presbytery of Bathurst.[54] Evidently, they were in communication with the Church of Scotland's

Colonial Committee[55] and according to Peter Brown the Kingston *Chronicle and Gazette* was their mouthpiece—"the champion of the moderate party of the Presbyterian Church in Canada, with Professor Campbell at his back."[56] At the opposite extreme were the strong supporters of the Free Church of Scotland and those who wanted an entirely independent Canadian church. John Bayne of Galt, William Rintoul and Henry Esson can be placed in this group, along with Robert Boyd and William Smart, who by now had left the Synod. At the very least, Smart and Boyd were in contact with the Free Church Colonial Committee.[57] The Toronto *Banner* and its irascible editor, Peter Brown, supported this "party."

There was also a "middle party," consisting mostly of evangelicals, whose sympathies lay withh the Free Church of Scotland but who hesitated at completely cutting the ties to the Auld Kirk. T. C. Wilson, Robert McGill, Mark Young Stark, and John Cook might be placed in this group.[58] One of the Free Church deputies, George Lewis, described Cook as "one of the ablest men" in the Synod, "a man of great candour, and very fit to be a leader at this crisis, had he more moral earnestness." He noted that Cook had a church, manse, schools and a prosperous congregation, and commented that "these things, I fear, will entangle."[59]

Mark Young Stark may be regarded as typical of those in the middle. Born 9 November 1797 in Dunfermline, Scotland, the son of a linen manufacturer, Stark was educated in arts and theology at the University of Glasgow. He failed to get an appointment in the Church of Scotland, emigrated to Canada under the auspices of the Glasgow Colonial Society, and was ordained to the charge of Dundas and Ancaster, 26 September 1833.[60] Fortunately, Stark's papers survive, and provide a glimpse into the evolution of his thinking, as he moved from a position of uncertainty to become the first Moderator of the Free Church in Canada. In February 1844 he intimated that there would be no split in the Canadian Church unless the issue were pressed by the Church of Scotland and the British Government. "If they force us to a declaration of our principles," he wrote, "to an adherence to the one party or the other as a condition of our retaining these privileges I believe there are few . . . who will not take the part of the Free Church." He still believed, however, that the Canadian Synod could retain its independence and receive ministers from both the Free and Established Churches.[61] Agitation from external parties continued and one month later Stark felt anxious about the situation in Canada:

> The conduct both of the Establishment and the Free Church towards us here has been very inconsiderate—they are both manifestly anxious by any means to hook us on to their respective parties and have been tampering with individuals rather than corresponding through official channels with us as a church—apparently unconcerned about us farther than that they may attach us as adherents to their own side of the question.

Yet still Stark persisted in his illusion of neutrality. Although he was concerned that there were "some hot and fiery spirits among us—

principally of the *Moderate* party who may give us some trouble,"[62] it was not until the opening of the Synod of 1844, when he was forced to a decision, that Stark abandoned the middle. Admittedly, these party groups are largely artificial. Never formalized in any sense, and existing only for a few months, they nevertheless represent the various positions and tendencies within the Synod on this issue.

A group of prominent laymen in Montreal actively supported the Free Church of Scotland. This Montreal Free Church Committee first met 6 January 1844 in James R. Orr's house in St. Paul Street, organizing themselves as "a Committee for the furtherance of the cause of the Free Church in this city and in the Province."[63] Present at this meeting were twelve men: William Bethune, John Redpath, J. R. Orr, Archibald and David Ferguson, William McIntosh, William Hutchinson, James Morrison, Evandor McIvor, Archibald McGoun, and Alexander and Donald Fraser. Soon afterwards, four others were added: Dr. Macnider, Adam Stevenson, Joseph McKay, and James Court, making a total of sixteen.

The leader of this group was John Redpath. Born 1796 in Earlston, Scotland, he was orphaned and emigrated to Canada in 1816. He began work as a stone-mason and was later involved in many of Montreal's business enterprises—the best known of which was his sugar refinery. On arriving in Montreal he first worshipped in the St. Gabriel Street congregation, but being an evangelical he was not sympathetic to the early Esson, and left with Mr. Black for St. Paul's. There he served as Superintendent of the Sunday School and in 1835 was ordained as an elder. He espoused the principles of the Scottish Non-Intrusionists, but, wanting to have the liberty to hold such views, he resigned as Superintendent at St. Paul's[64] and returned to the St. Gabriel Street congregation. He was able to do so because "he found that Mr. Esson and the majority of his congregation occupied common ground with him on the questions involved in the Free Church controversy." However, he was not happy with the "spiritual atmosphere" in St. Gabriel Street and left after only a short time there. His Free Church Committee, nevertheless, had in its purview the formation of a new congregation which would "adequately represent the revived spiritual life of the Free Church, as well as its merely political views."[65] That congregation became the Côté Street Free Church.

The social dimensions of the Disruption in Montreal have received recent attention. One commentator has argued that "the Disruption in Montreal was the result of a movement of artisans, traders, and rising manufacturers in opposition to the established mercantile elite who supported the Church of Scotland."[66] However attractive this thesis may be, there is a good deal of evidence to cast doubt on it. The situation in Montreal was complex, and ultimately resulted in two separate Free Church congregations being established. Indeed, a detailed analysis of Free and Kirk supporters suggests that social origin and occupation are not reliable guides to behaviour in a religious conflict.[67]

Redpath and his committee not only organized their own congregation but they helped diffuse Free Church ideas throughout the wider community. This was done in part by encouraging the Free Church deputies who were visiting the United States in the spring of 1844 to come to Canada.[68] This was precisely what the supporters of the Auld Kirk feared. Alexander Mathieson of Montreal, in a letter of 10 November 1843, probably to the Church of Scotland's Colonial Committee, expressed the fear of "the appearance of an emissary among us to excite the discussion of this question."[69]

Yet the necessity of sending representatives to Canada was not lost on the Free Church and they communicated with their American deputies accordingly.[70] In the winter and spring of 1843-44 the Free Church of Scotland sent a contingent of four ministers and one layman to North America in an effort to gain financial and sympathetic support. The most prominent of these deputies, and the first to leave Scotland,[71] was William Cunningham, a man who had already proved himself to be an able debater in the church courts and an accomplished pamphleteer during the Ten Years' Conflict. Following the Disruption of 1843 he taught church history and was later Principal of New College, Edinburgh, He was a man of great scholarship, though most of his work was published posthumously, including his two-volume *magnum opus—Historical Theology*. "As a theologian," one observer of the Scottish scene has noted, Cunningham was "the most eminent of the group of Evangelical divines of his age."[72] The rest of the deputation consisted of Henry Ferguson, a merchant and Free Church elder from Dundee whom Thomas Chalmers had hand-picked,[73] Rev. William Chalmers, Rev. George Lewis of Ormiston and, the most important as far as Canada was concerned, Dr. Robert Burns of Paisley,[74] long-time secretary of the Glasgow Colonial Society and later minister of Knox Church, Toronto and Professor in Knox College, Toronto.

The deputation went first to the United States, dividing the work in two: Lewis of Ormiston concentrating on the Southern states, Burns and Cunningham on the North. Cunningham had left Scotland in December 1843 and stayed in North America for more than four months. He travelled to New York, Philadelphia, Boston, Richmond, and Baltimore, and in Washington was to have preached before Congress had not illness prevented his doing so. He also visited Princeton, New Jersey, where he stayed with the eminent Old School Presbyterian theologian, Dr. Charles Hodge.[75] Various sums of money for the Free Church were collected in both the North and the South. A minister in New Brunswick, New Jersey, reportedly gave $500, and two congregations in New York contributed upwards of £1000.[76] The Rev. George Lewis was in attendance at the 1844 Old School General Assembly in Louisville, Kentucky where the suggestion was made that collections for the Free Church be raised in locations which the deputation would be unable to visit. Some Old School Presbyterians were suspicious of the Free Church, suspecting some members of being hostile on the issue of fellowship with slaveholders. Ironically, the acceptance of money from Southern contributors prompted charges throughout 1844-46 from American and British Abolitionists that the Free Church had accepted 'blood-stained' money.[77] In all, the Free Church deputies raised about $9000 in the Southern States and about $3500 in the North. The amounts might well have been larger had more deputies been able to canvass larger areas.[78]

Cunningham had been invited to visit Canada but ultimately only Dr. Robert Burns made the trek north.[79] Burns had left Liverpool on Monday, 8 January 1844 and arrived in New York on 7 February. Soon afterwards he joined with Cunningham and the two travelled together for about two months. Burns travelled up and down the Eastern Seaboard throughout February and March, going as far south as Richmond, Virginia, and visiting Baltimore, Philadelphia, Princeton, New York, New Haven and Boston. He then travelled west through New York state and finally arrived at Niagara on 10 April where he was met by Robert McGill and Alexander Gale, two ministers of the Canadian Synod. Thus began a nearly two-month tour of Canada West and East and the Maritime provinces. He stopped in most of the major centres, including Toronto, Hamilton, Dundas and Cobourg. On 19 April he arrived in Kingston and was met by an "active committee." This was one of the more significant stops on his itinerary. In anticipation of Burns' visit, John Machar of St. Andrew's Church had intimated to his sister, "Receive them kindly we shall some of us assuredly do, but as we are yet in a Church in connection with the Established Church of Scotland,—to be honest, we must be determined to act consistently with that title in our intercourse with them."[80] Burns was actually refused entry to St. Andrew's but spoke to a large crowd in the Wesleyan Methodist Church. His visit probably helped force a confrontation between a number of Queen's College students who were sympathetic to the Free Church of Scotland, and Dr. Thomas Liddell, Principal of Queen's. One of these students, Lachlan McPherson, later recalled that in Liddell's view "if we held Free Church principles we could not consistently continue to enjoy the benefit of Queen's College and therefore as honest men we were bound to take our hats and walk off!" Though Liddell attempted to smooth over these remarks, ultimately most of the theological students left Queen's and the student body declined drastically.[81]

In Brockville and Prescott Burns was met by delegates from the surrounding churches "to confer with him as to the future proceedings of the Church in Canada."[82] Burns then went to Cornwall, Lachine and Montreal before proceeding to Quebec City. In Montreal he visited John Redpath, met various people at Henry Esson's and spoke to a full house in the American Presbyterian Church on 30 April. The following day he met privately with individuals and on Thursday, 2 May he spoke to about seventy people at a public breakfast at Rasco's Hotel. According to a report in the *Banner* he "expressed his regret to find the friends of evangelical principles among the Presbyterian Clergy of Canada so disunited among themselves, and exposed the gross inconsistency" of those who claimed to uphold the principles of the Free Church, but for fear of losing their endowments remained connected to a Church which had given up those very principles. [83] After visiting Quebec City Burns travelled to Halifax via Boston and after a tour of the Maritimes set sail for Britain on 3 June aboard the *Britannia*.

While in Canada, Burns put together a pamphlet consisting of three parts: a letter which Cunningham had written to Henry Esson dated Boston, 9 April 1844; a letter from David Welsh as Convener of the Free Church's Colonial Committee to the Moderator of the Canadian Synod; and a new section written by Burns himself. Published in Montreal by J. C. Beckett, it expressed in strong language the necessity of the Canadian Synod declaring its allegiance to either the Established or the Free Church of Scotland. Cunningham thus argued that:

> the Colonial Churches have such a connection with the Mother Church, in virtue of their Ministers being licensed and ordained by her, that it would be morally dishonourable in them to abstain from substantially taking a side in the great contest for principle, which is now waging again, as in days of old, in Scotland, the selected battle field for maintaining the Crown rights of the Redeemer. [84]

Burns, for his part, asserted that "it appears to me that you are bound in honour and conscience to declare that the Free Church, as adhering to these principles, is the genuine representative of that venerable church to whose standard you adhere; and that with us, therefore, you desire to maintain the closest brotherhood." The Canadian Synod, he declared, cannot maintain this connection to the Church of Scotland "without serious injury to your spiritual interests as a church." Welsh's letter was even more forceful. He declared the present position of the Canadian Synod as "in the eyes of all, equivocal, unsatisfactory, and liable to grave misconstruction, and as, in the judgment of many, betraying a marked and serious inconsistency." The Canadian Synod's attachment to the Church of Scotland, he asked, was "it not such a connection, as may render the Synod to some extent partaker of her sins?" The Canadians must declare their allegiance to the Free Church of Scotland; to continue its connection with the Established Church will be perceived as either approval or as "a sacrifice of divine truth to interest and expediency." The Church of Scotland had a "violated constitution" which "they can no longer respect, and whose sinful subserviency to the secular power they must deplore and condemn." [85] Such challenges to take sides in the conflict, coming from men who were respected, if not revered, in the Canadian Synod, undoubtedly pushed many towards decisive action.

Henry Esson of St. Gabriel Street Church, Montreal, also wrote a pamphlet, which was published just before the opening of the Kingston Synod. He argued for a wholehearted identification with the Free Church, asserting that the Canadian church must take the high road of principle, and eschew all connection with the Church of Scotland. In part, this was a question of consistency, of remaining faithful to its previous resolutions: "For have we not given the kiss—the embrace of a disciple to the Free Church, and shall we, Judas-like turn the next moment to betray her and her cause? God forbid."[86] Those in the Synod who had already pledged their loyalty to the Establishment, "they will take their place in history by the side of the Presbytery of Strathbogie, or the patron and presentee of the Presbytery of Auchterarder."[87] He concluded with the warning that "if we separate our cause from that of the Free Church, we take away our vital influence and commit a suicidal act. The day that we conclude our union with the establishment, will sound our death knell."[88]

Many in the Synod were no doubt moved to take a stronger stand for the Free Church by such writing. Welsh's letter, in particular, strengthened John Bayne of Galt, who was concerned over the possible loss of Clergy Reserves money.[89] Burns' tour undoubtedly encouraged the Free Church's supporters already in existence, though whether he won any converts to the cause is more difficult to ascertain. Certainly he upset those who desired peace for the Synod. Thus John Machar wrote on 11 June 1844:

> The Deputation has been here, and the consequences are just what was anticipated. It is easy to excite strife among brethren;—far easier than to unite them in the bonds of love. A storm has been raised which may not soon be laid. Wounds have been inflicted upon a Church ill able to bear them, and which half a century may not heal.[90]

Between the arrival of Dr. Burns in April and the opening of the Synod on 8 July, Canadian Presbyterians were active on many fronts. The Toronto *Banner* continued to state the case for cutting all ties with the Established Church of Scotland. In an editorial of 17 May Peter Brown asserted that if this connection were not severed "a door will be opened for interference of the Civil Courts as in Scotland." He thus argued that ministers from such churches as the Free Church, the Associate Synod or the Irish Presbyterian Church might be prevented by the civil courts from taking up charges in the Canadian Synod. A call was issued for the mobilization of congregational opinion, for resolutions to be forwarded to both Presbyteries and the Synod, and for sound elders to attend the meeting of Synod. Brown also suggested that help would be forthcoming from the Free Church of Scotland.[91]

The Montreal Free Church Committee also remained active. John Redpath wrote to Dr. Burns on 28 May 1844 informing him that a memorial was being sent to the Free Church's Colonial Committee requesting both a minister and evangelist.[92]

Congregational meetings were also held in various Upper and Lower Canadian centres. Some congregations were, of course, content to insist on a change in the Synod's title, assert that the Canadian Synod was independent, or to attempt to avoid letting the issue divide the Canadian church.[93] Others were more vocal in their support of the Scottish Free Church. A meeting in St. Andrew's Church, Toronto, which was chaired by Isaac Buchanan and attended by George and Peter Brown, took a passing swipe at the Temporalities Bill and passed a resolution insisting that if the Synod did not terminate its relationship with the Established Church of Scotland then they would regard the congregation's connection with the Synod to be at an end.[94] Another congregational meeting, this time in St. Andrew's Church, Cobourg, declared its "particular affection for the *Free Church of Scotland*, recognizing in her, their *Parent Church*—and a true Church of the Reformation—inasmuch as she has come so boldly forth in defense of great principles, and renounced her temporal advantages, that she might, under the guidance of her King and Head, be better able to maintain them in their purity and integrity."[95] Indeed, on the eve of the Disruption in Canada the *Banner* listed seventeen congregations which had "declared for entire independence."[96]

It was not always so at the Presbytery level. The Montreal Presbytery voted 11-3 to stay with the Established Church of Scotland until both parties agreed to cut the ties,[97] and a meeting of the Toronto Presbytery on 25 June adopted a series of resolutions declaring that the Canadian Synod was in fact independent, and that while it respected the Free Church and would have fellowship with it, it did not feel compelled to go beyond this.[98]

Some ministers and laymen looked forward with keen anticipation to the July meeting of Synod. This however was not a universal sentiment. Writing to his sister in March 1844, John Machar, minister of St. Andrew's Church, Kingston, intimated that:

> The Synod meets here in July, and here, we are told by the newspapers, the battle must be fought. The meaning of which is just this:—the poor Presbyterian Church of Canada, her ministers and people, who have not a single reason for separation, but every reason to preserve union, must, for some days, oppose each other, and then separate, to hinder each other's work, instead of unitedly advancing the Kingdom of their common Lord.[99]

On the eve of the meeting of Synod, Stark wrote to his mother that, "I feel very anxious in regard to the result of that meeting—opposing parties are beginning to run very high so much so that I fear it may be difficult if not impossible to find any medium ground on which they will both meet." His concern at this point was for unity in the Synod as "necessary . . . to the support of an effective Presbyterian Church order in this country" to "oppose the growth of irreligion and immorality around us."[100]

The Synod of 1844 opened 3 July in St. Andrew's Church, Kingston, with John Clugston as retiring Moderator preaching from the text "We are troubled on every side." Difficulties arose almost immediately over the composition of the Roll, normally a routine matter. The commissions of two elders from the Kingston Presbytery were in dispute, and oddly enough, Smart and Boyd were in attendance, despite having already seceded. Only one of the elders was permitted to stay, and Boyd and Smart did not participate.[101]

Those great points of controversy which had been debated for the past three years came to the forefront almost immediately. The subordinate church courts had been active in petitioning Synod, the ultimate issue being the relations of the Synod to the Established Church. It was, however, considered inappropriate to rush heatedly into debate, and so part of the second day was spent in prayer, and a "friendly conference" held in the afternoon. As William Bell, minister of Perth, commented, "Friday and Saturday were spent in various attempts to preserve peace and unity, but without success." Nor were the Free Church of Scotland's deputies very far from the scene. William Chalmers, Free Church of Scotland minister at Dailly, was in attendance at the Synod on the Saturday evening, and according to Bell "very impudently interfered, which led to a kind of tumult, painful to every lover of peace and order." The next day Chalmers preached in the Methodist church in Kingston where a number of Synod ministers were in attendance.[102]

The debate had opened with John Cook acting as peacemaker. He suggested that common ground first be established and thus set forth eight propositions which all might agree with. Four of these were agreed to unanimously, namely, that Canadians were free to select their own ministers, that the civil authorities had never interfered with the church courts (though one person viewed that as a distinct possibility), that no legal obstacles stood in the way of church extension and that "the alleged causes of disruption at home do not exist here." Those statements which were more contentious concerned the Church of Scotland's jurisdiction; six members of Synod thought that the Kirk exercised some jurisdiction over the Canadian church; seven felt that it at least claimed such a right; and three suggested that it was entitled to such control.[103] What this exercise accomplished is far from certain. In any event, a committee of leading ministers and elders, representing most points of view, was set up to "consider and report on" the Synod's relation to the Church of Scotland. Not surprisingly, this committee failed to reach unanimity.

The main part of the debate took place on Saturday, Monday, and Tuesday. Although five separate series of resolutions were at one point under consideration, the heart of the matter lay in a choice between resolutions sponsored by either John Cook or John Bayne. There were similarities between the two. Both asserted that the Canadian Synod was independent, both spiritually and ecclesiastically. They differed in the matter of the relation to the Church of Scotland. Cook's resolutions left the door open to fellowship with the Kirk, even to the point of receiving its ministers. Bayne's resolutions insisted on slamming that door shut, and dropping the offending phrase "in connexion with the Church of Scotland" from the Synod's title. Bayne's motion also had a more positive attitude to the Free Church, asserting that the Disruption in Scotland was "vital and fundamental" and "inseparable" to the "purity and efficiency of any church of Christ."

On Tuesday, the Synod voted 56-40 to accept Cook's resolutions and added to them, without a formal vote, Hugh Urquhart's motion that it was unnecessary for the Synod to debate "the practical bearings of those principles which have so unhappily divided the Church of Scotland." Nearly all those who voted against Cook's resolutions recorded a formal dissent.

At 8:00 A.M., Wednesday, 10 July Mark Young Stark wrote to his wife, describing the "deplorable step which we were constrained to take in bringing resolutions to the vote which must lead to a disruption." He also intimated that a meeting of Bayne's supporters was scheduled for 9:00 A.M., with the Synod beginning at 10:00 A.M. Stark also remarked, interestingly enough, in reference to the Kirk supporters that "I understand there is war in their camp already" and anticipated seeing Clugston, McGill and possibly Cook coming over to their side.[104] As it was, only Clugston eventually ended up in the Free Church camp. In December 1844 Stark condemned the inconsistency of those who had sided with the Free Church supporters before the Disruption and yet who remained in the Kirk Synod and became opponents of the Free Church. "Many of them went much farther in condemning the conduct of the Church of Scotland than I did," he argued, but when "our church property and our endowments were endangered, now their tone is completely altered."[105]

Some two weeks after the Disruption, Stark remarked that "I was prepared to make great concessions but after the necessity for disruption was evident I felt it to be a relief to my conscience that I was no longer called upon to do so but could give full expression not only in words but practically to the principles I maintain."[106]

The supporters of Bayne's motion were not in attendance when the Synod opened on Wednesday, 10 July. Instead, they met elsewhere in what must have been a planning and strategy meeting. Their absence, according to William Bell, "enabled us to conduct our business with facility, and in peace." That evening Bayne and his followers "arrived at the church, in a body, and gave in their protest; then withdrew in the same manner."[107] Bayne had presented his reasons for dissent from the previous day's decision, and had declared that he could no longer remain as a minister of the Synod.[108] Thus he argued that the Synod had failed to "testify against the defections and corruptions" of the Established Church of Scotland and had refused to sever the "peculiarly close and untenable connexion" with that denomination. He presented seven reasons for dissent, arguing that the Synod had failed to give sufficient support to the Free Church of Scotland, and that it had maintained ties to a church which had committed grievous errors. He thus asserted that:

> by continuing the peculiar connexion . . . it is our conscientious belief, that in respect of the premises, sin, in matters fundamental, has been done by this court; and that . . . we can yet no longer with a clear conscience, hold office in the Presbyterian Church of Canada, in connexion with the Church of Scotland.[109]

Thus the Canadian Free Church had its inauspicious beginning. The ministers who joined it in 1844 were not radically different from those who remained with the Kirk Synod. They had a common educational and social background, being drawn from the Scottish middle classes, and having attended the same universities. Although the majority of Free Church supporters came from the newer-settled regions of the Province, from the Presbyteries of Toronto, Hamilton, and London, there were strong pockets of support in Montreal, Kingston, and Belleville. It was ideology, not social background or geography which was the determining factor. Those who were sympathetic to an evangelical theology, whose imaginations were captured by the ideal of a renewed and reformed church, were those who responded most readily to the call of the Free Church.

Chapter 3

CONSOLIDATION AND GROWTH

With less of a dramatic flourish than its Scottish counterpart, but with almost as much feeling and conviction, the Free Church in Canada was born. Thus in July 1844 a handful of ministers and elders gathered in temporary accommodation in Kingston's Wellington Street Wesleyan Methodist Church and constituted themselves as the Synod of the Presbyterian Church of Canada, doing so as "Office-bearers in the Church of our Lord Jesus Christ in Canada."

The problems which confronted this new church were not unlike those faced by any other group of seceders attempting to organize a denomination. Financial resources for the construction of new buildings and the payment of ministers' stipends were essential. More ministers were needed if the immediate pastoral requirements of Free Church sympathizers were to be met and if the church was to grow. Yet shared theological convictions and strong ties to the mother Free Church of Scotland would have provided a strong sense of identity and would have ensured unity of purpose and action.

Nineteen ministers and five elders were present at that first Free Church Synod. At that time two separate "Protests" were tabled: the first, by John Bayne of Galt, was signed by twenty ministers and nineteen elders; the second was presented by J. M. Roger and William Reid.[1] Robert Boyd, who had seceded before the Synod of 1844, conveyed his regrets for having resigned "precipitately and without a due regard for Presbyterian order" before the meeting of Synod. After adhering to the Protest he was admitted as a minister of the Synod.

Though they established themselves as an independent church, the Free Church retained the essential structure of the Church of Scotland Synod. Four presbyteries were organized: Hamilton and Toronto with fourteen ministers and congregations; Cobourg with four; Kingston with

---

Reference notes for Chapter 3 are found on pp. 152-53.

three, and Montreal with two.[2] Within a year a dozen more ministers and half a dozen students had left the Church of Scotland Synod to join the Free Church.[3] Committees were formed to examine the office of Deacon, and to study the feasibility of a Sustentation Fund. In both of these matters the Canadians were, consciously or not, following the example of their parent church. It was also decided that the Synod would publish its own magazine. This became *The Ecclesiastical and Missionary Record*, which, under the successive editorships of Alexander Gale, William Rintoul, John Burns, and William Reid, fulfilled its function as the official mouthpiece of the denomination. Many Free Church members undoubtedly continued to read Peter Brown's Toronto *Banner* for opinion, information, and criticism, until it was abandoned in 1848. The *Record* continued throughout the Free Church period to give extensive coverage to Canadian, American, and European religious news. Readers of the *Record* would indeed feel themselves part of a world-wide evangelical and Free Church movement as they read of the advances of the Free Church in their native Scotland and of its missionary endeavours in places like India. Later, another Free Church periodical appeared. The *Canadian Presbyter*, published in Montreal, was edited by Rev. Donald Fraser of Côté Street Church, and Rev. A. F. Kemp of St. Gabriel Street Church. Designed as a quarterly review and literary magazine, it attempted to act as an apologist for Calvinist theology and presbyterian polity.[4]

The Synod met again in October 1844, this time in Toronto in the United Secession Church. It was quite apparent that the new church would last and was attractive to other colonial Presbyterians. A deputation from the small Presbytery of Niagara, seeking union, was received and a committee set up to confer with them. There were no theological obstacles in the way of union and it was recommended that there be immediate cooperation on common interests and evangelicism, and that the union talks continue.

Also in attendance at this Synod were three deputies from the Free Church of Scotland—Andrew King of St. Stephen's, Glasgow, John Macnaughton of the High Church, Paisley, and Mr. McMillan of Cardross. They were the first of many to cross the Atlantic since the formation of the Canadian Synod, and their presence signified the close attachment of the Canadian and Scottish Free Churches and helped strengthen the cause in the Canadas—particularly in the area of theological education, as King was to become the first Professor of Theology in the Canadian Church. The third group to send a deputation was the Missionary Presbytery of the United Associate Synod of Scotland. The Free Church Synod regarded this as "an earnest of greater union amongst sound Presbyterian Churches in this Province."[5] It was this group with which long and serious negotiations were carried out during the next seventeen years, and with which a union was consummated in 1861, forming the Canada Presbyterian Church.

The Free Church Synod also received a communication from the Church of Scotland Synod suggesting that two committees be established—one to deal with disputed property and one to negotiate a re-union. The first committee might have done some useful work in helping to avoid litigation, but it accomplished next to nothing. Property disputes were accordingly settled in either of two ways—by the seceders voluntarily relinquishing any claim to the building, even though they might have been in the majority, or by litigation.

The prospects for negotiating a re-union between the Free and Church of Scotland Synods were dim, though some like John Cook of Quebec City believed the secession would be only temporary. Accordingly he counselled a Mr. Ironside of Amherstburg to remain in Peden's congregation, at least until the Kirk Synod met in September. Cook argued that "I am most unwilling that any thing should be done in congregations or church courts, which by stirring of party feeling or personal unkindness, might lessen the reasonable hope of a speedy reunion."[6] Although the Free Church Synod did agree to form a committee on re-union, the Church of Scotland Synod made negotiation contingent on the Free Church ceasing "operations which cannot be regarded in any other light than that of hostility,"[7] a provision which the Free Churchmen termed "unseemly and absurd."[8] The conditions thus set by the Kirk Synod, the act of that Synod in declaring the seceders to no longer be ministers of the Presbyterian Church of Canada in Connexion with the Church of Scotland, or of the Church of Scotland in Canada,[9] and the "Remonstrance" which they sent to the Free Protesting Church of Scotland, surely made negotiations very difficult. A Committee of the Free Church, consisting of Gale, Esson, Rintoul, Stark and J. F. Westland, an elder, did meet with one Justice McLean and Robert McGill in Toronto on 26 November 1844, but they made it clear that there could be no re-union unless the Kirk Synod broke all ties "real or nominal" with the Church of Scotland.[10] As one commentator put it: "tempers were too hot. The 'separated brethren' felt that those remaining had denied the Lordship of Christ over the Church, while a good many of the Kirk ministers felt that the others had been unnecessarily demanding."[11] The Free Church, for its part, insisted that the Church of Scotland Synod dissolve its connection with the Established Church of Scotland and alter its title accordingly. When the latter refused to do so, the re-union talks were broken off. As for the disputed property, the terms drafted by the Free Church committee for Canada West were refused by their counterparts in the Kirk Synod.[12] Re-union with the Kirk Synod on the basis of anything less than Free Church principles was unattainable, and undesirable. More pressing needs than an elusive re-union faced the new church.

It was essential for the new church to provide for the education of its students and to ensure a steady supply of new ministers. The numbers of trained ministers who might be expected from Scotland and Ireland would not be large. For these reasons it was necessary for the Canadian church to establish its own seminary: Knox College. Its beginnings were tentative and inauspicious; most of its early professors were temporary appointments from the Free Church of Scotland. Yet it did serve its purpose, growing in numbers of students, permanency of staff and buildings, and financial security, and by 1859 it had contributed to the education of nearly one-third of the ministers on the Roll of Synod.[13]

With the addition of Canadian trained men to the ranks of those from Scotland and Ireland, the number of ministers and congregations grew substantially. In October 1844 the Synod consisted of 32 ministers and 53 congregations. Ten years later there were 92 and 107, a tripling of ministers and a doubling of congregations in a decade. The initial four presbyteries of 1844 had expanded to eight by 1854: Brockville, Perth, Montreal, London, Hamilton, Toronto, Cobourg, and Kingston. The largest was London with 20 ministers; the smallest, Brockville with only four. On the eve of the Union with the United Presbyterian Church the eight presbyteries contained 158 ministers and congregations. This growth was not confined to the western parts of the province; there was substantial growth near Kingston and Perth.

Part of the explanation for this growth undoubtedly lies in the inactivity of both the Church of Scotland and the Canadian Kirk Synod. The Church of Scotland was relatively slow to respond to the Canadian situation.[14] Thomas Clark, as Vice-Convener of the Church of Scotland's Colonial Committee sent a "Letter of Sympathy" to the Moderator of the Canadian Kirk Synod, which was received on 20 September 1844.[15] However, it was not until June 1845, more than one year after the arrival of the Free Church deputies, that the Church of Scotland sent three deputies to North America—Dr. Simpson of Kirknewton, Dr. John MacLeod of Morven and Rev. Norman Macleod of Dalkeith. They left Liverpool in June 1845, went first to Nova Scotia, then to Prince Edward Island, Boston, Canada East, and finally to Canada West, visiting Perth, Markham, Kingston, Belleville, and Toronto.[16]

The Canadian Kirk Synod itself responded almost immediately to the Disruption of 1844, with an Answer to the Protest of John Bayne and his followers,[17] but was still not satisfying all of its constituents. Writing from Toronto on 3 March 1845 to his brother John, Oliver Mowat confessed that:

> I verily hope, John, that the ministers who may be sent out from "Queen's" will exhibit more zeal and judgment, in their office, than most of them who have preceded them in it in Canada. With our Mr. B. here I am becoming more and more dissatisfied every day. The Free Church is increasing in numbers, and in usefulness every day. Ours increases neither in one nor the other: indeed I fear it is retrograding in both. Every now and then I am learning some new fact in favour of the former; and quite as often some new fact in derogation of the latter.[18]

Earlier, Mowat had confided to his brother that "the friends of the old Synod have certainly a strange way in general of showing their attachment to it—that of looking on while it is attacked on every side, and without raising a finger in its defence."[19]

In the same period that the Free Church Synod was experiencing such dramatic growth, the Kirk Synod showed signs of substantial decline. According to the census figures for 1842 the Church of Scotland had 77,929 adherents in Canada West, constituting 16% of the population. In 1851 it had dropped to 59,102 or 6.2% of the population—a decline of almost 25%. By 1851 the Free Church had at least 70,000 adherents or about 7.5% of the population. By 1861 it had approximately 150,000 adherents or 10% of the population, while the Kirk Synod had 108,963 or 7.8% of the population. The only other denomination in Canada West to experience such growth was the Wesleyan Methodist.[20]

From the Disruption of 1844 until the Union of 1875 the Kirk Synod had failed to keep pace with either the growth of the country at large or of the other churches. "Thus in relative terms it was losing, for not only did its total membership and impact decrease proportionately to the other churches, but a good many of its best and most energetic people tended to attach themselves to the other more active ecclesiastical bodies." The Kirk Synod has been described as "although by no means dead, it manifested the symptoms of almost a comatose state."[21] Dr. Robert McGill of St. Paul's Church, Montreal, one of the Kirk Synod's more prominent ministers, asserted in 1852 that:

> It requires no gift of prophecy and only a little skill in the statistics of life in men and churches, to predict that, unless we shall be more successful than we have been in increasing our power from healthful and legitimate sources, twenty years will not pass before the Church of Scotland in Canada is a shapeless shadow, a heterogeneous thing which its parent will refuse to own.[22]

Undoubtedly, the Free Church, with a natural clientele among Scots and Ulster Protestants, succeeded in attracting some members away from the Kirk Synod, even in the years following the Disruption of 1844. Moreover, being more evangelical theologically, and thus more missionary-minded, the Free Kirk was prepared to move into new areas of the province and organize congregations under the aegis of Home Missions.

Although Dr. Robert Burns, after a missionary tour to Owen Sound, complained that "the modest timidity of the Free Church in Canada has kept us back in instances not a few," the Free Church was relatively successful in the field of Home Missions. This is perhaps partly attributable to their having a missions strategy, though even here Burns argued that "the distribution of our mission supplies has been regulated by local considerations more than by an enlightened and comprehensive survey of fields already 'whitening to the harvest'."[23]

The responsibility for Home Missions was divided between the Presbyteries and a central committee of the Synod. The task of the central committee was restricted to distributing, in an equitable manner, those missionaries who were available at any given time. The specific conduct of Home Missions was the responsibility of each presbytery. Each presbytery was to establish its own home missions committee, ensure that the necessary funds were procured, divide the Presbytery into missionary districts, and make annual reports to the Synod. Each of the missionary districts was to be under the supervision of one of the ministers of the Presbytery whose responsibilities would include visitation, congregational organization, and making provision for Sabbath worship—which was in turn carried out by missionaries, catechists or elders under the superintendence of the minister.[24]

Though this basic plan was retained, the Synod of 1847 formulated a more elaborate scheme for Home Missions. That year an overture had come before the Synod, calling for a restructuring of the Home Missions scheme "with a view to the prosecution of missionary operations throughout the land with greater vigour, unity, and efficiency."[25] According to this scheme the Presbytery would select particular locations and designate them as "Preaching Stations." The stations chosen, along with the vacant congregations in a particular region, would be grouped together as a Missionary District. Each District was to be supervised by a minister and would have a missionary if possible. The Presbyteries were enjoined to visit each district, giving explanations of the plan, organizing and setting up committees in each district, and impressing upon the people there the need for them to support this ministry. These local committees were, in turn, to make up a roll of adherents, visit families, collect offerings and conduct worship. Reports and statistics were to be kept by all concerned. Moreover, under these new provisions, the Synod determined that any minister, licentiate, or probationer who was admitted to the Free Church, who did not come to the church with a specific call from a congregation, would normally be expected to devote his first year to home missions. However, there were many exceptions made to this rule and it was ultimately abandoned—which some perceived as an abandonment of the home mission field. It is not clear whether this scheme was carried out in all its detail by each Presbytery, yet by July 1850 it was reported that there were approximately 150 mission stations in the Synod.[26]

In any event, one practice which seems to have been most successful was that of missionary tours throughout the provinces by ministers of settled congregations. These tours would have been particularly crucial in the years immediately following the Disruption of 1844, when it was necessary to rally and organize those Presbyterians who desired to be identified with the Free Church. Ministers would thus tour the province, explain the position of the Free Church and the reasons for the secession, and help organize a congregation in a particular locality.[27] Undoubtedly, in many cases, the prospect of regular worship services and pastoral care would have been sufficient to attract people to the Free Church. One indefatigable traveller was Dr. Robert Burns, who was absent for weeks on end, visiting the various regions of the provinces, preaching and dispensing the Lord's Supper. Describing one of these visits Burns wrote:

> Whenever I have been called to address a congregation on these visits, I have made it a rule first to preach the Gospel of the grace of God to sinful and dying men: and thereafter, if it is deemed proper in the circumstances, to address the hearers on their duties as a congregation connected with the Presbyterian Church.[28]

Such evangelical preaching had apparently particular results in Glengarry County. There, ministers from the Free Church of Scotland who were able to speak Gaelic, like Rev. Mr. MacLeod of Logie-Easter, saw encouraging results from their ministry. According to one report, "the District of Glengarry, long steeped in the frigid lethargy of a formal moderatism, has sensibly felt the influence of gospel truth, when proclaimed with the soul-stirring energy of a minister of Christ, so devoted and so much in earnest as Mr. MacLeod."[29] Glengarry seems to have been a classic example of the failure of the Kirk Synod, and the aggressive and evangelical thrust of the Free Church. At the time of the Disruption of 1844 only one of nine ministers joined the Free Church. Subsequently, two Kirk Synod ministers returned to Scotland. The Free Church through the work of its deputies was able to make inroads into the area. By 1847 they had reportedly five large congregations in the region, and five or six more in the embryonic stage. In a letter dated Cornwall, 13 October 1847, Rev. J. Fraser, one of the Scottish Free Church deputies, declared, "Give us labourers, and we will spread on every side. Our principles have gained a firm footing in the district: our stations are impregnable. The Free Church has sprung into full development in Glengarry, like a gourd in a tropical clime. The Lord pour our his blessing on our newly-cultivated soil!"[30] This seems to have been the start of a revival in the years 1847-48 in Glengarry[31] and perhaps prepared the ground for the Glengarry revival of 1862.[32]

Besides its aggressiveness and evangelical spirit and theology, there were perhaps three other reasons why the Home Missions of the Free Church were successful: they eschewed Scottish exclusiveness; they were cognizant of their own spiritual shortcomings and this prevented them from becoming smug and complacent; and they realized that missions were a concern for the whole church, and not just a clerical pursuit. In the first place, there is some evidence that Free Church ministers were aware of the dangers of assuming too Scottish a tone. Andrew Ferrier thus remarked that "there is a disposition among Presbyterians who are not from Scotland, to feel themselves overlooked when Ministers, or other officebearers, perhaps altogether through inadvertancy, make notices or remarks which seem to give a mere Scottish aspect to the Free Church in Canada." Noting that the Kirk Synod had a very Scottish tone to it, he urged the Free Church to be "a Church for the Province at large."[33] Mark Young Stark in his pastoral address of 1844 charged the Kirk Synod with being too narrowly Scottish and not broad enough to include Presbyterians from other countries. "She has been little better than a Church for the Scotch," he declared, "or rather . . . the Scotch of the Establishment."[34] Moreover, in an editorial of January 1851 the *Record*, while conceding that the Free Church had a primary obligation to Presbyterians, nonetheless argued that:

> we are fully persuaded, that it will not be well with out Church, unless she identify herself out-and-out with the evangelization of the whole land—and do her utmost endeavour, in an enlarged and truly Catholic spirit—to supply the faithful ministration of Gospel ordinances to every portion of our population, willing to receive them at her hand—without reference to language, or previous religious connexion.[35]

The Free Church seems to have done this, as is evidenced by its missions to blacks in Canada West and to the settlers at Red River; its support of the French Canadian Missionary Society and other interdenominational societies (such as the Toronto City Mission, the Upper Canada Religious Tract and Book Society, the Upper Canada Bible Society and the Toronto Sabbath School Union), its serious contemplation of a mission to Germans, North American Indians, and Vancouver Island, and its support of the Jewish and Foreign Missions of the Free Church of Scotland.[36]

Support for Foreign Missions was greatly stimulated by the tour of Dr. Alexander Duff to Canada in the spring of 1854. Duff, who was probably, at the time, the Free Church of Scotland's most famous missionary, was best known for his work among the Hindus of India. A former Moderator of the General Assembly of the Free Church of Scotland, and a serious candidate for the Principalship of New College, Edinburgh, Duff pressed home the cause of foreign missions in the principal towns of Canada West and East. The results of Duff's tour have been described as "startling":[37] givings to missions increased dramatically, and within two years the Canadian Synod was sponsoring its own missionary in Bancoorah, though this was short-lived and was abandoned because of the Indian Mutiny of 1857.[38]

In the second place, Free Church consciousness of its own spiritual failings kept it from becoming complacent. The Synod of 1845 adopted various resolutions concerning the state of religion within the Church and the need for Presbyterial visitation. One of these resolutions pointed to the deploringly "low state of spiritual religion among themselves, and the people generally, the formality, worldliness, coldness and indifference which abound."[39] In an editorial of November 1854 the *Record* asserted that there were too few candidates for the ministry coming forward, and ascribed this to "the low state of religion among us, and the great influence which secular and material things are allowed, at the present day, to exert upon the mind."[40]

An August 1858 editorial in the *Record* argued that most of the new congregations in the Free Church are "healthy, vigorous, self-sustaining. . . which may truly be regarded as an accession to the moral and spiritual strength of the Church."[41] At the same time, the Report on the State of Religion for 1858-59 asserted that "there is reason to fear that the spiritual life of the church in general is low, and such as calls for humility, and earnest prayer to God for a time of refreshing from His presence." This realization was particularly acute and troublesome in light of recent evangelical awakenings in Britain and the United States.[42] "A serious concern for the future welfare of our Canadian Church ought to be awakened," the report asserted, "should we be altogether past by at such a time."[43] By 1860, though no general revival had been seen, some improvement was perceived, though "much worldliness and immorality in various forms abound in the country, and much indifference and apathy among the professed followers of the Saviour."[44]

There is evidence that the fulfilment of the Free Church's mission was not seen as an exclusively clerical pursuit but was to be an integral part of the life of all its members. The *Record* thus argued:

> the work of spreading the Gospel of Christ, is not the duty merely of ministers and missionaries, or of such as hold official stations in the church, but the work of the whole church, and of every individual member of it. Every one on assuming a profession of Christianity, gives up himself and all that he has to the service of the Lord, thereby pledging himself to put forth all his power for the glory of the Saviour, and the advancement of his Kingdom in the world.[45]

At least one presbytery, that of London, had a Committee on Lay Agency, under the supervision of the presbytery's home mission committee. In conjunction with this, one Mr. W. Clarke had been appointed lay agent, at a salary of £100 *per annum*, with responsibility for visitation, congregational organization, Sabbath Schools, and the distribution of religious literature.[46]

Despite its relative success, the Canadian Free Church was not without its own internal problems. Dr. Robert Burns was frequently in the middle of such quarrels. The irascible pastor of Knox's Church, Toronto, had problems in his own congregation over the composition of its Kirk Session[47] and in 1853 clashed with Dr. Michael Willis over evidence which they had both given in a Toronto police court in the case of one George Isaac Lublin who had attempted to raise money for Jewish Missions in Toronto.[48]

Separation from the Church of Scotland Synod did not require the establishment of new types of structures for the Free Church. Presbyteries and a Synod were organized according to the same principles as before, and a theological college was established in Toronto to train the church's future ministers. To these structures and institutions, however, the Free Church brought a renewed missionary zeal and a vision for evangelism. Under the aegis of a clear and comprehensive Home Missions strategy evangelism was actively pursued by clergy and laity alike. This zeal, vision, and strategy, coupled with the relative inactivity of the Kirk Synod, seems to account for the Free Church's remarkable growth in the years 1844-61.

Chapter 4

THE FREE CHURCH MIND

Coelum non animum mutant qui trans mare current
— Seneca

The Scottish evangelical Calvinism which the Free Church espoused provided them with a consistent world-view which was easily transported to a different geographical setting and applied to a new set of circumstances. This set of beliefs has already been considered in some detail. Yet it remains necessary to examine the transfer of ideas and to see how Canadian Free Churchmen responded to particular cross-currents in theology, philosophy, and science, and to see what steps they took to guard theological orthodoxy.

In common with virtually all presbyterians the Free Churches of Scotland and Canada looked to the Westminster Confession of Faith as their theological charter. With the Larger and Shorter Catechisms this Confession defined the central doctrines of the faith with lucidity, precision, and force. Originally drafted by "The Assembly of Divines at Westminster, with the Assistance of Commissioners from the Church of Scotland" and approved by the Scottish General Assembly of 1647, it had for some two hundred years been the accepted "subordinate standard" of Presbyterians worldwide. In the eighteenth-century Church of Scotland, however, the Moderate Party attempted with some success to modify this strict confessionalism. Yet in the 1830s the emergence of young Evangelicals like Robert Smith Candlish and William Cunningham led to a revival of scholastic Calvinism which was carried over into the Free Church of Scotland.[1]

All ministers, elders, and deacons were required by ecclesiastical law to sign a statement affirming their acceptance of the Confession and the "Doctrine, Worship, Discipline and Government" of the church. Indeed, the seccond of the questions put to office-bearers at the time of their ordination asked:

Reference notes for Chapter 4 are found on pp. 153-55.

48

> Do you sincerely own and believe the whole doctrine contained in the Confession of Faith . . . to be founded upon the Word of God; and do you acknowledge the same as the confession of your faith; and will you firmly and constantly adhere thereto, and to the utmost of your power assert, maintain and defend the same, and the purity of worship as presently practised in this Church?[2]

The central doctrines of the Confession, as seen by the Committee of the Synod of 1844 which conferred with the Niagara Presbytery over a possible union, were "the divine sovereignty, the decree of election, and the imputation of the righteousness of Christ."[3] While this might appear gloomy and fatalistic, there was room within this confessionalism for a warm-hearted evangelical piety, and an aggressive missionary impulse.[4] As Principal Michael Willis of Knox College expressed it, "no sovereignty on God's part, is at all at variance with our immediate duty and privilege, of accepting the common salvation which is proferred to us in the most unrestricted terms."[5]

In their preaching Free Church ministers emphasized the doctrines of sin, redemption, and new life in Christ. Mark Young Stark, preaching from Colossians 3:1-3 "If ye then be risen with Christ," explored the themes of the fall of mankind, original sin, regeneration, conversion, the substitutionary atonement and imputed righteousness of Christ, and sanctification.[6] Similar views were expressed by Michael Willis who spoke of "saving faith" in the following terms:

> My dear friends, we must not rest in simple historical belief, a mental entertainment of the message concerning Christ, though that is very precious and valuable, and nothing good can be got without it. We must not rest in a mere intellectual assent; we must commit our souls to Christ, we must come to Him, we must rest upon Him, we must welcome him to perform in us all that belongs to His office as Saviour, not only as having died for us, but as now teaching us by His word and Spirit, that he may reign over us and make us wholly His. That is the faith which gives life.[7]

In dwelling on these particular tenets, Canadian Free Churchmen were in line with much of British evangelicalism, as described by Roger Anstey and Ian Bradley. Thus Bradley has noted, for example, that "the doctrines of the depravity of man, the conversion of the sinner, and the sanctification of the regenerate soul represent virtually the sum total of the theology of early nineteenth-century Evangelicalism."[8] The conviction that unconverted sinners would spend eternity in Hell, and the desire to obey Christ's Great Commission, were powerful motivations fuelling Free Church missionary activity.

There was also a deeply pietistic dimension to Free Church evangelicalism. Peter Brown, editor of the Toronto *Banner*, and the Free Church's most articulate layman, wrote of prayer:

> Prayer to God, what comfort there is in that word! Communion with God! Can it be that the High and Holy One, who rules the mighty universe, will deign

to hold communion with a worm of the dust!—that He who is from eternity will condescend to listen to the sighs of a creature of dust and ashes!—that He who cannot look on iniquity without abhorrence, will yet dwell with sinful men, if they are of humble and contrite hearts! It is even so, and who will not eagerly lay hold of the invaluable privilege? Who would refuse an invitation to the palace of an earthly king? Few indeed; but how many will turn a deaf ear when the King of Kings invites us to banquet with him.[9]

Many of these characteristics were common to evangelicals in Scotland, England, and the United States. At the same time the Free Church's immediate roots were in Scotland, and the Disruption of 1844 had certainly facilitated the transfer of Scottish theological ideas to British North America. This was particularly true in the case of Knox College, all of whose professors were born and educated in Scotland. Indeed, Burns and Willis, its two most prominent, were very recent immigrants to Canada, both having arrived following the formation of the Free Church. It is instructive to attempt to trace the theological influence imbibed by a generation of Canadian ministers, through examination of professors' reports to the annual meeting of Synod, and college notices printed in the *Record*, outlining courses of lectures and subjects for examination. This may appear to be exalting the preachers over the people, until it is remembered that preaching was central to the presbyterian heritage, was one of the (if not the) chief functions of its ministry, and was regarded as the chief means of spreading the gospel message. The pulpit was thus the principal means of diffusing ideas throughout the denomination. Central to this process was the Free Church's theological seminary, where a generation of Canadian ministers was trained.

Henry Esson taught Moral Philosophy from 1844 until his death in 1853. An 1845 prospectus for a course on the "Philosophy of the Human Mind" indicated that he regarded "mental and metaphysical science" as "having their proper and perfect work as the handmaid of Divine Revelation." His analysis of the nature of man was to encompass the *sensitive, intellectual,* and *emotional,* understanding by this last the various original active springs or principles, including the moral faculty, by whatever name it may be designated, as the supreme and governing power." Proceeding to a study of Logic, Ethics, and Natural Theology, Esson wanted to demonstrate "how insufficient are all that man's knowledge and powers can effect in the enlightenment of the understanding, and the regulation of the will, without light and grace from on high." He also proposed to lecture on the "moral condition of man" using Butler, Abercrombie, and Chalmers, with supplemental readings from Reid, Beattie, and Brown.[10]

William Rintoul lectured briefly on Hebrew and Biblical Criticism. His topics for 1846 included "structure and contents" of the Bible; authorship, stylistic differences between books; texts and manuscripts; ancient and modern versions; the inspiration, "authenticity and genuineness" of scripture; interpretation; "difficulties"; and "difficulties in the Bible compatible with its inspiration—these gradually lessening with the progress of Biblical science and the advancement of the Gospel age"; and "the Transcendant importance of a thorough knowledge of the holy Scriptures to the Christian Minister—the subordination of the critical to the devotional study of the Scriptures."[11]

Dr. Robert Burns lectured in Systematic Theology and later in Church History. In 1846 his lectures in Systematics were to include the following subjects:

> ancient and modern theories regarding the being and perfections of God, as contrasted with the system of the Bible; imperfections of natural theology. General character and claims of revelation; internal evidences and outline of proofs at large; objections grounded on mysteries and supposed opposition to reason examined and refuted. Doctrine of the Trinity; divinity of Christ; incarnation; mediatorial scheme; modern views on the atonement, its nature, extent and issues; justification by imputed righteousness through faith; divinity, personality and work of the Holy Spirit; on good works and the place they hold in the Christian system.[12]

Dr. Burns was one who was influenced by the Scottish Common Sense philosophers. In a printed letter to the College Committee of 23 March 1848 he praised them for their refutation of Hume and Berkeley. "The world is under infinite obligations to such men as Reid, Stewart, Campbell, Beattie, and others," he asserted, "who exposed the baselessness of the theory, and appealed successfully to primary principles of human belief, as ultimate facts in the arrangements of God." He further asserted that "I tremble when I think of the readiness with which the exploded theory has been received; because I look upon it as not only destructive of all the evidence for final causes, in proof of the existence of God, but as directly subversive of all belief in the existence of any beings in the universe except ourselves."[13]

In 1856-57 Burns taught both Church History and Christian Evidences. The outline of his lectures in Church History indicates that the focus of his course was Old and New Testament history—little time was devoted to post-Patristic Christianity. His outline included a consideration of "the Mosaic History of Creation and of the Deluge"; "The Common Origin of the Human Family"; "the history of the work of redemption under various dispensations"; inter-testamental history; "a condensed view of Jewish antiquities"; an "Examination of the theories of Eichhorn, DeWette, Strauss, and others, regarding the history of our blessed Saviour, and analysis of the Acts of the Apostles"; and the New Testament church from Pentecost to Constantine.[14] It is notable that Burns included in his course a consideration of some recent German New Testament scholarship. In his Church History course for 1857-58 he included the medieval, reformation, and modern periods.[15]

A number of Burns' introductory lectures in Church History were published in the *Record* and from these one can discern his conception of the scope and intent of his subject. In an 1848 lecture he defined Church History as:

> the history of God's arrangements with our world, for displaying his own glory, and securing the salvation of his people: the history of successive dispensations of grace in behalf of guilty man: the history of the doctrines, the worship, the institutions of the visible Church: the history of the effects of true religion on the literature, the arts, the civilization of the species: the history of the relations established betwixt the varied sections of the Church and the civil communities of men: in a word, the history of the contest betwixt truth and error for the mastery. On such a history much precious instruction may be grafted, and the historian and herald of the Churches, may become also the minister of God for the salvation of his people.[16]

Church History, as so conceived, had both a didactic and apologetic value. In this regard, Church History helped in "the establishment of the truth of the Gospel by arguments derived from its rapid progress and success"; it described "the history of the fulfilment of prophecy"; it provided "a map of the human mind and of the human character," and it encompassed "an enquiry into the causes of error, and such an enquiry is of great advantage as supplying in many cases the means of exposing and refuting the error itself."[17]

Burns also taught Christian Evidences in 1856-57. For texts he used Butler's *Analogy*, Paley's *Evidences*, and the work of Whateley on evidence. The subjects dealt with in this course included:

I. Sketches of various theories of infidelity ancient and modern—chiefly the latter—as embracing Atheism, Pantheism, and Development theories—and the different forms of Deism as at present in vogue.

II. The existence, attributes, and government of God—argument *a priori* of Dr. Clarke—argument of Descartes, estimate of the argument in regard to clearness and conclusiveness. Argument from Design—replies to objections by Lord Bacon, Descartes, Hume and others—Illustrations from works of God—from mind—from adaptations—from succession of events. Development theory—Geology—argument from *Conscience*.

III. Evidences of revelation—possibility—necessity and probability of revelation—objections of Newman and others as to the *mode* of revelation—Miracles, Prophecy, Rapid Propagation of the Gospel—Internal Evidence—undersigned coincidences. Genuineness—Authenticity—Inspiration of the Sacred books—Replies to popular objections.[18]

Although we know little of Burns' specific approach to these subjects, it seems clear that much of his time was spent in the field of what would be called apologetics—that branch of theology which is concerned with providing a rational defence for the Christian faith. Like other Scottish, American, and Canadian theologians, he adopted the principles of the Common Sense school as a means of refuting the philosophical skepticism of David Hume. He also introduced his students to some of the other principal theological disputes of the eighteenth and nineteenth century. The deistical controversy was examined via the Anglican anti-deist writers Samuel Clarke, William Paley, and Joseph Butler. Their arguments would be used to defend "revealed religion" against the critiques of the deists. He also seems to have followed their division of Christian evidences into "external" and "internal"—the former encompassing "Miracles, Prophesy, Rapid Propagation of the Gospel"; the latter bassed on what Lefferts Loetscher has called "the high spiritual and moral calibre of the biblical writers."[19] The more recent challenge of the Oxford Movement was considered through examining the thought of John Henry Newman.

Dr. Michael Willis lectured on Systematic Theology and Biblical Criticism, in 1854-55 using the Westminster Confession of Faith and Calvin's *Institutes* in Latin for the former, and Horne on hermeneutics for the latter. In 1856-57 Willis also used Hill's system of theology.[20] In the area of hermeneutics Willis was aware of what was being done in the German universities—praising some scholars and cautioning against others. He thus argued that

> Though I think the writings of their critics and philologists have been overpraised; yet they have brought some valuable accessions to the illustration of the evidence of our faith, and to the exposition of the sacred books, in opposition to the assaults of rationalism, and it is well that we should keep up some acquaintance with the Olshausens, the Hengstenbergs, the Hugenbachs [*sic*], and others, who have assisted to stem the torrent of a wild and licentious criticism, as well as philosophy, which threatened to sap the foundations of Christianity.

Willis then went on to commend the study of Systematic Theology as an antidote to certain hermeneutical excesses:

> there is, we think, a danger of magnifying hermeneutical science to the deprecation of theological systems—of attaching by far too much importance to the assaults of modern infidelity, or neology, and letting ourselves down from the tone of confidence with which we are entitled to speak of long-established truths; as if the whole of Christianity were yet a question, and the very safety of the citadel were compromised by some small affair of a various reading, or some conjectural emendation of occasional clauses.... It enhances in our opinion, the value of dogmatic theology, when we see the Ernestis, and Tholuks, and Rosenmullers and Heinrichs of Germany, compromising truth in so serious a degree even while opposing themselves with success to certain devices of the common enemy; pulling down with the one hand, while they build up with the other; not because their criticism is valueless, but because their knowledge of the analogy of faith is defective.[21]

Though the Free Church as a whole was firmly wedded to a Calvinistic orthodoxy, one of its professors has been charged with departing from that stand. D. C. Masters has thus argued that "the most distinguished of the early teachers at Knox College was also the shakiest in his theology."[22] More recently, Leslie Armour and Elizabeth Trott have argued that

Young's decision to leave Knox may well have been influenced by his convictions about freedom and reason, though they stop just short of suggesting that he "must have always been in the wrong church."[23]

Born in 1818 in Berwick upon Tweed, George Paxton Young had been educated at the Edinburgh High School, the University of Edinburgh and the Free Church Theological College. He was ordained to Martyr's Church, Paisley and in 1847 emigrated to Canada. He served as Minister of Knox's Church, Hamilton from 1850-53. In 1854 he left Hamilton to become Professor of Mental and Moral Philosophy. Two years later, with the addition of Dr. Robert Burns to the faculty, Young was given the responsibility of teaching Exegetical Theology.[24] Yet in 1864 Young left Knox College because he could not fully subscribe to the Westminster Confession of Faith. As Masters put it: "By 1864, philosophy and higher criticism had landed him in a position in which he could no longer accept orthodox Presbyterian doctrine."[25] Indeed, as early as 1860 Young was seeking the Chair of Logic and Metaphysics in Queen's College, Belfast.[26] After leaving Knox, Young served with the Ontario Department of Education. He returned briefly to Knox College before taking up the Chair of Logic, Metaphysics and Ethics in University College, Toronto.[27]

In 1854 Young published his *Miscellaneous Discourses and Expositions of Scriptures*—a collection of sermons which he had preached at Hamilton. According to Masters, they "indicate that already he had begun to introduce into Canada historical and critical methods of analysing the Old Testament, that were being developed in Europe."[28] Apparently this book also indicates that Young had been influenced by H. F. W. Gesenius, one of Germany's leading Hebraists who taught theology at the University of Halle.[29] In light of the Free Church's concern for theological orthodoxy, the question immediately arises as to why Young's views were not detected, and Young himself subjected to church discipline. The church had not hesitated to expel ministers on previous occasions for heterodox views. Robert Peden, for example, minister at Amherstburg, had been expelled for holding unsound views on the atonement.[30]

In November 1854 a review of Young's book appeared in the Free Church's in-house organ, *The Ecclesiastical and Missionary Record*. The review was favourable and there was no mention of Young employing "higher critical" methods. The sermons were described as "discourses of great excellence, rich in evangelical sentiment, and pervaded by a spirit of earnest piety." Moreover, "the author reveres the authority of the inspired record, and has too deep an appreciation of excellency of the divine truth to permit his travelling out of his way to deal in barren abstractions or in the nice refinements of metaphysics."[31]

An examination of Young's *Miscellaneous Discourses* confirms this view. They were Calvinistic, evangelical and orthodox. In a sermon entitled, "The Traitor Unmasked, or Incidents of Our Lord's Last Passover," based on the text John 35:21-38, Young declared "*what an encouragement*

does this passage furnish to sinners to put their trust in Christ!" He went on
to assert that:

> God was glorified in Him. He fully satisfied divine justice. He magnified the
> law and made it honourable; so that, on the footing of His finished work, God
> can pardon sinners, and bestow upon them the blessings of eternal life,
> without a shadow falling upon any of the perfections of His nature, or the
> slightest injury being done to His moral government. No sacrifice less than
> the blood of Emmanuel could have sufficed to take away sin; but this
> infinitely precious offering has been made, and every sinner, however guilty,
> who puts his trust in Christ, is assured, on the word of Him who cannot lie, of
> obtaining forgiveness, sanctification, peace, and complete redemption. The
> invitation, addressed to every creature under heaven, is "Believe on the
> Lord Jesus Christ, and thou shalt be saved." Let me urge this upon uncon-
> verted sinners. It is my duty, brethren, as a minister of Christ, to use every
> persuasion in my power to induce you to avail yourselves of the rich provi-
> sions of saving mercies brought to your hand in the Gospel; and this I would
> discharge, not merely as a duty, but in the spirit of friendly affection, and out
> of love to your immortal souls. AS THOUGH GOD DID BESEECH YOU BY US, WE
> PRAY YOU IN CHRIST'S STEAD, BE YE RECONCILED TO GOD.[32]

John Irving has suggested that it was Young's rejection of the Scottish
Common Sense philosophy which led to his theological problems of 1864,
citing J. G. Hume's remark that Young "saw that many of the doctrines of
the Presbyterian Church were moulded in the thought and phraseology of
this philosophy and so he found that he could not teach what he regarded as
erroneous."[33] It is clear that Young, like his colleague Burns, used Common Sense writings in his classes. Thomas Reid's *Essays* and Sir William
Hamilton's *Philosophical Writings* were used as texts in the Junior and
Senior Philosophy classes,[34] though the *Record* pointed out but did not
explain that "the doctrine taught by the Professor is widely different from
the views of Dr. Reid."[35] This would seem to be consistent with the pattern
developed by Scottish evangelicals like Thomas Chalmers, who employed
the Scottish Common Sense philosophy largely as an apologetic tool in
combatting Humean skepticism, but who also infused it with their own
evangelical theology.[36] Moreover, in his classes on Exegetical Theology,
Young used the commentary on Ephesians of the orthodox Charles Hodge
of Princeton Seminary.[37] This suggests that Young was more orthodox
during his Knox College career than is sometimes thought. Indeed, if his
philosophical and theological views were undergoing a transition in the
years 1854-64, it seems that he kept them very much to himself and never
let them become the focus of public discussion.

Though the main theological influences at Knox would seem to have
been British, there are some connections between the Canadian Free
Church and Princeton Seminary. Dr. Robert Burns had been part of the
Scottish Free Church's deputation to the United States in 1844 and had
visited Princeton, though the irascible Burns did not fail to irritate his
hosts. On 21 March 1844 Charles Hodge wrote to William Cunningham

that "Dr. Burns preached a delightful sermon in our chapel last evening. I believe we are all disposed to let him abuse us and our domestic institutions as much as he please, if he will only preach the gospel as purely and spiritually as he did last night."[38] Burns was also a friend of the Professor of Church History at Princeton, Dr. James W. Alexander. The Free Church *Record* gave frequent and favourable reviews of the *Biblical Repertory and Princeton Review*. As Dr. Burns commented on the occasion of the death of Dr. Miller: "It is to these noble theologians at Princeton we are indebted for that treasury of sacred literature and sound theology, 'The Princeton Review,' a periodical which no seminary of theology should be without." As well, Knox students studied Charles Hodge's commentaries on Ephesians and Romans.[39] This connection with Princeton Seminary was fully consistent with the Free Church's evangelical Calvinism. Throughout the nineteenth century, under the leadership of Archibald Alexander, Charles Hodge, and Benjamin Breckinridge Warfield, Princeton was regarded as a bastion of Calvinistic orthodoxy.

The only internal challenge to the Free Church's Calvinistic orthodoxy was the case of Rev. Robert Peden. Peden was born *c.* 1816 in Kilmarnock, Scotland, and educated at the University of Glasgow and the United Secession Theological Hall. He emigrated to Canada and was admitted to the charge of Amherstburg in the Kirk Synod in 1844. That same year he signed Dr. John Bayne's Protest and joined the new Free Church Synod.[40]

Peden's views came to the notice of the church at large in 1847 with the publication of his book, *A Hidden Gospel; the Cause of the Loss of Souls* (114 pp.). The *Record* began to review his book in December 1848. In the eyes of the reviewer Peden had denied the doctrine of particular redemption and held unsound views on conversion. "We would earnestly and affectionately warn our friend," he wrote, "against the more than questionable tendencies of his present views."[41] This review was continued in the February 1849 issue of the *Record*. Objections were raised against Peden's views of election and his downplaying of creeds and confessions. The reviewer asserted that "we do not at all sympathize with those ultra views which would hesitate as to a free and frank invitation to sinners to come to Christ. We are not aware of anything in the view we have set forth of the doctrine of election, that militates against this." "The decrees of God," he argued, "are not meant to influence our conduct at all; it is with the revelation of God only we have to do." Clearly the reviewer was attempting to argue a consistently Calvinistic position over and against Peden's watered-down version.[42] In the March 1849 issue of the *Record* Peden replied to the charge that he advocated the doctrine of universal redemption. Distinguishing between atonement and redemption, Peden argued that:

> there is an unlimited sufficiency in the ransom of the whole world, while I as assuredly believe that none will enjoy the blessings of redemption, but those

who put their trust in the finished work of Christ. . . . Because all do not, and will not enjoy the blessings of redemption, to say that the meritorious work of Christ was neither sufficient for them, nor intended for them, is virtually to say that there was really *no Gospel* to be preached to them, or if it were preached to them, *the very fact of their dying in impenitence is a proof that it was false*, for Christ never died for them—never did or endured anything for them on the cross, and therefore, the very fact of their dying impenitent, would shew that if Christ had ever been exhibited to them as a Saviour *able* to save them, and *willing* to save them, it was false, for they were neither included in the ransom, nor was any price ever paid for them.

Peden based his case scripturally on such passages as I John 2:2; 2 Cor. 5:14; I Tim. 2:4-6, and quoted at length from Thomas Chalmers in attempting to defend his position. In closing his letter he asserted that:

> A universal atonement is necessary to a universal offer, but redemption in the sense of deliverance is only enjoyed by those who put their trust in the atonement, and consequently redemption is particular, as it is restricted in its enjoyment only to believers, just as justification and sanctification are restricted only to such,—and thus it is that a Gospel for every creature, is only redemption to those who believe. [43]

In replying to Peden's letter the editor of the *Record* maintained that Peden had espoused views which were both unscriptural and inconsistent with the Westminster Confession of Faith. Moreover,

> while plausibly appearing to set off to advantage the grace of God, or the grace of the Saviour, they indeed detract from both; reducing the scheme of salvation to a thing uncertain and contingent; and contradicting all that the Word of God sets forth of a covenant of redemption; and of a commutative satisfaction of the Divine law, as implied in the work and death of the sinners' surety.

The reviewer went on to argue that:

> the real question is this:—was the atonement a price paid and accepted for all men alike? or, was it in respect of destination, a meritorious and effectual satisfaction only for many? The question is not of the intrinsic value of Christ's blood. We perceive that Mr. P. blends together the universal destination of the atonement, with its sufficiency (which we delight to affirm no less than he)—to avail every one who shall trust in it. No one denies that the blood of Christ is, in respect of inherent value, sufficient not only to have atoned for all men, but for all creatures—angels as well as men. But, either it was, according to the will of God, a price for all, or it was not. If it was, then the salvation of all must follow: if Christ was made sin for every individual of the human race, justice requires that all shall be "made the righteousness of God in Him." But if Christ was not a sacrifice for all to the effect of securing the deliverance of all; then, in a strict sense, and the only sense relevant to the question, his death was no *price* whatever, and nothing was purchased by it. [44]

In Peden's scheme, the work of the Father in election was separated from the work of the Son in redemption, which in turn was divided from the work of the Holy Spirit in regeneration and effectual calling. Nor, from the reviewer's point of view, was such a doctrine of definite atonement at all inconsistent with the free offer of the gospel.[45]

Robert Peden and his critics were reactivating an old debate in the history of the Christian Church—that of the nature and extent of the atonement of Christ.[46] This debate had been a lively one in Scotland, both within the Church of Scotland and in the secessionist churches. Within the United Secessionist Church, James Morison of Kilmarnock had espoused a view of universal atonement and had been deposed from the ministry.[47] In all likelihood, Peden was a follower of Morison.[48]

Because of his views Peden was called before the Presbytery of London. He failed to appear and instead sent a letter. The Presbytery examined his book and announced that it contained "doctrines at variance with the word of God, and the standards of the Church" and served Peden with a libel. In response to this libel Peden appeared before the Presbytery. The Presbytery sustained their libel, but on account of the wide circulation of Peden's views, sent the case to the Synod "for their judgment, in the hope, that the dangerous and most *pernicious* doctrines advocated by Mr. Peden, may be the more effectually discouraged and condemned."[49]

The case came before the Synod in 1850. Peden appeared and defended his position, admitting that he did hold some of the doctrines he was credited with, and denying that he held others. However, his speech to the house convinced the Synod that he held these other doctrines as well. A Committee was appointed "to meet with Mr. Peden, and endeavour to convince him of the unscriptural and dangerous nature of the doctrines which he holds."[50] After further debate and consideration of the report of this Committee, the Synod sustained the reference from the Presbytery of London and issued a lengthy statement on the atonement. In this they upheld the doctrines of election, effectual calling, regeneration, unmerited grace, and justification by faith. As for Peden's views, they were:

> at direct variance with the aforesaid doctrines, subversive of the fundamental truths of the Gospel and fitted to prove injurious to the souls of men, and in particular that he holds:
> 1. That Christ made atonement in the same sense for all mankind, thereby denying Christ's covenant relation to his people, and effectual satisfaction to justice on their behalf.
> 2. That the fallen sinner does not require a special subjective work of the Holy Spirit in his heart, to enable him to believe in Christ to the saving of his soul.
> 3. That the work of the Spirit in enabling a sinner to believe in Christ unto salvation, is the same in nature and energy, with that which takes place in the heart of a sinner, who resists the Spirit and remains in unbelief and a state of enmity towards God.

4. That faith is a mere intellectual act, and that in a sense which is
inconsistent with the doctrine, that saving faith implies a vital spiritual
principle in the heart, and that its principle acts are of a moral and
spiritual nature, consisting in particular of the "accepting, receiving
and resting upon Christ alone for justification, sanctification and eternal
life."[51]

The Synod suspended Peden, cut the tie between him and the congregation of Amherstburg, and gave to the Presbytery of London the responsibility of dealing with him "with the view of convincing him of the unscriptural
and dangerous nature" of his views. If he refused to abandon these views or
submit to the Presbytery's authority, the Presbytery could depose him.[52]
In actual fact, Peden was eventually deposed. The congregation at
Amherstburg split into two and a property dispute ensued.[53] Those supporting Peden were organized as the Evangelical Union Church—the
name which the Morisonian churches in Scotland used.[54] The Peden case
closed, then, with the Free Church affirming its Calvinistic orthodoxy and
slamming the door on Morisonianism.

Like the Scottish Common Sense philosophy, certain strands of Victorian science were eminently useful in defending the faith, and thus were
complementary to the Free Church's evangelical Calvinism. While the one
provided a necessary antidote to David Hume's skepticism,[55] the other
illustrated and confirmed the work of the Creator. As Carl Berger has
reminded us, natural theology asserted the existence of "an overall design
in nature, a rank and order in the chain of life, and a regularity in the
operation of laws, all of which were evidence of a transcendent guiding
intelligence."[56] At the same time, however, natural theology was never
regarded by evangelicals as wholly adequate in providing answers to their
basic theological questions about the nature and workings of God. Still, it
was important for them to see that the "book of nature" harmonized with
the Word of God. Mark Young Stark, for example, in a lecture on the
Scottish Free Church geologist Hugh Miller, asserted that:

A revelation from God cannot, when properly understood, contradict true
science. God revealed in nature and in his word must ever be consistent with
himself; and so, as science has advanced, and the Bible has been better
understood, the latter has derived many indubitable confirmations of, and
testimonies to its truth from the investigations of scientific men. It is ignorance which causes the antagonism.[57]

Stark's lecture was delivered before the Y.M.C.A. in Dundas, Cobourg,
and Montreal, and printed as a pamphlet. Here was a good example of a
Free Church minister, on the intellectual hustings, preaching the essential
harmony of the Bible and science.

Despite its attempts at popularization, the Free Church in Canada
never developed a separate or systematic response to nineteenth-century
science. Predominantly concerned with geology, it drew upon various

British scientists and theologians, particularly Thomas Chalmers, William Buckland, and Hugh Miller, in an attempt to harmonize the recent evidence for an old earth, with the first chapters of the Book of Genesis. At least until the beginning of the eighteenth century, it was commonly understood that the earth was no more than six thousand years old. Subsequent scientific research challenged this view and prompted a reexamination of the traditional interpretation of Genesis 1 and 2. Two attempts at harmonization are of particular relevance to the Canadian Free Church: the first by Thomas Chalmers, the second by Hugh Miller. Both of these were Church of Scotland Evangelicals who were subsequently prominent in the Free Church of Scotland, Chalmers as first Moderator of the General Assembly, and Professor of Divinity in the Edinburgh Free Church College; Miller as editor of the Edinburgh *Witness* newspaper.

Chalmers' view was that God's creation of the heavens and the Earth preceded the six-day creation. The precise dating of the original creation was not revealed in scripture. In this way, Chalmers could maintain his views on Biblical inspiration and at the same time "could quite nicely fit all the geological activity exposed in the rock record into this presumably vast stretch of time prior to the six days, which Chalmers maintained were truly ordinary days of recreating the Earth from the chaotic condition that followed the original creation."[58] Some comments which William Rintoul made in 1848 point to a similar understanding. "While the world, as now arranged, was the work of a few days," he wrote, "its present arrangement was preceded by a state of darkness and confusion, beyond which it discloses nothing but the sublime fact, that the world was not eternal—that it had a beginning."[59]

Chalmers, William Buckland, and John Pye Smith, despite their differences, had also posited a restitution theory in which "the long periods of time required by geology could adequately be accounted for by assuming that the first two verses of Genesis 1 described a condition that lasted an indeterminate amount of time and preceded the six days of creation."[60] The other popular attempt at harmonization was the "day-age theory" in which the six days of creation were not equated with periods of time of twenty-four hours, but "should be considered as time periods of indeterminate length."[61] Defended by geologists such as Benjamin Silliman of Yale and John William Dawson of McGill, the day-age theory was given classic expression by Hugh Miller. Interestingly enough, theologians like Charles Hodge of the American Old School Presbyterians, and James Orr of the Scottish Free Church, found this theory attractive.

In Stark's commemorative lecture on Hugh Miller, already mentioned, we find an exposition of the day-age theory. Stark began by criticizing Lamarck's developmental theory, arguing that it questioned "the doctrine of the immortality of the soul, because if there be no intermediate acts of creation from the calling into existence of the original monads, or first elements of being, then, in what does man differ from the brute, except in being merely a higher development of dying, perishing creatures." This view, Stark argued, was "atheistical in its tendency, in so far, that if man be not an immortal creature, it matters little to him whether there be a God or not." Yet in Stark's mind, the results of contemporary geology had helped to destroy theories such as Lamarck's.

Stark also made a number of comments about the age of the earth and the creation of man. He suggested that there were geologic ages prior to the creation of man. He rejected the idea that the earth was created as it is with the fossils already in place. The "days" of creation in Genesis 1 and 2 "must have been lengthened periods of time in which, under the inscrutable economy of God, our planet was preparing for its present dispensation, and the reception of man." Moreover, nature provided a mirror of humanity "created in the image of God—having become fallen, corrupt, and degenerate, and this in analogy with the deteriorating process, which is ever operating in nature, according to a universal law, written in the Record of the Rocks, those marvellous, but indisputable chronicles of the Earth's history." God's eternal decrees, he declared, were "engraven . . . in unmistakable and indestructible characters on the face of nature."[62] As for the Mosaic flood, Stark followed Miller in postulating that it had not been universal, but had only covered those sections of the earth inhabited by humans.

While the day-period theory was attractive to Stark, it did not receive universal acceptance within the Free Church. A review in the Free Church *Record* of William Dawson's *Archaia* rejected the "day-period hypothesis" in favour of one in which God's creation of the world was encompassed within a series of creative acts, "in all the departments of organic life up to the time when man appears." The first chapters of Genesis thus contain "a representation of the creation in the form of six literal days in which there is comprehended in epitome all that is necessary for us to know concerning the origin of the physical phenomenon of the universe." In the reviewer's mind, such a view "releases the text from its supposed figurative signification, and Geology from the necessity of discovering certain distinctly marked periods of the creation of the vegetable and animal Kingdom."[63]

From its inception the Free Church was committed to a particular theological system—that of evangelical Calvinism. Thus in the classroom and in the pulpit they emphasized the doctrines of God's sovereignty, Christ's substitutionary atonement, and justification by faith alone. They maintained the Calvinistic view of particular redemption and limited atonement and deposed one of their ministers, Robert Peden, for his rejection of them. On the other hand, the orthodoxy of George Paxton Young, despite suggestions by modern commentators, was never in question.

As might be expected the roots of Free Church theology were British—the Westminster Confession, Paley and Butler, George Hill and Thomas Chalmers, and the Scottish Common Sense school. At the same time they were in touch with the writing of Princeton theologians like Charles Hodge. These two streams would have complemented each other. Thus the Free Church never developed an indigenous theological tradition. They were importers and transmitters rather than innovators.

In their role as apologists for the Christian faith some members of the Free Church saw fit to react to current scientific thinking in the field of geology. Although the denomination as a whole never articulated a particular position on these matters, those who did comment drew on British roots in formulating a reply. In particular they looked to the Scottish journalist and amateur geologist Hugh Miller, and to Thomas Chalmers for guidance. Whatever the specifics of their responsibility, they were careful to assert that religious belief and true science were never in conflict. In short, the Free Church emerged from these controversies with its orthodoxy intact.

Chapter 5

TRANSFORMING THE NATION

Political involvement was a necessary expression of the Free Church's theology. Armed with strong moral sentiments and a profound conviction that a righteous God judged the nations, they acted the part of crusaders in a holy war against intemperance, slavery, Sabbath-breaking and Popery. In so doing they were consistent with their Scottish Covenanting traditions and their Evangelical heritage.

Rejecting the idea that "spiritual" courts should not be involved in political controversy, a suggestion put forth by some Free Church office-bearers during the 1850 debate on the Clergy Reserves and Rectories, the bulk of the church regarded the political arena as a legitimate and necessary place for Christian activity.[1] "Ought Christians to meddle with politics?" the Record asked in an 1856 editorial. "Certainly they ought. Why should the ungodly alone have control of these matters? If Christians stand aloof, it need not be wondered at if our Courts of Parliament and Municipal Councils reflect, not the virtues, but the vices of the people." Addressing, then, the specific issue of the election of aldermen, councillors, and school trustees, the editor argued that "pious as well as intelligent men" must be selected because they "can do much to protect the Sabbath, to repress intemperance, to discourage the horse-race and circus, and promote education." Christian principle, moreover, must replace mere party considerations. "It is high time that God should be acknowledged in politics," he argued, "rulers are instruments employed by God for important ends," and "is it not then a direct insult to the Almighty, to select for his service, men who are notoriously his enemies?"[2] Not only should Christians in general be involved in politics, but ministers must also address themselves to public issues, yet at the same time avoiding becoming a "political agitator, or partizan." Many political questions:

Reference notes for Chapter 5 are found on pp. 155-58.

have a most important and direct bearing on the progress and influence of true religion; and it will not do for ministers to avoid these, under the plea that they lie beyond the limits of their peculiar province. Some of these questions we may specify, such as Education, Popery, Temperance, Slavery. There is no doubt that all these important questions have suffered greatly from this very cause, namely, from a tendency on the part of some ministers to shrink from the responsibility of assuming a distinct position, and giving from the pulpit a certain sound. For this, however, the people are at least as culpable as ministers.[3]

While recognizing their political involvement, many Canadian historians have made an uncritical identification of the Free Church with the Reform Party in the united Canadas. Thus P. B. Waite, citing the Toronto *Leader*, has argued that "the Free Kirk of Scotland, though its adherents numbered only 8 per cent of the population, was the strongest of all the Protestant sects in political energy and almost wholly Reform in politics."[4] Part of the reason for this correlation is the notion that the embodiment of a Free Church politician was George Brown of the Toronto *Globe*. Accordingly, Donald Creighton has written that during the election of 1844, John A. Macdonald "knew . . . that the Scots Presbyterians, upon whose united support he might have counted, had been divided by the 'Great Disruption' between 'Old Kirk' and 'Free Kirk' with the Free Kirkers following the Reformist lead of George Brown and the Toronto *Globe*."[5] Brown and Macdonald, then, personified the Free Kirk and Old Kirk respectively:

> In temperament, character, and convictions, he [Brown] was almost the exact antithesis of Macdonald. A Reformer, a stiff Free Kirker, an ardent voluntaryist who abominated any connection between church and state, a passionately serious dogmatist to whom all compromise and accommodation were alien and difficult, Brown contradicted Macdonald's instinctive habit of thought with the whole force of his downright, positive nature. The two men were almost certain to clash.[6]

That many Free Churchmen were Reformers cannot be denied. Indeed, even in Scotland, most Non-Intrusionists and Free Churchmen were on the Whig/Liberal side in politics.[7] However, the Free Church was not bound by George Brown's political interests and involvement. While many of the Free Church members who sat in the Legislative Assembly and Council were Reformers—William Notman, Joseph C. Morrison, and Adam Ferguson[8]—not all were, at least not all the time. Malcolm Cameron and Isaac Buchanan, both of whom were as active in the Free Church as George Brown, do not fit easily into the Reform mould.[9] At the same time, it is necessary to distinguish between the political activities of individuals, and those of the entire church as expressed by the Synod. In the latter case six political and social issues were addressed during the late 1840s and 1850s: Clergy Reserves and Rectories, King's College, Intemperance, American Slavery, Sabbath-breaking, and Popery.

The question of the Clergy Reserves and Rectories almost immediately confronted the new church. The former, it will be remembered, were established as part of the Constitutional Settlement of 1791, when it was decided to set apart one-seventh of the land in Upper Canada "for the support and maintenance of a protestant Clergy."[10] The precise meaning of this phrase helped exacerbate the controversy for the next half-century. The Church of Scotland Synod, on the strength of its position as one of the Established Churches of the British Empire, agitated for and eventually received a share of these reserves.[11] By 1840 a solution to the Reserves question provided for the Methodists and even the Roman Catholics to share in this patrimony.[12] It was into this situation that the Free Church was plunged following its organization in 1844.

The Canadian Free Church was indeed in an awkward position. Their parent body in Scotland, having severed the connection with the Established Church of Scotland because they felt that they could no longer maintain this position at the same time as being faithful to the Headship of Christ over His Church,[13] had nonetheless not relinquished the establishment principle. As Dr. Thomas Chalmers had declared to the first General Assembly of the Free Church of Scotland:

> The Voluntaries mistake us, if they conceive us to be Voluntaries. We hold by the duty of Governments to give of their resources and their means for the maintenance of a gospel ministry in the land. . . . Though we quit the establishment, we go out on the Establishment principle; we quit a vitiated Establishment, but would rejoice in returning to a pure one.[14]

The Canadian Synod was in a similar situation. They were not opposed to government endowments as such, and firmly held to the principle that governments and nations have a responsibility to acknowledge God in their activities and legislative decisions.

The specific question of Clergy Reserves came before the Free Church Synod at its October 1844 meeting. At that time a Memorial was drafted and forwarded to Governor-General Metcalfe, notifying him of their secession from the Kirk Synod, their reasons for doing so, and seeking a response to the questions:

> whether or not in this position,—maintaining as they do unchanged their Standards of doctrine, discipline, government and worship,—her Majesty's Government will be disposed to continue those allowances from Government enjoyed by some of their number, and secured to them personally, they believe, by a late Imperial statue, and which, indeed, some of them enjoyed before they were admitted into the Synod of the Presbyterian Church in connection with the Church of Scotland.[15]

Indeed, in the election of 1844, various politicians like Francis Hincks, Malcolm Cameron, and the Conservative H. M. Jessup attempted to gain Free Church support by aiding the efforts to receive a share of the Clergy Reserves.[16] By the time that the Synod met again in Cobourg in 1845 it had received a reply from the Office of the Provincial Secretary: in the opinion of the Crown's Law Officers, "said allowances could not be continued on account of the new position in which the Synod stand."[17] Accordingly, the Free Church Synod assumed, for the most part, a position of practical non-endowment. Though a cumbersome phrase, it more accurately describes the Free Church's position than that of voluntaryism. In actual fact, four former United Synod ministers who were now members of the Free Church retained their government allowances under the provisions of the Act of 1840: Robert Boyd, William Smart, James Rogers, and Duncan McMillan each received about £63 *per annum*.[18] Boyd and Smart kept theirs until 1855 when they commuted for about £650 each; Duncan McMillan voluntarily relinquished his around 1846.[19] The editor of the *Record* attempted to justify this situation by asserting that: "As for these three brethren, the Synod has not thought fit to interfere with their own judgment in the matter; seeing their allowances are held by them on purely individual grounds, and not by any engagement to which this Church is a party, and must become void at their death."[20]

Following the election in 1848 of a Baldwinite Reform Ministry, the Free Church again had to make a decision concerning accepting government endowments. There existed at that time a surplus of £1800 from the Clergy Reserve Fund for which one could apply. There was some difference of opinion within the Church as to the most appropriate course of action for the denomination to take. A report in the *Record* indicated that a minister in the Presbytery of Brockville had applied for, and received, an allowance;[21] an Overture from the same presbytery called upon the Synod to "adopt such measures as may secure a just proportion of said fund to the ministers of the Church."[22] Various congregations also applied for money.[23] On the other hand, some members of the Free Church laity like the Browns of Toronto had finally adopted an anti-endowment policy, particularly in the wake of Sir Robert Peel's grant to the Roman Catholic college at Maynooth, Ireland.[24] Moreover, an editorial in the *Record* argued that if the Free Church "after her recent experience of the Lord's goodness, were to go back to take a Government allowance in the company of the present recipients of them, then would her glory be indeed departed."[25] Thus when the Synod met in Toronto in 1848 it passed a series of resolutions, affirming the duty of the civil magistrate to protect and support the church, but asserting that the question of using public funds to support the church was a secondary matter and might be settled "on the grounds of Christian expediency." Having set the ground rules, the Synod declared:

> That, however justifiable the retention of endowments received under different circumstances may be, the Synod looking to the conduct of the Government of this country in now offering endowments to religious bodies without reference to the distinctions between truth and error—to the divisions and

jealousies which the acceptance of endowments in present circumstances would occasion—to the strong feeling which prevails throughout the Church that their acceptance would tend to diminish the usefulness of ministers and the liberality of the people in contributing to the support of the Gospel—and to the evil influence which an irreligious Government might exert through the dependence upon the State, which such endowments would occasion—the Synod is of opinion that it would be deeply injurious to the interests of the Presbyterian Church of Canada, and to the cause of the Redeemer in this land, to accept in present circumstances of any grant of public money from the Government.[26]

Thus the Synod refused to accept allowances from the Government and forbade all ministers and congregations from taking independent action in this matter. Moreover, they set up a commission which, along with the Presbyteries, was to deal with "erring Congregations, and to endeavour by affectionate dealing with them to induce and persuade them to give up the false position which they have assumed and especially to return without delay any money which they may have received from the government."[27]

The Free Church's opposition to the Clergy Reserves and the Rectories did not remain a matter of internal discussion, but became one of the foci for Free Church political action. At the Synod of 1850 Dr. Burns put forward a motion calling for the lands held as Reserves and Rectories to be appropriated for education—Academies and Common Schools—"and that in both, the Word of God shall be distinctly recognized as the basis; and as the guardian of education." The Synod passed Burns' motion, defeated one which regarded the discussion as involving a spiritual court in a political question, and set up a committee to draft a memorial which could be presented to the Government.[28]

For a time, however, in 1849-50, various Free Church members were divided on the Clergy Reserves issue—though more on tactics than on ideology. Thus Dr. Burns sided with Lesslie of the *Examiner* and Malcolm Cameron in their more radical Clear Grit attitude, over and against Willis, Gale, and the Browns who supported the Baldwin/Lafontaine position. However, by 1851 the Free Churchmen were united in advocating immediate government action on the reserves.[29] In that same year they supported J. C. Morrison's bill to repeal the rectories by annulling the 1791 Constitutional Act. This action succeeded in placing an obstacle between the Reform ministry and the Free Church which, in the words of one commentator, made them a "solid block, hostile to the government." When in 1851 the Clear Grits supported the Hincks/Morin governments in their equivocal stand on the reserves, Cameron became *persona non grata* with the Free Church.[30]

A Committee of Synod was appointed throughout these years 1850-55 to make known the Free Church's position on these matters. In 1851 a petition from this Committee was presented in the Assembly by Hon. James H. Price.[31] In June 1853, an editorial in the *Record* asserted that:

when it is manifest that State endowments, as in our case can only be enjoyed at the expense of civil peace and prosperity, and of charity and confidence and co-operation and hopeful prospects of union among the several sections of the evangelical Church, we find it difficult, without imputing very unworthy motives, to understand how any man, or number of men, can be induced to ask or take or retain such ill-omened advantages.

Moreover, under the present system both "truth and error, evangelical religion and anti-christian superstition" are supported.[32]

Some members of the Free Church, like Hon. Adam Fergusson of Woodhill, James Shaw, and Peter Brown, were involved in the Anti-Clergy Reserve Association.[33] As well, others worked behind the scenes at election time. Though he lost badly, Isaac Buchanan, who had supported Metcalfe in 1844, ran against Allan MacNab in Hamilton on an anti-reserves platform.[34] MacNab was not trusted by such Free Churchmen as George Paxton Young. In July 1854, Young wrote to Buchanan suggesting that the latter get the Hamilton *Banner* to pressure MacNab to make known his views on the issue.[35] Young had tried to get George Brown to run against MacNab and had written to George's brother Gordon that, "It would be a great triumph for your brother to unseat Sir Allan."[36] Finally, when the new clergy reserve bill was being discussed in 1854 the Free Church expressed its disapproval of the clauses allowing ministers and churches to commute their shares.[37]

The Free Church opposed the existing constitution of King's College, Toronto, and made repeated calls for an end to its "sectarian character." Accordingly, a petition from the Commission of Synod, dated 10 October 1845, called for the establishment of a University of Toronto "to be entirely freed from all sectarian attachments, and made exclusively a School of Literature and Science on the broadest base, and on the most liberal principles." Moreover, the management of the college should be vested in a group elected by the Legislature. Their oppositions to King's was based, not only on a desire to see its patrimony benefit the whole community, but also on the fact that it was currently dominated by the Church of England—"a sect hostile to evangelical truth and charity."[38] A committee of Synod was formed in 1848, with Dr. Burns as Convener, to watch over any bill to amend King's charter and to petition Parliament on the matter.[39]

One of the Free Church's most outstanding critics of King's College was Dr. Robert Burns. In a series of open letters to Governor-General Elgin, published in the *Banner* in 1847-48, he put forth his position. He argued against any partition of the funds of the college; to do so, he asserted, would be "unpatriotic and pernicious." The financial affairs should be distinct from the "literary" department and should be overseen by an independent board which would be responsible to the Legislature. Nominations to chairs should be made by a board of governors or trustees chosen periodically by the Legislature and "representing different colonial interests." The "test" should be kept as it is. However, while all chairs of theology and theological education should be excluded this "will not be understood as excluding all practical religion on principles generally acknowledged."[40] He was accordingly critical of any attempts to prevent religious observances from being authorized by the college authorities. "There seems to be *less danger* to be apprehended," he maintained, "from leaving a wide discretion on this subject to the existing managers of the Institution than by an authoritative exclusion of religious forms in every shape." Indeed, he argued that:

> It appears to me altogether preposterous to legislate *at all* for the education of the people in the absence of religious sanctions. And can there be any sense of moral obligation independently of the being of God and man's responsibility to him? Can sound morals be separated from the fear of God and the sanctions of the Divine law? Can Christianity and the Holy Scriptures be set aside without practically setting aside all visible religion? And can that education be safe which is wholly detached from all religious associations? Yea, are we entitled to banish from all schemes of College reform that which is placed in the very front of the Charter of erection?

Religion was thus the handmaiden of education. To suggest that one could inculcate a set of moral precepts apart from God's revealed will in Scripture, was, to Burns, absurd. Burns eschewed what he called sectarianism (meaning denominationalism) and, advocating instead a common Christianity, asked, "is there no medium between exclusively sectarian opinions, and the shoreless sea of godlessness?"[41]

Robert Baldwin's University Bill of 1849 aimed at the creation of a single degree-granting, non-sectarian, provincial university. It abolished the Chair of Divinity and prohibited both religious tests and clergymen from serving as either Chancellor or President. While theological colleges were allowed to affiliate, they were barred from sharing its endowment.[42] Because it helped end the domination by any one religious denomination of a university which was regarded as the common property of all the citizens of Canada West, the Free Church was reasonably pleased with its provisions. The editor of the *Record*, while defending the bill against charges that it was "ungodly and unchristian," did complain that it was not explicit enough about Christianity. Yet he did argue that "if the bill pass into law, and be made to operate against the religion of the Saviour, then must the guilt lie in the community at large, and especially the professedly christian part of it."[43] Moreover, "if it became law, and be worked by good men, it will be worked in favour of religion."[44]

Baldwin's bill, however, did not achieve its aims. Queen's and Victoria Colleges survived, and the Anglicans under Bishop John Strachan established their own church-based college, Trinity. A further attempt to solve the University Question, Francis Hincks' bill of 1853, made the University of Toronto an "examining body" while leaving the actual teaching to University College. It also provided for affiliate colleges to share any surplus which the endowment fund might accumulate.[45]

The issue of dividing the University College endowment among denominational colleges reappeared in 1859-60.[46] The bulk of the Free Church was still opposed to any such division. This is not surprising, as University College "seemed more an adjunct of the Free Church than a national institution."[47] A petition from the Knox College Board of Management argued that the endowment could not be divided "without endangering the whole system of national education, fostering religious strife and jealousy in the community, and virtually lending the national sanction and support to systems of religious error."[48] Dr. Willis, on the other hand, supported dividing the endowment.[49] Always a strong believer in the principle of church establishment, Willis also envisaged government money extricating Knox College from its financial difficulties. Indeed, he felt so strongly about the issue that he temporarily resigned from the College and the Synod.[50]

Although the movement to end the High-Church Anglican dominance of King's College has been termed "secularization" this term is apt to be misleading when applied to the Free Church attitude. Certainly they wanted an end to sectarianism. At the same time, they saw Christian men operating the system and teaching the courses. "We see no infidelity or antichristianism in the Common School Act, or the College Bill," declared the *Record* in June 1849, "so long as they allow religious men to conduct the system of education which they severally originate, in harmony with Christian truth, and in subordination to it."[51]

The Free Church advocated a strict observance of the Fourth Commandment—"Remember the sabbath day, to keep it holy." They were careful to point out to their own members and adherents their responsibilities and duties concerning this aspect of God's law and engaged in public and political agitation in an attempt to suppress Sabbath-desecration—particularly in the post offices and on the canals and railroads. So vigorous were their attempts to ensure a proper observance of the Lord's Day that the Toronto *Leader* in 1857 was prompted to remark that "those Free Church fanatics are advocating the abolition of the Sabbath Day!"[52]

A good illustration of the Free Church's attitude to the Sabbath was their Pastoral Address of 1853. This outlined what was regarded as the Biblical basis for their views on the Sabbath, arguing in part that "It is enshrined in the very heart of the decalogue, and is surrounded by commands which are looked upon as universally binding."[53] Thereafter it delineated both "public abuses" and "social abuses" of the Sabbath. In the former category were labour in the post office, and on the canals, stages, steamboats, and trains.[54] The government, it asserted, had been "converted into a gigantic Sabbath desecrator, setting an example which, if followed by all classes of the community, would speedily annihilate the Sabbath." Because of such abuses others were also forced to work on the

Sabbath, thus depriving workers of "rights which we deem sacred, and . . . [consigning them] to a slavery as unnatural as it is unnecessary." Under the category of "social abuses" were listed social visiting; travelling, including "pleasure excursions" and business travel; harvesting crops; "indulgence in light reading" whether the "polluting pages of some novel," newspapers, history or science books or even religious literature; letter reading and writing.[55] Instead, the entire Sabbath day was to be devoted to "the exercise of God's worship, excepting only such portions of it as acts of necessity and mercy may require."[56]

Private abuses might well be the focus of discipline by Kirk Sessions; public abuses, however, necessitated political action. Individuals and congregations were encouraged to petition Parliament, organize associations, sponsor lectures and circulate tracts. In Kingston, for example, Rev. R. F. Burns was prominent in the Sabbath Reformation Society. Indeed, he has been described as "the outstanding leader of the sabbatarian cause" in Canada West. His Sabbath Alliance, which was founded in 1852, organized demonstrations in Toronto, and after a series of defeats in the Parliament, was successful in 1859 in securing the Sunday closing of saloons.[57]

The Free Church *Record* published a model petition for the use of their readers, which was addressed specifically to the problem of Sunday labour in the Post Office.[58] George Brown repeatedly presented these petitions in Parliament where he met regular defeat until 1860 when Sunday work in the Post Office was voluntarily abolished.[59] The Free Church also maintained a committee on Sabbath observance which corresponded with its Parliamentary counterpart.[60]

The Sabbath question was intimately related to the larger issue of national responsibility and God's judgment upon nations. Citing Nehemiah 13, the *Record* in 1850 asserted that "if we quietly and passively submit to the perpetuation of a great national outrage against the Lord of the Sabbath, need we wonder if He visit us with national judgments." As well, it was asserted that "the Sabbath supplies a thermometer by which the religious temperature in individuals and communities may be tested. Just in proportion as it is observed or neglected will religion flourish or decline."[61]

The Free Church's "War Against Vice"[62] embraced not only sabbath-breaking, but also extended to such "worldly amusements" as the theatre and dancing, and to the sin of intemperance. However, not all Free Churchmen regarded drinking as necessarily sinful. Thus, in the Synod of 1847, during a debate on a case from the Côté Street Church, Montreal, in which the Kirk Session had disciplined a man for trafficking in liquor, John Bayne put forth a motion which, while commending the Session for its "zeal . . . and their efforts to promote purity of communion," yet

> urge upon them the importance of avoiding every thing which might have the least appearance of an arbitrary or capricious application of general rules in

the exercise of discipline, more especially with reference to matters in which difference of opinion may exist, even among Christians, as to the line of distinction between what is lawful and what is unlawful.[63]

Yet, by the early 1850s the Free Church had taken a decided stand on the side of total abstinence. Indeed, some of the Free Church's college students organized The Knox College Temperance Society which was described as a "total abstinence association."[64]

There seems to have been two principal reasons for the Free Church's advocacy of temperance. By many intemperance was regarded as a sinful practice, one which if engaged in by church members brought shame to the church and was an obstacle to evangelism. Secondly, intemperance was seen as a social evil—causing great harm to individuals, families, and society itself—and was "the main source of crime in our land."[65] Thus Rev. P. Gray of Norval, in an article based on the text Romans 14:21: "It is good neither to eat flesh, nor to drink wine, nor any thing whereby thy brother stumbleth, or is offended, or is made weak," railed against intemperance as "a deadly enemy of the gospel of Christ, and . . . one of the sorest plagues to our fellow-creatures as denizens of this world."[66] Or as the editor of the *Record* argued in 1849, only the gospel can make a drunk sober, but "men can strive against a common enemy, and by enforcement of external prudential rules, may be co-workers with the Author of the great remedy—may be the instruments in His hand, of promoting the moral regeneration of perishing souls."[67] Accordingly, the Free Church was involved in lobbying the legislature for a law to suppress totally "the importation, manufacture, and sale of intoxicating drinks as a beverage."[68] In April 1853 Malcolm Cameron's bill was commended to the readership of the *Record* as "more stringent than the famous Maine law, and so much the better. Nothing short of it will suit Canada."[69]

The Synod of 1853 admonished Kirk Sessions to be more diligent "in dealing with those who, by intemperance or tippling habits, bring a reproach on the Church, and on the cause of Christ" and called upon all ministers, office-bearers, and members "to pursue such a course, in regard to the use of intoxicating drinks, as shall bear the most decided practical testimony against the sin of intemperance, remove temptation from themselves, and free them from the serious responsibility of countenancing the use of intoxicating drinks by others."[70]

The following year the Synod resolved "to adopt and advocate the practice of total abstinence from intoxicating drinks as a beverage, as essential to the full influence of the Church in the world as well as on its own adherents."[71] Thus, although some Free Church ministers and members may have continued to drink moderately, the official position was one of total abstinence. Nor was their position one peculiar to themselves, as they participated with other evangelical churchmen in such associations as the Toronto Temperance Reformation Society,[72] and the Montreal Temperance Society where John Redpath was a leading member.[73]

In most discussions of the temperance movement in mid-nineteenth-century Ontario great stress has been given to American influence, to regarding temperance as a means of social control, and as embodying middle-class bourgeois values.[74] F. L. Barron, for example, has argued that the working classes were the primary objects of the temperance and Sabbatarian crusades. They were intended to keep the workers sober and punctual, while for their advocates, the principles they embodied helped in "defining the means to middle class status." Yet the Free Church's concern was not addressed exclusively to the working classes. Indeed, in 1847 the Session of Côté Street Church, Montreal, refused to allow any of its members to take communion who "trafficked in wine and spiritous liquors" and were supported by the Synod in this. Clearly, in this case the object of the discipline would have been a member of the merchant class. While the Free Church was alive to the social costs of intemperance, they were also concerned about the obstacles which it placed in the way of evangelism, and about the shame and dishonour which in their view it brought to Christ and His church.

Temperance and Sabbatarianism were not the only crusades with which the Free Church was involved. Like many other Victorians, on both sides of the Atlantic, they were forced to respond to a revived Roman Catholicism. The Free Church took a decided stand in opposition to "Popery" both on theological and political grounds. Not only did they regard it as wrong theologically and biblically but they also saw it posing a serious threat to civil and religious liberty.[75] In 1848 the *Record* described Popery as "the masterpiece of Satan's policy in the world. For while it is essentially opposed to the Religion of the Son of God, it yet counterfeits it in all its prominent features; and so it has a shew of Apostolicity, Catholicity, and unity."[76] In August 1850 the *Record* argued that: "If we would secure civil and religious liberty for ourselves and our posterity, and deliver our country from the blighting influence of Rome, let us labour, not as some would, for the destruction of Romanists, but with spiritual weapons let us seek the destruction of their system."[77] This was certainly a prime motivation in the evangelism of French Canada. An editorial in the July 1853 *Record* thus commented that:

> Surely, however, the political influence which they wield, the manner in which that influence has of late blasted measures that we would have hailed with joy, and the mournful scenes connected with popery, which we have witnessed, will lead the members of our Church in Canada West to strive to do something in order to remove the ignorance and superstitious blindness of the *habitans*. This motive we mention as a selfish one, secondary to the ever-binding command of our Saviour—to preach the gospel to every creature, and to be added to the desire engendered in the heart of every true Christian, to give to others also a share of what he possesses, of the knowledge of the true God, and Jesus Christ his Son, for this is life eternal.[78]

Accordingly, the Free Church was a warm and active supporter of the French Canadian Missionary Society. In 1857 the Society's officers and committeemen included such Free Churchmen as John Redpath, James Court, D. Fraser, and A. F. Kemp.[79] For many years the Society was designated as one of the Synod's annual collections and was commended as assisting "the advancement of sound Protestantism in opposition to soul-enthralling and soul-ruining error."[80]

Sir Robert Peel had already outraged Protestant sensibilities by his endowment of a Roman Catholic college at Maynooth, Ireland. As Peter Brown expressed it: "England, Protestant England, as a nation is about to renounce all distinctions between right and wrong in matters of religion, and is forming a State alliance [with] the man of Sin. We stand amazed."[81] If they were outraged by the actions of 1845, they were infuriated by the Papacy's decision in 1850 to restore the territorial diocesan system to the English Roman Catholic Church—something which had not been done since the Reformation.[82] This "Papal Aggression" of 1850-51, coming in the wake of Puseyite inroads into the Church of England, had all the makings of a worldwide Popish conspiracy. Indeed, Dr. Robert Burns, participating in a debate in Simcoe on the Clergy Reserves and Rectories question, declared that "an alliance *will be* formed between the High Church body of the West and the Papists of the East, to crush the liberties of our land." Moreover, Burns, in reflecting on his actions in Scotland in 1829 in opposing Catholic Emancipation, asserted that "assuredly the present aggressions of Popery are just the filling up of what the friends of Protestantism then anticipated."[83] At the Synod of 1851 a series of resolutions on this subject were moved by Dr. Burns. It was asserted that Popery was "a system of Religious Error and Ecclesiastical Despotism, at war with the civil interests of mankind." It characterized the recent attempts to set up a Hierarchy in Britain "as a direct assumption of Papal supremacy, . . . to be resisted by every constitutional means, on the part of a Protestant Government." It also condemned such dangerous trends as the endowment of Roman Catholic schools and colleges, and any claims to restore the Jesuit Estates. Finally, it called Protestants to unity, spirituality, and prayer, and for Ministers to educate their people against "the Errors of Popery."[84]

The wider Protestant community of Toronto responded to the Papal Aggression with the Protestant Alliance.[85] Backed by George Brown, this group aimed at a transdenominational group united to oppose Popery, and

> to maintain and defend, against all its encroachments, the scriptural doctrines of the Reformation, and the principles of religious liberty, as the best security, under God, for the temporal and spiritual welfare and prosperity of this Province; and further, by scriptural means, hereafter to be specified, to aim at the conversion of Roman Catholics to the pure faith of the gospel.[86]

The Free Church *Record* warmly supported such a Movement, as "not only expedient, but necessary." "It is high time," the editor asserted, "for something being done for uniting Protestants in an intelligent, scriptural, mild, but still firm opposition to Popery, as being a system directly opposed to the social and political, as well as to the moral and spiritual interests of any community."[87]

In 1853, in the wake of the Gavazzi riots in Quebec City and Montreal, the Synod defended "that distinguished Italian refugee" and called upon the Legislature "to discriminate carefully betwixt those matters of conscience which no public law can reach, and those systems of priestcraft which are based on allegiance to a foreign power, and are in their tendency inimical to the rights of loyal subjects, and the interests of public morals and of the public safety."[88]

The Corrigan murder case in St. Sylvestre, Canada East, and Bishop Charbonnel's pastoral of January 1856, evoked harsh sentiments from the Free Church, as it did from many Upper Canadian Protestants.[89] The *Record* accordingly declared in March 1856 that "The time has come, when Protestants can no longer make concessions, or temporize with Popery. It is time that the Protestantism of the country were thoroughly roused, and practical measures adopted for checking the encroachments of insidious Jesuits and grasping Ecclesiastics."[90]

In short, the Free Church viewed a revived Roman Catholicism as a threat to the political, social, and religious interests of Canada. The Montreal-based *Canadian Presbyter*, for instance, argued that to separate Church and state or "religion from the conduct of public affairs" was not only wrong, and virtually impossible, but would not obliterate such a threat. Asserting that George Brown himself held this mistaken idea, it argued for denying support to Roman Catholicism, "not on the poor footing of the separation of Church and State, but on the ground of an intelligent disapproval of the whole system of Popery, as detrimental to the highest interests of the State, or Common Weal."[91]

In the minds of many Free Churchmen there were definite links among these four issues: Clergy Reserves, Temperance, Sabbath-breaking, and Popery. Affirming as they did that nations were responsible to God for the conduct of their affairs, and that God blessed those individuals and nations which honoured Him, and visited with His judgments those who did not, they had a powerful motivation for speaking out on these issues. An editorial of January 1854 thus pointed to these four issues and asserted:

> Let us all, under a deep sense of our responsibility, combine our energies and prayers, in order to remove the evils and vices which, alas, too extensively prevail among us, and to render our country moral—sober—religious. Then we may expect, that "God, even our own God, will bless us," and that we, as individuals, as families, and, as a community, shall experience the blessedness of those "whose God is the Lord"![92]

Moreover, the Free Church Synod railed against the evils of slavery, and against their American Presbyterian brethren who tolerated it. Free

Churchmen were prominent in such ventures as the Anti-Slavery Society of Canada—Dr. Michael Willis acted as its President[93]—and as a denomination they operated a mission to free slaves and other blacks in the western sections of Canada West.

The Free Church conscience was outraged by the "Double Shuffle" of August 1858.[94] The *Record* denounced Macdonald's actions, declaring that "we . . . cannot but look upon it as fitted to demoralize the community, and familiarize the public mind with trickery and perjury." "If such corruption prevails at the fountain," they asked, "what can we look for in the streams?"[95] The *Canadian Presbyter* was even more outspoken. Declaring the right of those who were "guardians of morals and piety" to protest against violations of the law of God, they denounced the actions of Macdonald's government as legally questionable, and as having "insulted the Majesty of Heaven by taking a deceptive oath." They also took the opportunity to lecture their "voluntary friends," arguing that "this is an instance in point . . . of what we mean by the magistrate, in his official capacity, having regard to the revealed Word of God." "Reverence for the thrice-hallowed name of God is the bulwark of justice," they asserted; "let this once be broken down, and our national glory as a God-fearing people will be destroyed."[96]

In many ways the Free Church adopted a strict attitude towards society. They eschewed various practices which they regarded as "worldly" and "carnal." The Presbytery of Kingston, for example, declared in August 1857 that:

> in their opinion, horse-racing, public balls, circuses, and theatres, are decidedly injurious to morality and vital godliness, and ought not to be engaged in, attended upon, nor in any way countenanced by the members of the Church, as staining the purity of christian character, offending pious brethren, and bringing scandal upon the Church, as well as endangering their own safety.[97]

The Free Church's political activities were, for the most part, restricted to questions of public morality—Sabbath-breaking,, Popery, Slavery, Clergy Reserves and Rectories, the University question, and temperance. These included many of the most important and controversial issues in mid-nineteenth-century Canada. The Free Church, however, sought influence, rather than power. Those politicians seeking Free Church support would find it to be a two-edged sword, for while it might help them gain office, it forbade the kinds of compromises which were often necessary to retain power.

The desire for moral reform was not an exclusively Free Church concern, but was shared by many Methodists, Baptists, and Congregationalists. Indeed, most moral reformation societies in mid-nineteenth-century Canada were inter-denominational and evangelical in character. At the same time, Free Churchmen, both clerical and lay, gave conspicuous leadership to these societies, including R. F. Burns in the Sabbatarian cause, Michael Willis in the Anti-Slavery Society and Elgin Association, George Brown in the anti-popery crusade, Peter Brown in the Toronto City Mission, and John Redpath in the Montreal Temperance movement.

Yet the Free Church in particular conceived of moral reform in the context of national responsibility and a covenanted nation. They drew these themes from their Scottish background and applied them to the Canadian scene.

Chapter 6

AN EDUCATED MINISTRY

> A good theological college is the sheet anchor of every
> Christian Church, the source, humanly speaking, of its
> internal purity and prosperity, and the mainspring of its
> evangelistic and missionary power.
>
> — *Record* (December 1848)

In 1844 the Free Church began with a contingent of ministers who had received their education abroad, in the universities and theological halls of Aberdeen, Glasgow, and Edinburgh. This was a situation that could not be expected to continue indefinitely, and could at best only hope to fill part of the requirements of an expanding church.

Despite its shortage of ministers the Free Church was very cautious in admitting those from other denominations. Ministers from the Kirk Synod who wished to join the Free Church had to do so by September 1844 by subscribing to one of its "Protests" of the previous summer. Hereafter, ministers from the Church of Scotland were effectively barred from entering the Free Church. The admission of ministers from other churches was regulated by an act which distinguished "the ministers and licentiates of Churches strictly and intimately in connection with this Church" from "all others making application to any Presbytery for admission into the Church." Never explicitly defined, the churches in intimate connection were undoubtedly the Free Church of Scotland and the Presbyterian Church of Ireland. A presumption of soundness and theological orthodoxy was made in their favour and they were easily and readily admitted. A more rigorous examination was required of all others.[1]

The slavery issue placed another restriction on the admission of ministers. Almost since its inception the church had protested against the evils of the institution of slavery and in 1845, 1851, and 1853 had both denounced it and chided the American Old School Presbyterians for their equivocal stand. In 1856 the Synod, responding to an Overture from the Presbytery

---

Reference notes for Chapter 6 are found on pp. 158-60.

of London, instructed its Presbyteries "in dealing with applicants for admission into the ministry of our Church from the United States, to satisfy themselves respecting the views of such applicants on the resolutions of 1853 anent Slavery."[2]

The New School Presbyterians posed a different problem. In 1858 and 1859 the question of "fraternal intercourse" with this church arose. A deputee from the New School General Assembly addressed the Free Church Synod on the principles and work of his denomination. Dr. Michael Willis convened a committee to investigate the New School and reported that, while appreciating the New School's stand against slavery, and admitting the existence of some common ground between the two churches, significant differences still remained outstanding "not so much on sovereign electing grace, or faith, or the work of the Spirit, as on the extent of the atonement, and the imputation of guilt and righteousness in the Adamic and Christian covenants."[3] For this reason a formal recognition was declined. The supply of British Presbyterian ministers was thus uncertain, the admission of American ones problematic. A native-trained ministry was essential. This was recognized by the *Record*'s editor who commented in October 1845 that the seminary was "manifestly under God, the great hope of our Church, and ought to be a chief object of our prayers and efforts—for it is abundantly clear that no adequate supply of labourers for the harvest of this land is likely to be obtained but from among the youth of this country."[4] Peter Brown reiterated these thoughts in the *Banner*, arguing that the college "lies at the very foundation of the prosperity of the Church. It is only necessary to give a glance at the evils which afflict a church, when the fitness and qualifications of those preparing for the ministry are not attended to."[5]

In mid-November 1844, then, class began in a "small upper room" in Richmond Street, Toronto, for the education of "young men of pious character and suitable gifts who may be aiming at the ministry."[6] What has been described as the "first regular College Hall" was located in James Street in a room containing "a long deal table, two wooden benches, a few chairs, and a range of shelves, containing Mr. Esson's library and some books kindly lent by clergymen and other friends for the use of the students during the session." In 1845-46 the college moved to Adelaide Street.[7] For a number of years afterwards, the college was housed in rented quarters on Front Street. By 1856 it had moved to Elmsley Villa at the head of Spadina Avenue, formerly the Government House during Lord Elgin's tenure of office.[8]

In the first year classes were conducted by Rev. Andrew King of St. Stephen's, Glasgow, one of the deputies of the Free Church of Scotland, now designated as Interim-Professor of Divinity. He was joined by Rev. Henry Esson, formerly minister of St. Gabriel Street Church, Montreal, and now Professor of Science and Literature. King taught systematic theology, using the first twenty-one chapters of the Westminster Confession of Faith as his text, and advanced Hebrew. Esson taught the preparatory class, involving Latin, Greek, junior Hebrew, philosophy, and ecclesiastical history.[9]

Student numbers grew steadily in the early years, but seemed to fluctuate latterly. In 1844 fourteen students were in attendance, six of whom were former students of Queen's College, Kingston.[10] By 1847 the college contained forty-four students; in 1853 there were fifty-two; in 1860 there were about forty; and in 1861 about forty-five.[11] The Roll of Synod for 1859 contained some fifty ministers who had attended the college for at least part of their education.[12]

Many of the lecturers in the early years were interim appointments: deputies from the Free Church of Scotland like Andrew King, Michael Willis, and Robert McCorkle, or ministers from within the Canadian Synod such as William Rintoul, Alexander Gale, and John Bayne. The first permanent addition to the faculty was Rev. Henry Esson, appointed Professor of Literature and Science in 1844, a position he held until his death in 1853. Rev. Robert Burns of Paisley, a former editor of the *Edinburgh Christian Instructor*, and the father of the Glasgow Colonial Society, was appointed Professor of Theology in 1844-45, a post he held concurrently with the pastorship of Knox Church, Toronto, until 1847 when the Synod divided the two positions. Burns thus gave up his chair and remained in the pastorate for the next nine years.[13]

The most important addition to the college faculty was Dr. Michael Willis. Described as "a scholar of some eminence" by D. C. Masters,[14] Willis was a man of pastoral experience, vast theological knowledge, and decidedly evangelical convictions. He had been raised in the Original Burgher Synod, one of the secessionist churches of Scotland, had taught theology in their Divinity Hall, and with most of them had joined the Church of Scotland in 1839. In 1843 he joined the Free Church of Scotland, though he seems to have had reservations about some of the more extreme claims put forth by its apologists.[15] In 1845-46 he served as Interim-Professor of Divinity. Though he returned to Glasgow in the spring of 1846, by late autumn 1847 he was back in Canada and was inducted into the Chair of Divinity on 16 December 1847.[16] Willis acted as Principal from this point on, though his official title was Primarius Professor of Divinity. His appointment as Principal came in 1857 on the eve of the college's incorporation.[17]

When Esson died in 1853 John Bayne of Galt was offered his position but declined,[18] and George Paxton Young was appointed, leaving the pastorate of Knox Church, Hamilton to teach mental and moral philosophy. Because of certain theological difficulties with the Westminster Confession of Faith Young later abandoned the teaching of theology and had an intermittent relationship with Knox College. He was to become prominent as Professor of Logic, Metaphysics, and Ethics in University College, Toronto.[19]

In 1856 a third theological chair was established and Dr. Robert Burns was appointed Professor of Church History and Christian Evidence. Professor Young was moved from evidences to exegetical theology, while Willis remained as Primarius Professor of Theology and Principal of the College.[20] A tutor was also temporarily employed to assist students whose previous education was deficient. In 1855, for example, the tutor was regarded as necessary because "the great majority of the young men who come to Toronto to study for the ministry are unable to profit by the Latin and Greek classes as at present conducted in University College." This problem was apparently solved as the tutorship was abandoned in 1857.[21]

At the same time a closer relationship was evolving between Knox and University College. Some students who intended to enter Knox College were attending classes in University College, and for this reason in 1856, the abandonment of the first year of the Arts course was considered.[22] In 1857 the opening and closing dates of the term at Knox were changed to 1 October and 1 April to correspond to those of University College.[23] Some Knox students were also being taught Hebrew outside the College in 1855, an arrangement not to the Synod's satisfaction.[24]

Some prospective Knox students also attended the Free Church's grammar school, Toronto Academy. Established in 1846 because of the perceived failure of the Provincial schools to provide an education with sufficient religious content, its first and only Principal was Rev. Alexander Gale, formerly minister at Amherstburg, Lachine and Hamilton. Gale was at the same time Professor of Classical Literature in Knox College. He was joined on the Academy faculty by Rev. Thomas Wightman, a future Moderator of the Free Church Synod, and Thomas Henning, formerly of the High School of Quebec.[25] Prior to the formation of the Academy, Henry Esson had conducted a school for boys which was abandoned in 1846. Toronto Academy was to be "conducted with the economy and vigour of a Scottish High School or Academy" while, like Dr. Duff's institution in Calcutta, it was to "be pervaded throughout with the influence of Bible Truth."[26] It was designed in part to provide a good education for those intending to enter Knox College, as well as helping "to educate those admitted to the College, whose early education had been defective."[27] Its curriculum included subjects like bookkeeping in addition to English, mathematics, and classics.[28] During its first two years, some 267 students attended the Academy. Two of William Lyon Mackenzie's sons attended, as did Thomas Moss, later Chief Justice of Ontario.[29] Although the administrative structure of the Academy had undergone some modifications by 1847 there was still an "intimate connection" between it and Knox College.[30]

This connection was severed officially in 1849, a move partly prompted, no doubt, by financial strains on the college. A new plan envisaged the Academy embracing "all evangelical denominations and the inhabitants at large." A proposal was thus made to raise £1000 by selling £5 shares in a joint-stock company.[31] Financial difficulties seem to have afflicted the Academy in 1850-52 and it faded out of existence after this.[32]

In content and scope the curriculum of Knox College reflected the Free Church's Scottish Calvinist tradition. In 1846-47 the course of study included Latin, Greek, Hebrew, mathematics, mental philosophy, moral philosophy, biblical criticism, rhetoric, evidences of natural and revealed religion, systematic theology, church history and pastoral theology.[33] In 1848, however, Burns and Esson clashed over this curriculum. In March of that year Burns issued a printed circular to the members of the College Committee, calling for the tightening of admission requirements and the hiring of an additional professor in "mental training, or philosophical education." He argued that the present system was deficient with regard to English composition, elocution, and philosophy. As for the latter, he wanted greater attention to "a plain common-sense view of the powers cand capacities of the human mind, with rules for their improvement" along with an examination of the nature of evidence, logic and the Scottish Common Sense critique of idealism. He also suggested that the curriculum include modern geology, Christian ethics and pastoral theology.[34] These proposals were put before the College Committee on 8 April 1848. Esson objected to them, arguing that they gave preference to logic over moral philosophy, were impractical, and also elevated the study of logic over that of psychology.[35]

By the middle of the 1850s the curriculum at Knox had reached a fairly settled state. That which was submitted to the Synod of 1855 followed a tripartite division between pre-arts, arts, and theology. The pre-arts or "Preliminary Class" was designed for students "who, on examination, are not found qualified to enter upon the course properly so called." It consisted of arithmetic, mathematics, English grammar, civil history, Latin and Greek. Undoubtedly, this was intended to replace the now-defunct Toronto Academy. The "Non-Theological" or arts course consisted of a three-year programme which, though including the study of classics, also reflected a Scottish emphasis on physical science and philosophy.[36]

In the first year students were taught classics, mathematics, and English composition; in the second year, classics, junior philosophy (logic and metaphysics), physical science (natural philosophy, chemistry or natural history) and history and English literature. The final year embraced senior philosophy (metaphysics and ethics), junior Hebrew, physical science (geology), history and literature.

The theological course also encompassed three years. In the first year it consisted of a study of evidences of natural and revealed religion, senior Hebrew, church history, and expositions of scripture. Systematic theology, church history, hermeneutics and Biblical history, and pastoral theology were taught in the second year. The final year involved more advanced study in systematic theology, hermeneutics and biblical criticism, and pastoral theology. This curriculum was not substantially different from that which had hitherto been followed. According to a report of the College Committee "the principal difference . . . is, that students in the first year of their theological course are, according to the scheme proposed, required to attend a class, to be conducted by Professor Young, for the critical exposition of scripture. In this class, selected portions, particularly of the Old Testament Scriptures, are read by the students in the original, and critically expounded by the Professor." Young's course would be preparatory to Dr. Willis' classes in hermeneutics and biblical criticism, taught in the second and third years.[37] Such a curriculum was not without its detractors. The Montreal-based *Canadian Presbyter* complained that "it may form sound theologians, and yet, egregiously fail in preparing accomplished and competent preachers and pastors." It recommended closer attention to modern language, literature and sermons (as an aid to better sermons); scriptural exposition, elocution, worship, church law and polity, and the "bearing of modern science upon Theology" and "the modern aspects of philosophical infidelity."[38]

During the course of their studies students were examined periodically as to their academic accomplishments and their spiritual health. The College Committee examined students before they were admitted to the College each fall. According to Rev. William Rintoul, Convener of that committee in 1844-45, these examinations "were not confined to their intellectual acquirement, but extended also to their views and experience of divine truth, and their motives for seeking admission to the ministry."[39] As the *Record* for May 1847 put it, the College Committee "admit at first, and continue in the Institution, only those who, in the judgment of charity, have had some experience of a work of grace in their hearts: while those who are attending the literary and philosophical classes are considered to be more strictly probationary students."[40] According to the interim rules passed by the Synod of 1859, at the close of each year's session the student had to apply to his professors "for certificates attesting the regularity of his attendance, his proficiency, diligence and general conduct, which certificates shall be presented to the Presbytery of the Church, by whom said student may be examined for license or for entrance upon the next year of the Curriculum."[41] Students were thus under the supervision of both the college and their own presbyteries, though the line of demarcation between the two jurisdictions was not always clear. Having satisfied the college's requirements the candidate was "taken on trial for license" by his Presbytery. He was examined in Greek, philosophy, theology and practical religion and then underwent what were called "public probationary trials." These consisted of further examinations in Biblical Hebrew and Greek, theology, church history, government and "personal Religion." There were also five set pieces which the candidate was required to read before the Presbytery: "a Latin exercise, a Greek critical exercise, a Homily, a popular lecture, and a popular sermon."[42]

Like many other college students at the time, those at Knox were involved in various student societies. According to a report in the *Banner* some students had established a Missionary Society which met monthly for the reading of papers on subjects relating to missions. This society was also involved in city mission work in Toronto. The city was divided into eight districts, each having four students assigned to it. Students distributed tracts (about 500 reportedly given out every two weeks),[43] established some 18 weekly prayer meetings, assisted with Sunday Schools, conducted services at the General Hospital and visited the immigrant sheds. During the summer vacation the tract distribution was continued by a group of ladies from Knox Church, Toronto.[44]

Following the completion of his studies and his licensure to preach the gospel, the licentiate (or probationer—the terms were used interchangeably) was normally required to spend one year on the Home Mission field. During this time he would be expected to preach, teach and act as a pastor, but would not be permitted to administer the sacraments, nor would he have a seat in the courts of the church. After completion of this year as a missionary, the probationer would then be allowed to receive a "call" from a particular congregation. This was an expression of a congregation's desire to have a particular man as their minister. According to Rev. A. F. Kemp of St. Gabriel Street Free Church, Montreal, "no particular form has been prescribed by the Synod for the election of ministers to vacant congregations. . . . All that the Church stipulates for is that full effect shall be given to voice of the Christian people."[45] After election by the congregation, and acceptance of a call, the Probationer would then be taken on trials for ordination. These were the same as those for licensure. The Presbytery on being satisfied by the trials would then set a date for the ordination, and issue an edict to the congregation concerned (at least two Sundays before the day for ordination) announcing the ordination and giving an opportunity "that if any of them have any thing to object to the life or doctrine" of the candidate, that they bring this to the attention of the Presbytery. On the day set for ordination, another opportunity to state objections was given. One minister of the Presbytery would then preach a sermon, outline the procedures followed hitherto, and put the ordination questions to the newly elected minister. These questions were part of a "Formula to be signed by Ministers, Elders, Deacons, and Probationers." Adopted by the Synod of 1845, they involved certain theological affirmations which were required of all office-holders. By this candidates indicated their acceptance of the Westminster Confession of Faith, the worship, discipline and government of the Presbyterian Church, and particular Free Church emphases concerning church-state relations and the rights of the people to choose their own minister.[46]

When the ordination questions had been answered affirmatively,

> the Moderator comes down from the pulpit and the Candidate kneeling is by prayer and the laying on of hands of the Presbytery set apart to the office of the ministry. After which the Moderator declares that in the name and by authority of the Presbytery he admits and inducts him into the pastoral charge of that Church; and along with the members of the Court, gives him the right hand of fellowship; addresses are then delivered to minister and people by the minister or ministers appointed.[47]

Because this was the normal procedure followed in the Canadian Free Church, it conflicted with one of the practices of the Presbyterian Church of Ireland. It seems that the Irish church was in the habit of ordaining its Probationers before sending them to Canada. An Overture before the Synod of 1858 drew attention to this and complained that it was "contrary to the principle and usage of Presbyterian Churches, to ordain, except to the cure of souls, unless when sending missionaries where the Gospel is not preached, and its ordinances cannot be otherwise administered according to the practice of the church sending them" and that "the circumstances of this Province are not such as to call for such procedure."[48]

Most ministers in the Free Church were responsible for a single congregation, though in some cases they might have charge over two. Congregational size varied according to locality. In 1859-60 the largest congregations in the denomination were Knox Church, Toronto, with 560 communicant members, Galt with 480 and Knox Church, Hamilton with 477. The smallest congregations contained approximately 50 to 100 members. Worship services were held on Sundays in the morning, afternoon, and evening. Most congregations had two services—one in the morning and a second either in the afternoon or the evening. Some had three services. It is worth pointing out that the average attendance was often higher than the communicant membership. In 1859-60, for example, the communicant membership in the Côté Street Church, Montreal was 350, while 750 attended its one Sunday morning service (the pulpit was vacant at the time). Knox Church, Toronto had 850 at its morning service and 670 in the evening.[49]

The Free Church, then, brought to bear on an underdeveloped educational situation the best theological traditions and educational standards which Scotland had to offer. Equipped with six years of demanding literary, scientific, and theological training, the Free Church clergy were among the best educated in the province.

Chapter 7

ELDERS AND PEOPLE

A popular impulse lies at the heart of Presbyterian church government. Congregations choose their own spiritual overseers—ministers and elders—and these in turn represent them in the higher courts of the church. At the same time there is a clear division of responsibility between the various offices and a pattern of authority whereby spiritual oversight and discipline is exercised. Within this nexus of authority the eldership plays an important part. Though a spiritual office, the eldership could also be a socially prestigious position to which many in the community might aspire. Yet interestingly enough, many prominent Free Church laymen, the most notable examples being Peter and George Brown, never seem to have been elders. On the other hand, such elders as John Redpath of Montreal, while they were important figures in business and society, also had the piety and knowledge requisite of this office.

The eldership, as an intrinsic part of Presbyterianism, was easily transferable from the Kirk Synod to the Free Church in 1844. This meant that many congregations which moved from one to the other did so with their Kirk-Sessions virtually intact. In other cases a reconstruction was necessary, as in Glengarry where the elders "who formerly acted resigned their office into the hands of the people, and the best of them were re-elected, along with two others, as elders in connection with the Free Church."[1] Where no session existed, or additions were necessary, the congregation was exhorted to "give itself unto prayer, seeking that the Lord, the searcher of hearts, may direct its choice to men of tried and proven piety, and such as may be expected to devote themselves prudently and zealousy to the work of the Lord in their particular sphere."[2]

No one system for the election of elders was demanded. A. F. Kemp of St. Gabriel Street, Montreal, recommended one in which each member of the congregation formulated a short list of potential elders, those with the most votes being considered elected.[3] If these men were then regarded as suitable by the existing elders, and if they agreed to hold office, they would be ordained. The date of the proposed ordination would then be announced and an opportunity for objections would be provided. On the day set aside for ordination a sermon would be preached, the ordination questions posed and the minister "shall then by prayer set them apart to the office of Elder (or Deacon) and along with the other members of Session give them the right hand of fellowship declaring them to be elders (or Deacons) of this Church."[4]

The only difference between this and the method adopted in the case of ministers was that the latter were ordained by the laying on of hands. This caused problems when one congregation ordained its elders by laying on hands. The discussion in presbytery and synod revealed differences of opinion. The *Canadian Presbyter*, arguing for an elevation in status of ruling elders, asked, "Why are hands not laid on ruling elders, unless it be to *lower* their office, and to mark them out as an entirely different *grade* of the ministry?"[5] No final pronouncements were made on the question, though it seems that the normal practice of ordaining without laying on hands was followed.[6]

Having been duly elected and ordained, the elders were to perform specific spiritual functions within their own congregations. According to an Overture approved by the Synod of October 1844, the primary responsibilities of the elders were

> to watch for souls, to rule in the Church, and especially and peculiarly to assist the Minister in the examination of candidates for sealing ordinances, in visiting the sick, instituting and conducting prayer-meetings, inquiring after the fruits of the preaching of the Word, superintending Sabbath-schools, promoting the observance of Family Worship, and in faithfully administering the discipline of the Church.

They were also to minister to mission stations and in their own congregations in the absence of a pastor.[7] "The church must no longer delegate her teaching functions in each congregation to one person," argued the *Canadian Presbyter*, "but commit them, as of old, to a body of faithful men 'apt to teach,' and able by sound doctrine both to exhort and to convince the gainsayers."[8] Moreover, such duties were to be carried out with diligence, faithfulness, judiciousness, impartiality, "with *tenderness, affection, real solicitude* for the best interests of the flock"; and "with a practical recognition of the responsibility to God, and simple *dependence on his grace and blessing*."[9]

In addition to performing the spiritual and pastoral functions required of them in their own congregations, elders were also expected to sit, debate, and vote in Presbytery and Synod. Each congregation was permitted to send one of its elders as a representative to Presbytery and to Synod. Fewer than fifty per cent of the elders designated to attend the Synod did so (Table 2, pp. 134-35), and many congregations even failed to designate a representative elder. Because of the expenditure of time involved in attending the annual meeting of Synod, only those elders who could be absent from their place of work for one week in June would be able to attend. In an attempt to ensure full elder participation at Synod meetings, the Synod of 1844 passed as an interim act the provision "that it shall be lawful for any Session legally convened, and after due notice given, to elect and appoint as their representative to the Synod, any Elder in good and regular standing in any other Session of this Church."[10] Some congregations did take advantage of this provision.

Elders were intimately involved in the exercise of church discipline. Each of the three levels of authority within the denomination, Kirk-Session, Presbytery, and Synod, had disciplinary functions. The Presbytery acted as a court of appeal for cases not satisfactorily resolved at the congregational level. The Synod had both judicial and legislative functions, acting as the supreme court of the church, and as a parliament enacting new legislation. Only the most significant and far-reaching matters ever reached the Synod. These would include moral misconduct by ministers, and all cases of alleged heresy. In general, questions concerning baptism, admission to the Lord's Supper, or immorality on the part of members would be resolved by the Kirk-Session. Care was taken to avoid arbitrariness, and strict rules were formulated to cover such matters as church censures, accusations, and witnesses. The following section from the draft Book of Discipline concerning "church censures" indicated their scope and nature:

1. The proper grounds of Church Censure, are breaches of the Divine law, which tend to bring discredit upon religion; or the maintenance of doctrines which are manifestly inconsistent with the fundamental principles of Christianity.

2. The proper subjects of Church Censure, are Church members; and its proper ends are the preservation of the Church's purity, the prevention of error, and immorality, and the reclaiming of offenders.

3. Charges against individuals which have long lain dormant; or where there is a manifest deficiency of proof; or where the precept in Matt. xviii. 15, has not been complied with; should not be investigated by Church Courts, with a view to the infliction of censure.

4. In receiving accusations, conducting processes, and inflicting censures, Church Courts should avoid the unnecessary divulging of offences, lest the spreading of scandal, should harden the guilty, grieve the godly and dishonour religion.

5. The censures inflicted by Church Courts are admonition, rebuke, suspension, deposition from office, and excommunication.

6. Scandals may come before Church Courts by *fama clamosa*, accusation, reference, complaint or appeal.[11]

It is possible, through a brief examination of Kirk-Session records, to see how discipline was conducted at the congregational level. In Prescott, Canada West, for example, one Isaac Boyd came before the Session on 30 January 1845, "to account for immoral conduct & absenting himself from public worship; & having been frequently admonished in private & entreated to return to the path of duty, & no hopes that he would do so, his name was taken from the role." After about a year and a half, we find that Boyd had been restored to church privileges.[12] In this and other cases of discipline, the goal seems to have been repentance and reconciliation.[13]

Some issues of discipline and practice had wide implications and were debated in the Synod. The case of trafficking in liquor has already been considered in another context.[14] One such issue was baptism. In 1850 the Synod passed a Declaratory Act on Baptism, to the effect that it should be administered to only those (and their children) "of whom there is good reason to believe that they are consistently professing the name of Christ, and obedience to him." Moreover, parents who desire to have their children baptized should not be neglecting the Lord's Supper. In general, baptism should be administered publicly, not privately.[15] The other major question concerning baptism to reach the Synod was that of Roman Catholic baptism—was it valid; and thus should converts from Roman Catholicism be "re-baptized"? An overture to the Synod of 1858 asked that "Romish Baptism is not to be regarded or treated as Christian Baptism, and to instruct Sessions to take action accordingly." This was sent down to the Presbyteries under the Barrier Act and rejected.[16] The question of marriage with a deceased brother's wife was also discussed; the Synod merely reaffirming the position of the Westminster Confession.[17]

The maintenance of internal discipline was essential to the smooth functioning of the church. Standards were enunciated and these were expected to be obeyed. Nor was this merely the foisting of middle-class or even clerical morality upon ordinary members, but the maintenance of what they understood to be Biblical standards of morality and conduct on members, elders, and ministers alike. Indeed, the two most notable cases of expulsion from the denomination were those of two ministers, Robert Peden and Andrew Ferrier, albeit for "heretical" views rather than moral lapses. Though strict, this discipline seems to have been fair, and for the most part did not disrupt the church.

The office of deacon was the third to which members might be ordained, but this was never successful within the Canadian Free Church, principally because of the undercurrent of tension between clergy and laity.[18] Its particular sphere of responsibility was financial. The Synod of October 1844 thus asserted that elders were not to be involved with the secular affairs of the church. Rather, deacons were to "take a general supervision of all the monetary and secular affairs of the Church, as in respect to the repairs of the edifices, and the expenses connected with these, the raising of funds for missions, Sabbath-schools, the Sustentation and other Synod funds, the supplementing the ministers' Stipend and so forth." It was suggested that pious young men, with business ability, might be suited for the office of deacon.[19]

The Synod of October 1844 also established a committee to study Deacons' Courts and the Synod of 1847, while calling for further study, did argue for the usefulness and scripturalness of this office, and recommended that Presbyteries and ministers encourage its adoption in congregations.[20] Nonetheless, little action was taken until the Synod of 1856, which received an Overture from the Presbytery of Montreal which attempted to delineate the functions and responsibilities of elders and deacons. At the same Synod, another Overture from the Presbytery of Hamilton drew attention to the fact that some Free Church congregations "do commit the management of their congregational affairs to pew-holders, pew-owners, or subscribers, instead of communicants; and whereas the tendency of such practices is to bring the Church into bondage to the world," that "the right of suffrage and management [shall be given] only to communicants in good and regular standing."[21] Both of these Overtures were sent down to the Presbyteries for study, were rejected by a majority of Presbyteries and were allowed to lapse.[22] They do, however, give evidence of a reluctance of Free Church congregations to commit their financial affairs into the hands of ordained office-bearers. Perhaps this was one more manifestation of a clerical/lay tension which had plagued both the Church of Scotland Synod since the Temporalities Bill and the Free Church since the attempts to institute a Sustenation Scheme. As A. F. Kemp described the situation: "A prejudice seems to exist in the minds of many ministers and members of the Church against this office, the result of which is that not one half of our congregations have entrusted the management of their pecuniary and secular affairs to these scriptural Office-bearers."[23]

In fact, an examination of congregational statistics indicates that Kemp is too generous in his estimates. In 1859-60, for example, only 27 congregations had Deacons' Courts, and of these some 16 had Managers or Trustees as well. The size of these Deacons' Courts ranged from 3 to 12. On the other hand, 140 congregations had Managers or Trustees which ranged in group size from 2 to 19.[24]

Although exerting a dominating influence, only a small number of the people of the Free Church would have been office-holders. The remaining members of the Free Church would have been involved in a plethora of church-oriented functions which would have undoubtedly had both a "spiritual" and a "social" aspect to them. For the children of members and adherents the most important of these would have been the Sabbath-school.

Most, if not all, congregations would have had a Sabbath-school. In 1859-60 it was estimated that the church contained 225 schools; 9460 pupils with an average attendance of 6967; 1196 teachers and some 22,276 volumes in church school libraries. The lessons taught could have come from a variety of sources: written by the pastor of the congregation himself; written by Rev. William Gregg for the Synod as a whole; or produced by the Edinburgh Sabbath School Union. As well, children might read *Nel-*

son's Children's Paper, the Presbyterian *Sabbath School Visitor* or the
Child's Paper. They might also sing children's hymns from the collection of
the Montreal Sabbath School Association of the Kirk Synod, or *Hymns for
Young Children* from the Old School Presbyterian Board of Publications.[25]
Occasionally, Sabbath-schools would hold Soirées, which combined some
sort of devotional with singing and refreshments.

For the youth and adults of the congregation, various Bible classes
were provided. In 1859-60 it was estimated that there were 160 classes with
a total average attendance of 2875. These were taught principally by the
ministers, but occasionally by elders.[26] Some congregations also contained
women's societies. Knox's Church, Toronto, for example, had in 1846 a
Female Association. With Elizabeth Burns as its Treasurer, and Elizabeth
Esson as its Secretary, it corresponded with the Female Colonial Committee in Edinburgh. Its main purpose was to raise money for missions and
bursaries, through the sale of "female work"—presumably knitting and
sewing.[27]

For many in the Free Church, such prayer meetings, bible classes and
associations would have provided, in addition to their professedly
"spiritual" function, a focus for social contact and interchange. At the same
time the weekly gathering for worship would have constituted the most
regular contact among members.

The mid to late Victorian periods witnessed a number of changes in
the worship and liturgy of the Scottish churches: the introduction of organs
and hymn-books; altered communion practices; and architectural changes.
In these matters the United Presbyterians and the Church of Scotland
were the most receptive to change, while the Free Church remained the
most conservative.[28] The Free Church in Canada, like its parent in Scotland, resisted most changes in worship and liturgy.

There was no formal service book or liturgy in the Free Church apart
from the *Westminster Directory for Public Worship*. This directory,
drafted by the Westminster Assembly, was passed by the General Assembly of the Church of Scotland, 3 February 1645 and by Parliament, 6 February 1645.[29] The order of worship according to the Directory was: Call to
worship; a brief prayer; scripture reading (reading Old and New Testaments consecutively and providing an exposition of the passage if necessary); singing of a psalm; a long prayer (the Directory set down the order for
such a prayer); sermon; prayer; psalm and a "solemn blessing" to close the
service.[30] It is difficult to determine how closely the Canadian Free Church
followed this order. The *Canadian Presbyter* complained in 1858 (with
particular reference to prayer) that while the Directory "still holds a place
nominally among the standards of Presbyterian usage," it has "practically
fallen into neglect" and "every one does what is right in his own eyes"—
some, for example, neglecting prayers for civil authorities, omitting the
Lord's prayer, or praying for a short or long period as seems fit.[31]

During the service, the congregation sat while singing and stood to pray.[32] The singing was led by a precentor. He might use a tuning fork to locate the proper note and would then often sing the first line of the psalm, which was then repeated by the congregation. Of the ten set tunes for the psalms the precentor might know only a few, and these he might embellish by "gracing"—"the addition of unauthorized shakes and quavers to the tune very much as the spirit moved him."[33] Congregational singing was often poor in quality and precentors often unskilled. The *Canadian Presbyter* complained, for example, that "Most frequently our precentor is one who can shout and make a noise neither musical nor melodious in its character, and who, in the selection of his tunes or in the mode of their expression, has little or no regard to the subject of the Psalm."[34] The staple diet for congregational singing would have been the metrical psalms. In addition to these, some congregations would have sung "paraphrases"—prose sections of scripture. These had been published in Scotland in 1781 and contained many which were antithetical to an evangelical outlook.[35] Within the Canadian Free Church they were criticized by both conservatives and innovators.

The *Record* probably spoke for many of the conservatives when it eschewed both paraphrases and hymns by writers such as Isaac Watts. The editor thus asserted that:

> One of the first steps in the defection of those churches which have departed from the faith once delivered to the saints, has been the superseding of the words of the Holy Ghost and substituting the words of man in the worship of God. There is cause for alarm, for the purity and stability of the Church, that disregards scriptural worship.[36]

Paraphrase, he declared, "admits of human opinions and sentiments being mixed up with the word of God." While admitting the need for a new version of the Psalms, he argued that "God has given in his word a *model* for prayer, while he has given a *system* of praise, complete, it must be esteemed, until cases in the experience of the Christian and the Church can be cited, to which nothing in the Scripture songs is applicable."[37]

The *Canadian Presbyter*, representing those who were calling for innovations in worship, criticized the paraphrases, but instead of regressing to exclusive psalmody, called for the production of a Free Church hymn book. Pointing to the hymn book of the United Presbyterian Church of Scotland[38] which was used by some of their congregations in Canada, it declared it to be "unquestionably greatly superior to our own paraphrases." It argued for a hymn book which would contain selected paraphrases (getting rid of those "which are a scandal to us as a Calvinistic Church, and of those that are manifestly defective in their statements of evangelical truth") and selected hymns (retaining only those "which are couched in the language of direct prayer and praise" and omitting "didactic and sentimental songs").[39]

The question of the use of instrumental music in public worship first came before the Synod in 1855. The congregation in Brockville had introduced an organ into their worship service. This the Synod disapproved of, declaring:

> that the introduction of instrumental music in public worship is not approved or permitted by this Church, and [enjoining] all Presbyteries to take order that no such innovation be introduced in any of the congregations within their bounds; but to take steps, so far as practicable, to encourage and cultivate the harmonious exercise of vocal praise.[40]

Yet two years later the Brockville congregation was still in possession of its organ, and apparently "the congregation is unanimous in their desire to retain the organ as an aid in leading the praises of the Sanctuary, and that the peace of the congregation has not been interfered with." Nonetheless, the Synod instructed the congregation to remove the organ and the congregation complied with this order.[41] Such sentiments against the use of organs would have been supported by Peter Brown and the Toronto *Banner*. He argued that the use of organs suppressed congregational singing, with the result that "the hearers leave the praise to be performed by the wood, the ivory and the brass."[42] The *Canadian Presbyter*, on the other hand, asserted that "It would, we believe, have been agreeable to many, if the Synod could have seen its way to grant the modest and earnest request of those gentlemen."[43] At the time of the Union of 1861 congregations were permitted to retain their previous forms of worship, which meant that United Presbyterian congregations would continue to use their pipe organs.[44]

Most Free Churches had at least two services each Sabbath day. In Knox's Church, Hamilton, for example, the Sabbath-school met before the morning service. This morning service began at 11:00 and lasted until 1:30 P.M. The afternoon service began at 3:00.[45] In Galt, John Bayne, for most of his ministry, had only one service—beginning before noon and continuing until nearly 3:00 P.M. When he began to hold a second service, he had to shorten the morning one so as to rest for the evening.[46] In the Côte Street Church, Montreal, services were held at 11:00 and 7:00 with the Sabbath-school meeting at 2:30.[47]

As for the celebration of the Lord's Supper, the Synod of 1848 declared that it "shall be dispensed at least once a quarter, and that ministers should, if necessary, dispense it without assistance from brethren in the neighbourhood, rather than not dispense it thus frequently."[48] There is evidence, however, that this was not always carried out.[49] Typically, the "communion season" would encompass meetings over a number of days. Fast and preparation days would be held on the Friday and Saturday prior to the communion service and a day of thanksgiving would follow it.[50]

The presence of prominent businessman and politicians in the Free Church gives a false impression of the social status of its average member.

Using the manuscript census returns, it is possible to gain at least a partial picture of the social composition of the denomination. In rural sections of the province the bulk of the church was composed of farmers. In Compton County, Canada East, for example, there were 1853 persons listed as Free Church Presbyterians in the Census of 1861. As such they were the largest Protestant group in the county, comprising about 18 per cent, and were the single largest concentration of Free Church members in the province. The vast majority of them were located in the six northern townships of Bury, Hampden, Marston, Lingwick, Winslow, and Whitton. Within these six townships the Free Churchmen made up the preponderance of the population. The overwhelming majority were farmers, with a scattering of "labourers."[51]

An examination of two towns suggests that many Free Churchmen were skilled artisans. In Guelph, there were 69 identifiable Free Churchmen, many of them heads of families. This number included 8 carpenters; 8 servants; 6 labourers; 6 tailors; 5 masons; 4 merchants; 3 tanners; 3 moulders; 2 shoemakers; and 2 saloonkeepers. According to Katz's occupational classification most of these would be found in the third rank.[52] A similar, though not identical, pattern emerges in the town of Perth. There a large number of Free Churchmen were skilled workmen, but it also contained a larger proportion of professionals. Thus they included a sheriff, a bailiff, a barrister, a dentist, a physician and 6 merchants, in addition to 9 carpenters, 8 cabinetmakers, 9 blacksmiths, 4 shoemakers, 3 tanners, 3 tailors, 2 wagon makers and 2 carriage makers.[53]

The membership of the Free Church comprised a fair cross-section of the communities in which they resided. In rural congregations this of course meant a preponderance of farmers. In urban situations, the congregations were made up of businessman, professionals and skilled artisans. The average Free Churchman tended to be a substantial citizen. Free Church membership, on the whole, probably resembled that of the Methodists and the Baptists. While the wealthy and powerful were more likely to be in the Auld Kirk, attitudes and not class formed the dividing line between the two churches. Class distinctions were less important in a strongly committed religious community than in conventional parishes. Membership in the Free Church was a choice dictated by a religiously-active conscience and not by a desire for social status.

Chapter 8

FINANCING THE ENTERPRISE

The formation of the Free Church in Canada was a major financial undertaking, involving the construction of new buildings, stipends for its ministers, and educational facilities for its students. Though formally committed to the principle of an established church, it was the internal resources of its people, and not government funding, which were necessary to launch and sustain this new enterprise. This, however, was not a disastrous situation. The Free Church community included wealthy businessman like Isaac Buchanan and John Redpath, and the support of the Free Church of Scotland's Colonial Committee and the Presbyterian Church of Ireland could be counted on. Financial solvency was achieved, but not without some hardship and retrenchment.

The most immediate financial needs were for church accommodation and ministers' salaries. The Disruption of 1844 had left a number of congregations without places of worship. In some cases the seceders, though they comprised the majority of the congregation, were prepared to relinquish any claim to their building. Alexander Gale's congregation of St. Andrew's, Hamilton, for example, declared that they would not "consent to occupy the Church for public worship at the hazard of unseemly litigation, or subject to the caprice or arbitrary pleasure of any individual or party, or to any interruption of the ordinary diets of worship in their minister."[1] Some congregations contested the title to the property and were successful, like Rev. John Scott's in London which won St. Andrew's from the Church of Scotland in a Chancery Court decision.[2] Others, like Mark Young Stark's congregation in Dundas, went to litigation and lost. In this case the Court of Queen's Bench found against them, in a decision based on the fact that the title deed contained the phrase "In Connexion with the Church of Scotland."[3]

Some congregations sought temporary accommodation with the Methodists, Congregationalists, or United Presbyterians while their own

Reference notes for Chapter 8 are found on pp. 161-63.

buildings were under construction. Such building projects were aided by donations from Isaac Buchanan. Besides making substantial contributions to Knox College, Buchanan, in the early years of the Free Church, offered £50 to ten new churches in Canada West. Certain conditions were, however, attached to this grant. These apparently included provisos that the managers of the property be elected annually by the congregation, that the local congregation raise £50 for building materials, and that the church be named Knox's Church.[4] The property must be held by and for members in full communion with the Presbyterian Church of Canada. By those terms Buchanan was attempting "to protect congregations against the interference of the church courts in our congregational temporalities."[5] One such congregation, the Free Temple Church in Chinguacousy, submitted their title deed to Rev. William Rintoul, to see if it met Buchanan's conditions. Apparently it did not, but they were prepared to amend it. As Rintoul intimated to Buchanan, "*entre nous*, they are pretty well imbued with an *Ecclesiastic-phobia*."[6] Buchanan's insistence on congregational control of property likely reflected his suspicion of clerical control and power. His offer of money probably came too late to induce any congregations to leave the Kirk Synod, but did strengthen those that had already left.[7]

Financial support for the ministry was another primary concern of the newly-formed Synod. One plan for providing such support which captured the Synod's imagination in the early years was the Sustentation Fund. Although ultimately abandoned, it engendered considerable debate and revealed the lay-clerical tensions at work in the Church. It was Chalmers in Scotland, forced to abandon the Establishment, who first conceived of a sustentation plan. The Sustentation Fund was Chalmers' method of realizing "the goal of a national territorial 'establishment,' based upon voluntary contributions."[8] Its purpose was to maintain a minimum stipend for each Free Church clergyman and through the workings of this plan to foster a sense of community throughout the church. In Scotland, considerable sums of money were raised and the plan was, on the whole, successful, thus contributing "the cement which held the Free Church clergy together during the initial years of trial" and providing "the foundation for the permanent Free Church financial constitution."[9]

The Free Church in Canada considered the matter of a Sustentation Fund at its initial meeting of July 1844. It established a committee to consider a Sustentation Fund for the whole church and Deacons' Courts for each congregation.[10] The Commission of Synod, meeting in Hamilton, 7 and 8 August 1844, again considered the matter and resolved to establish a Board of Trustees to oversee the Sustentation Fund. The first board consisted of Isaac Buchanan as President, along with five laymen, three ministers, and the local board chairmen who would sit *ex officio*. These trustees were responsible for general oversight and encouragement, and the collection and distribution of money.[11] The avowed purpose of this plan was to supplement, raise, or equalize ministers' stipends to "a respectable minimum."

The Synod of October 1844 rejected this plan on the grounds that it was only a "supplementary fund"; and that "a common sustentation fund, sustained by the exertions of all the congregations, and one on which all the ministers shall depend, is to be preferred."[12] The Free Church of Scotland deputies, King and Macnaughton, argued in favour of such a fund, and this was undoubtedly a factor in influencing the Synod's decision.[13] The Commission of Synod was given the task of finalizing such a plan.

Subsequent trustee boards included a number of prominent Canadian businessmen. In 1845 the President was Isaac Buchanan; the Vice-Presidents were John Redpath and Andrew Jeffrey; the Treasurer, James McIntyre and the Secretary, James Walker. For the years 1846-48 John Redpath served as President, Andrew Jeffrey of Cobourg and James Gibb of Quebec City as Vice-Presidents, and William P. McLaren and James Walker as Treasurer and Secretary.

The new plan, as developed by the Commission of 29 October, was intended to raise the salaries of ministers in poorer congregations by drawing upon the resources of the wealthier ones. A common fund would supersede local stipendiary arrangements. Congregational giving might be raised by pew rents, Sunday collections or periodic contributions. Each congregation would have an association with a group of collectors. The local affairs would be under the superintendence of the Deacons or Managers. An elaborate method of calculating salaries was developed. The minimum salary was set up at £100 *per annum*. For the purposes of calculation this was represented by the number 10. For every £20 over £100 given by a congregation, its number was raised by 1. For example, the proportional number of a congregation contributing £120 was 11; if it contributed £140 its proportional number was 12. The total contributions to the fund would be added together and divided by £100 to give the number of the multiplier. To calculate the total stipend for each congregation one had to multiply the proportional number by the multiplier. The system worked as follows.

Congregation	Contribution	Proportional #	Stipend
A	£100	10 × 13	£130
B	£100	10 × 13	£130
C	£120	11 × 13	£143
D	£140	12 × 13	£156
E	£200	15 × 13	£194
F	£240	17 × 13	£221
G	£400	25 × 13	£325
	£1300	1300 ÷ 100 = 13 (multiplier)	

Source: *Record*, Oct. 1844, 19-20.

The plan, as finally approved by the Commission of 14 November, contained lengthy and detailed regulations for the collection and distribution of money, but the most controversial sections were those dealing with Deacons' Courts. Deacons were to be elected by the members in full communion of each congregation, and were to be ordained *ad vitam aut culpam*. Deacons' Courts were to consist of both elders and deacons, were to meet at least quarterly, oversee the collections and, according to Article 6, "manage the property and all the temporal affairs of the congregation." It was this last provision which, as we shall see, was the downfall of the Sustentation scheme.

Besides such provisions, the scheme contained some which appear to the modern reader to foster social distinctions and elitism. There were to be no seat rents in congregations participating in the Sustentation Fund. Instead, members and adherents were to give according to their ability. However, seats were to be allotted according to how much one gave—the more given, the better choice of pew. Accordingly, the regulations set down that:

> To prevent unnecessary shifting of seats after the first allocation, the seats of the church shall be divided into two, three, or more classes, according to the order of preference: a corresponding classification shall be made of the contributors; and those holding seats appropriate to the class to which they belong shall not be required to change them—the change only being made from class to class. [14]

Adherents of any congregation were to be allocated seats on the same principles—but only after seats had been allocated to all the members. The Deacons' Courts did, however, have the authority to allocate seats "irrespective of the sums contributed by members or adherents, in cases of poverty, or also in cases of deafness or other infirmity," though if seven members complained, such preference was to be overruled "so that no partiality may be allowed." Every term the names and amounts contributed were to be printed and circulated. Regular Sabbath collections were to pay for local congregational expenses—lighting, heat, repairs, poor relief, etc. A special subscription or a public collection could be taken up for any extraordinary expenses, though permission for this should first be given by a general congregational meeting. The actual method of distribution was not substantially different from that of the Commission's scheme.

The avowed purpose of the Sustentation Fund was: to raise minister's stipends in poor congregations by drawing upon wealthier congregations; to allot stipends "in some proportion to the importance of their congregations, and the probable expenses of the style of living required of them"; to avoid gross inequalities of stipend between ministers, and to stimulate liberal givings. [15]

Considerable opposition was voiced against this sustentation plan. Peter Brown and the Toronto *Banner* were among its most vociferous opponents. Brown's opposition was based on a fear that the rights of congregations were going to be superseded by a central board. "The question is," he wrote in April 1845, "whether a strong, central, irresponsible power, absorbing the control of the property and affairs of the Church is to be erected, which will in due time dry up and wither the energies of that Church, or whether the congregations are to have that control in their own hands."[16] Brown was particularly incensed by the proposal to place the management of congregational finances in the hands of a Deacons' Court which would constitute "a religious oligarchy . . . possessing all the property and all the power."[17] Whether Brown ever fully understood the plan is not certain. In all likelihood, however, he saw it as another Temporalities Bill in which clerical control of finances and property was sought.[18] Admittedly, the plan was complicated, and as one elder put it, "However simple the scheme may have been, in reality it was, we believe, too complicated in appearance, ever to obtain general sanction."[19] The congregation of Knox's Church, Toronto, was also opposed to the scheme. They had already made separate arrangements with Dr. Robert Burns for the payment of his stipend, and he would have to be consulted before the congregation could participate in the plan.[20] They described the plan "as arbitrary in its details, most dangerous to the rights of the Christian people in its principles, and likely to be ruinous to the best interests of the church in operation."[21]

In the early months of 1845, Isaac Buchanan and the editor of the *Record* attempted to rescue the sustentation plan from what they considered to be misrepresentations and inaccuracies propagated in the press. Buchanan tried to distinguish the principles of the scheme from its details—the details would not be forced upon congregations, they were merely recommendations. The principle, he insisted, was that congregations "agree to hand over to the public Sustentation fund all the money raised annually, by whatever *machinery* this is done (whether by Managers or Deacons, whether from seat rents or voluntary subscriptions), after paying the necessary congregational expenses."[22] Buchanan also retreated from the infamous Article 6, referring to its "unfortunately equivocal wording" and arguing that, "It is now apparent to me that the *property* pointed at the foregoing, is the *property* of the *Sustentation Fund alone* but it certainly is a pity that more care had not been taken clearly to explain this originally." The Deacons' Court, he insisted, would not hold title to the congregational property; "their interference can only by in the management of those temporal beings which each congregation voluntarily bestows on the whole Church, from time to time."[23] The *Record* insisted that the property was not to be vested in the Deacons, but that it was their responsibility "to *take care of* the property of the congregation, and to collect and apply the monies required for the various religious objects authorized by the Church, rendering an annual account to the congregation of their proceedings, and being liable to the regular discipline of the Church in case of malversation in office."[24]

The *Record* was also insistent that the details of the plan were only recommended to the congregations: "Common sense would teach any *honest* and truth-telling man, that any more was as absurd as it was impossible.—The Synod have not the power nor the legal compulsators of a Board of Police, either to issue mandates or to enforce them as some miserable terrorists seem or pretend to imagine."[25] Those attempting to promote the Sustentation scheme were thus forced to retreat. Indeed, a circular from the Sustentation Board of 3 March 1845 omitted all of the articles concerning the Deacons' Courts and other details of the plan.[26]

The question continued to be debated for five years, but to no avail. At the Synod of 1849 the Sustentation Board, considering that its mandate had ended, tabled its books. Accordingly, the Synod passed a resolution that because of the inactivity of congregations in this matter "it hence appears that this Church is not prepared as a whole to sustain a general scheme for providing for the support of the ministry." The Presbyteries were then admonished to ensure that the financial needs of its ministers were cared for.[27] Similar advice had been given to presbyteries two years earlier when they were told

> to use their utmost endeavours, in all future settlements, to secure that an adequate provision has been made for the maintenance of the ministry, and where congregations are known and acknowledged to be well able to support the ministry, that the provision intended be somewhat proportional to the ability which God has given to such congregations.[28]

In cases where an adequate stipend was forthcoming, the Presbytery was to proceed with the settlement; where it was not sufficient, the case was to be referred to the Synod.

In 1850, the Synod, conscious of the need to assist weaker congregations, decided by a vote of 31-18 to set up a committee to investigate the reasons for the failure of the Sustentation Fund and to consider either a supplementary plan or one which combined a sustentation with a supplementary plan. In the meantime, it was given to presbyteries "to promote and establish within their own bounds, as they may severally see fit, funds for sustentation of the ministry, or for the aid of weak congregations."[29] The following year the Agency Committee reported that there was not enough interest in a plan for the "common support" of ministers. Although the establishment of presbyterial sustentation boards was recommended, very few were set up.[30]

Although the presbyteries were given the responsibility of overseeing the financial support of their ministers, by and large this matter remained in the hands of the individual congregations. Not all congregations adopted the same method. In 1858, for example, 30 congregations used seat rents alone; 51 used subscriptions; 20 used a combination of rents and subscriptions, and 12 used some other combination of rents, subscriptions, collections or other means. The congregation at Buxton was entirely supported by the Synod. Such congregational control had obvious advantages. It also meant, however, that there was sometimes a great disparity among the stipends, though admittedly those congregations which were the largest numerically, paid the largest stipends.

A minimum stipend of £100 *per annum* was set in 1844 when the Sustentation Fund was under discussion. In 1855, however, seven ministers were being paid less than the minimum—the congregation at Ste. Therese being the lowest at £46. In that year 50 ministers received between £100 and £149; 13 received between £150 and £199; 6 received between £200 and £299; 2 received between £300 and £399; and 2 received £400.[31] The average stipend was £120.

In 1856 the minimum stipend was raised to £150 *per annum*. The statistical returns for 1858 showed that the average stipend in the church was $504 or £126—less than the minimum. The average contribution per member was estimated at $3.50 for the stipend, $8.00 for all purposes; the average for each family was $1.75 for the stipend and $4.00 for all purposes.[32] In 1858, the Committee on Statistics noted that "The statistics also clearly show that it is not those congregations which pay the largest stipends and contribute most largely to the funds of the Church that are in reality the most liberal, for some of the smaller struggling congregations contribute more than these on an average per member."[33]

The returns for 1859 indicate that $64,857 was promised as stipends to the ministers of the church, whereas $55,568.57 was actually paid. The total value of church property rose in the years 1855-59. In 1855 it was estimated at between £60,000 and £70,000, and in 1859 at $450,000, though of the latter amount there remained as a debt about $80,000 loaned at 6% interest.[34]

Thus each local congregation had substantial financial responsibilities. Deacons, Managers and Trustees were the chief financial officers. They were responsible for the construction and maintenance of church buildings, and the ministers' stipend. Congregations were also expected to contribute to the various funds and stated collections of the denomination, and to the presbytery's home mission fund. These stated collections were for projects administered by the denomination itself, such as the various college funds, and the Buxton Mission, and for funds external to the denomination like the Foreign and Jewish Missions of the Free Church of Scotland and the French Canadian Missionary Society. Collections for most of these projects were received on specific Sundays at quarterly intervals during the year.

There was no one financial officer for the denomination during the early years. In 1844 James Shaw was appointed Treasurer of the Synod Fund, but by 1847 each of the church's funds had its own treasurer: John Laidlaw for the Synod Fund; Samuel Spreull for the Bursary fund; John McMurrich for the College Fund; Daniel McNab for the Home Mission Fund; John Redpath for the Foreign and Jewish Missions of the Free

Church of Scotland; and W. P. McLaren for the Sustentation Board. However, by 1849 it appears that the Agent had become the chief financial officer. In 1848 the Committee on Public Accounts had recommended that the Agent for the Sustentation Fund also be designated "Agent for the General Scheme of the Church." As such, it was his responsibility to correspond with Presbyteries and congregations, oversee the collections, and endeavour "to bring out the liberality of the people to the schemes of the Synod." His salary was to be paid out of the funds of each scheme in proportion to the time given to each.[35] The following year John McMurrich and John Laidlaw resigned as the treasurers of Knox College and the Synod Fund. John Burns as General Agent and Treasurer of the Church was given the responsibility of publishing the *Record* and was given the mandate of supervising the church's various projects with the assistance of the Agency Committee.

The 1844 establishment of a theological college in Toronto was, at least financially, the single most ambitious scheme undertaken by the Free Church.[36] The administrative structure of Knox College was simple and straightforward. General oversight was vested in a committee which was appointed annually by the Synod. In 1844 its mandate was "to provide for the accommodation of the professors and students, to superintend the raising of funds, and generally to watch over the institution."[37] This committee consisted of various ministers and laymen in addition to the professors and treasurers who sat *ex officio*.[38] The professors themselves constituted a separate committee with responsibility for curriculum and the college's internal discipline.[39] As well, when the Synod met each year it usually appointed committees to deal with various aspects of the college business. Normally these committees only sat during the Synod and were disbanded at its close. In 1846, for example, two temporary committees were formed: one to discuss incorporation, buildings, funds, a boarding house and an academy; and a second to draft admission requirements and to discuss curriculum.[40] Occasionally a committee's mandate would exceed the duration of the Synod, as in 1848 when a committee to draft a constitution for the college was established, but did not report until 1849.[41]

This college committee thus had both financial, academic, and administrative responsibilities. The college's finances were encompassed in three separate funds: the Ordinary College Fund, the Bursary Fund, and the Building Fund. The Ordinary Fund paid the professors' salaries and the general operating expenses. Its principal source of money was congregational collections and givings. The Bursary Fund provided money for students on the basis of both merit and need. Congregational and individual donations comprised the bulk of this money. Isaac Buchanan, for one, was a consistent supporter. In 1860-61 the Prince of Wales, on a visit to Toronto, toured the college and later donated $800 to be invested and the money used for prizes. In 1854, when the Synod resolved to build a college it set up a committee to publicize it, to collect subscriptions, and to select and purchase a site. An examination of the building fund for 1857-58 reveals three main sources of funding: congregational givings; individual donations; collections from England received by Rev. Donald Fraser, and—the largest amount—givings from Scotland and Ireland collected by Dr. Robert Burns.[42]

During the embryonic years of the Free Church the financial affairs of the college were cause for much concern. Fortunately, the expenses were not very great and the capital expenditure minimal. Dr. Burns had brought a substantial number of books with him from Scotland[43] and this formed the nucleus of the college library. In the early years those pastors from Canada or Scotland who lectured were not paid salaries by the college—they had to live off their stipends as pastors or were paid by the Free Church of Scotland's Colonial Committee. Only Esson as a permanent appointment would have received a salary.[44]

Still, the college did have periods of financial crisis when there was not enough money in the treasury to meet immediate expenses but appeals to the people of the church seems to have met the immediate need. Indeed, by 1854 the Synod resolved to dispense with the £300 which the Free Church of Scotland had contributed each year since its opening.[45] As the editor of the *Record* triumphantly announced in December 1854:

> We have, through the goodness and favour of the Great Head of the Church, reached the position of manhood and independence so far as resources are concerned. Hitherto we have been fostered and aided by the Church in Scotland. But we have now by our own act assumed the responsibility of sustaining our Theological Institute, as we have been sustaining our other schemes.[46]

Thus, despite what D. C. Masters refers to as "a chequered career in its early period"[47] Knox College had by 1854 seemingly achieved a position of stability and independence.

The College had experienced financial difficulties before— particularly in 1848-49—but the move in 1856 to Elmsley Villa placed strains on the College as a whole. The Synod of 1857 was informed that congregational contributions to the Ordinary Fund were not meeting its expenses and the suggestion was made that additional money be raised by subscription.[48] The College Report for that same year noted that "the Treasury proves inadequate for the present staff of Professors, at the same time that the value of their stipends, by the well proven change in the rate of living, has become less, much less than before."[49]

By 1858 the Ordinary College Fund was still operating with a deficit, which had grown from £40 in 1856 to £210 in 1858 and in this latter year about £400 was estimated as the "actual deficiency for current expenditure." By the following year, however, the fund seems to have been extricated from this financial difficulty by some shrewd financial manoeuvring. An office for the Agent and Editor of the *Record* was to be set up in the College buildings, and an amount equal to the cost of the office credited to the Ordinary College Fund. A decision was made not to liquidate the mortgage at the present time, a legacy from the estate of James Gibb of Quebec City was applied to the Ordinary Fund on a temporary basis, and contributions from congregations were reportedly increased. No deficit was reported from 1858-59 and the cumulative deficit was reduced from £438 to £392. Yet in October 1861 there was still about £2600 to be paid on the College buildings. This was due in January 1862.[50]

The incorporation of the College was discussed as early as 1850 but not until buildings were purchased and new construction contemplated was the matter viewed with any urgency.[51] Debate over the matter once again revealed clergy/laity tensions within the church. Isaac Buchanan and others had fears about the property being deeded to the Synod. Samuel Spreull, for example, asked Buchanan in 1854, "Can we trust all to the Synod?" adding that "I think Church Courts should have little to do with Brick and Mortar."[52] Buchanan, for his own part, seems to have favoured a system in which congregationally appointed trustees held the property, and he even asserted that "I see no difficulties in the college trustees and the synod being two entirely independent bodies" though he foresaw a crisis "if either the Clergy or Laity push their pretensions too far."[53] Mark Young Stark wanted the property deeded to the Presbyterian Church of Canada "while it maintains the principles of the Protest" of 1844. He asserted that "we do not want to attach our property to a *name* but to the principles of our Church."[54] In 1856 the College property was temporarily conveyed to Messrs Reid, Jeffrey, Redpath, Ferrier, and McConkey "for such proposes as the Synod shall hereafter determine."[55] Moreover, it was agreed that any Trust Deed must bind the college property "to the principles of this Church" and that trustees were to be elected by the Synod from lists of names proposed by congregations.[56] The following year the Synod passed a "Draft of An Act to Incorporate 'Knox College'"[57] which was amended and passed through the Provincial Legislature and given Royal Assent on 24 July 1858.[58] The Act which was finally passed by the Legislature was considerably shorter and less detailed than the draft of 1857. It omitted the statements of theological principle, and the details of management which the Draft of 1857 contained, but did provide that:

> It shall be lawful for the Synod of the Presbyterian Church of Canada, at its next ordinary meeting after the passing of this Act, to declare by a resolution or a By-Law to that effect and record in the register of proceedings of the said Synod, the Theological doctrines and principles which shall be taught in the said College, or what are the books and documents in which the said principles and doctrines are contained; and such declaration so made and recorded shall be irrevocable in so far as the said College shall be concerned, and shall be held at all times thereafter to contain the Theological doctrines and principles to be taught in the said College, and for the propagation of

which the property now held for the said College, or hereafter acquired for the same, shall be appropriated, and to no other.[59]

It also provided for the subsequent passage by the Synod, of "rules and by-laws for the government of the said College" and for the constituting of a College Senate and a board of management.[60] These changes were made to accommodate the objections of several Free Church members of the Provincial Legislature, who had objected to the bill containing the principles and doctrines which were to be taught in the college. This was seen as asking Parliament to give "legislative saction to teach and confirm our principles" which would also give the legislature the power to change those very principles. Moreover, these M.P.P.s wanted to maintain a consistent stance in opposing "Popish incorporations."[61] Accordingly, the Synod of 1859 resolved that the "principles and doctrines to be taught in Knox College . . . shall be such and such only as are consistent with and agreeable to . . . 'The Westminster Standards,' and shall comprise all theological learning consistent with the said Standards." The Confession of Faith's chapter on the Civil Magistrate was, of course, interpreted in the non-Erastian sense as agreed to by the Synod of 1854. Moreover, the Westminster Standards were to "be taken and understood with such other, or further directions and rules as to Church government, discipline or worship, as may from time to time be prescribed or ordained by the Synod of the said Presbyterian Church of Canada, with the concurrence of a majority of the Presbyteries of the said Church."[62] Various "Regulations for the Government and Administration of Knox College" were also presented to the Synod of 1859 and finally agreed to by the Synod of 1860.

These regulations established both a Board of Management and a College Senate. The Board was to consist of thirty-five Ministers and Elders of the church, appointed annually by the Synod "and its members shall hold office until their successors be appointed." It was to have a Chairman, Secretary and Treasurer, and "shall have the whole management of the financial affairs of the said College, shall receive and disburse all its money, keep and manage all its property, and transact all its business relating to property and money committed to its care, by the Synod or otherwise, and shall exercise all the powers, in regard to property and money, vested in the Corporation of Knox College, by the Act 22 Vic., cap. 69." The Board was also to be responsible for the boarding facilities and was "to take general cognizance of all matters pertaining to the interest of the College, and co-operate with the Senate in maintaining its discipline."[63]

The Senate was to consist of the Principal, Professors, and seven members of the Synod, appointed annually by the Synod and was to "be entrusted [with] the reception, academical superintendence and discipline of the Students, and of all other persons within the said College." It was also to "take a general inspection of the whole internal arrangements, of the

College and of the studies of the Students, and shall place said Students in
that year of the curriculum to which they may be certified by Presbyteries."[64]

While Knox College may have dominated the Synod's financial con-
cerns, the church was also responsible for a number of other projects. One
of these, the Ministers' Widows and Orphans Fund, functioned as a life
insurance plan. First brought before the Synod in 1846 by a group in
Ancaster, the concept was readily approved, though it was not until 1852
that a plan was formulated. Expanded to include orphans, it contained an
elaborate set of regulations. According to these, each minister would pay
an annual rate of £2 to the Treasurer by November 1. Penalties and
ultimate dismissal from the plan awaited the negligent or any who retired
from the ministry for any reason other than old age or infirmity. Annuities
would be paid to widows and orphans twice yearly—on 1 May and
1 November, on presentation of a certificate from the Presbytery Clerk,
Minister, or the Session Clerk. Ministers from other denominations who
joined the Free Church would only be permitted to participate if between
45 and 60 years of age, and would have to pay a yearly rate of £6.

The Treasurer of the fund was responsible for collecting and managing
the money, making investments, paying the annuities, and reporting
annually to the Synod. A Committee of Management, appointed yearly by
the Synod, was given general oversight for the fund, and was to act as an
advisor to the Treasury. Presbytery Clerks were to provide the Treasurer
with annual statistics concerning the marital status of the ministers in their
Presbyteries, the number and ages of their children, and any changes by
death or marriage. The plan was to be reviewed by the Synod at least every
five years, and any disputes between the committee and the annuitants
were to be settled by mutually acceptable arbitrators.

The annuities were to be paid according to the following scale:

Widows with no children — £30 *per annum*
    "   " 1 child   — £35 *per annum*
    "   " 2 children — £37, 10s *per annum*
    "   " 3 or more — £40 *per annum*

Families of 1 orphan   — £10 *per annum*
    "   " 2 orphans — £15 *per annum*
    "   " 3 orphans — £20 *per annum*
    "   " 4 or more — £25 *per annum*

Children would not be supported beyond the age of 14. Widows would be
supported for life or until they remarried, and no family could receive more
than £40 *per annum*.[65]

William Reid was appointed Superintendent of the Fund in 1854, a
post he held concurrently with the Agency for various other schemes of the

church, and with Editorship of the *Record* and Clerkship of Synod. The money in the fund was derived from congregational givings and collections, ministers' rates, and interest on the fund's investments. The financial statement for 1860 indicates that the fund was solvent, with total revenues of $6704.07, annuities disbursed of only $910 and a total in the fund of almost $28,000.[66]

On the eve of the Union with the United Presbyterians a new set of regulations was adopted. The rates for ministers were increased and made proportional to their age upon entering the fund. Ministers were required to join the fund within four years of their ordination or forfeit the right to do so. Those who ceased to act as pastors, professors, or missionaries would only have one-half of their money returned.[67] The ministers of the United Presbyterian Church would only be admitted to the fund when their congregations raised "a sum equitably proportional to the capital now possessed by this Synod."[68]

The Ministers' Widows and Orphans Fund was, on the whole, financially successful. It also serves to indicate the mutuality of feeling existing within the church, and its awareness of its responsibilities towards the dispossessed among its members.

The Colportage and Publication Plan was an example of a scheme which, though sound in intention, was financially unsuccessful and was for this reason abandoned. The idea for this project first came before the Synod in 1855 and was approved in principle. Presbyteries were encouraged to begin their own colportage plans, and the Synod established a committee to "mature a scheme for a general Board of Publications and Colportage."[69]

By 1856 it was reported that Presbyteries had been distributing "sound Theological literature"; thousands of families had been visited "with most of these the Colporteurs have held religious conversations"; and thousands of books had been sold—provided mainly by Nelson and Sons, Carter and Brothers, and the Presbyterian Board of Publication in Philadelphia. An elaborate plan for the organization of this scheme was also presented and approved. The Synod thus expressed its concern for "the vast importance of encouraging a truly Christian Literature in the rising Provinces of Canada, to counteract influence of a pernicious kind."[70]

According to this approved plan, a board consisting of 24 persons would be responsible for the "publication of works pertaining to the History, Discipline, Government, Doctrine and General Religious Literature of our Church" and for the distribution of other works. The Board would have a Convener, elected by the Synod, as well as a Secretary, Treasurer, Agent and an Executive Committee of seven members. The Executive Committee would scrutinize books and manuscripts for publication, help the Presbyteries supervise the colporteurs, and give general oversight.

The Agent would be responsible for the book depository, orders, correspondence, and would recommend colporteurs for election by the

Executive Committee. There was also to be a standing committee on publication. All publication to be distributed must be stamped, and none could be stamped unless approved by the general council. [71]

The report to the Synod of 1857 revealed problems with the scheme. Rev. W. Inglis, a minister without charge in the United Presbyterian Church, had been hired as Agent at a salary of £200 plus accommodation. Rental of a house in Hamilton as the book depository seems to have been the beginning of the difficulties. According to the report, "the history of our effort is one of progress from bad to worse." Some were unhappy with the Committee, and one Presbytery even passed a resolution against the Board. Indeed, the work stopped for a while. The Committee then decided to discard the office of Agent. Mr. Inglis was paid £100 and retired. Mr. S. Armstrong, a former colporteur from the Presbytery of Hamilton, was then engaged. He agreed to work part-time at the depository, which was now moved to a small rented room, and would receive £90 *per annum* in addition to travelling expenses. With Armstrong's appointment matters seemed to have improved. He was reported to have worked 138 days as a colporteur. During that time he had visited 900 families, "held religious conversations, or engaged in devotional exercises" with about 400 families and sold about 2168 books. Despite these signs of improvement, the financial picture was not promising. The Synod of 1857 resolved accordingly, that "considering however that some difference of opinion exists in regard to the propriety of the Church engaging in so extensive a scheme of Colportage, as the Committee contemplated, [to] instruct said Committee to undertake no farther liabilities than may be necessary for the working out of the present plan pursued by the Committee." [72] At the Synod of 1858 the decision was made to terminate the present plan, dispose of the inventory, and liquidate the debt. [73] In 1860-61 a special collection was necessary to help pay the debts, though these were still unpaid on the eve of the union with the United Presbyterians. In retrospect, it would seem that the plan failed because those in charge overextended themselves in terms of stock on hand and the size of their depository, and failed to collect their outstanding debts quickly enough.

The Home Missions of the Free Church also had financial needs and responsibilities. While those in the various missionary districts were expected to contribute financially, the presbytery itself was to have a home missions committee and a home-mission fund. The money for this fund was to be raised by contributions and collections at both Preaching Stations and among the settled congregations of the presbytery, [74] though donations were also forthcoming from both the Free Church of Scotland and the Presbyterian Church of Ireland. In turn, the Synod's Home Missions Committee was responsible for the distribution of missionaries, helping to set salary rates and distribute any money which it received. A general Home Mission Fund at the Synodical level was to have been established.

Never in regular operation, such a fund was superseded by the Presbytery funds. [75]

The salaries of those involved in home missions were slightly less than the minimum that settled ministers were to receive. In 1851 the salaries were to be set at £100 *per annum* without board or £80 with board for ordained missionaries and probationers; and at £50 with board for catechists. Travel within presbyteries would be paid by the Preaching Stations; that between presbyteries would be paid by the Presbytery which received the missionary. [76] As with ministers' stipends, the amount actually paid often did not attain the minimum set by the Synod. The Home Mission Report for 1848-49 revealed, for example, that missionaries were not well paid. In the Presbytery of Kingston six missionaries received £26/13/4; in Toronto, twelve received £20/17/8 each; and in Hamilton, seven received £42/17/4. [77] By February 1859 the Home Mission fund of the Presbytery of London had a debt of $1013. [78] Knox College students who supplied local pulpits during term were to receive, in 1857, at least $4.00 in addition to their expenses. [79]

The Free Church was also responsible for the financial health of the Buxton Mission in Kent County. This mission was operated by the Free Church in the Elgin Settlement, a community of refugee black slaves from the pre-Civil War United States. Both the mission and the settlement had been founded by the Rev. William King, a Free Church minister, originally from Ireland. Financially, the mission and the settlement were separate, the latter being the responsibility of a Toronto-based incorporated stock company called the Elgin Association. [80]

At the same time, a church was organized, consisting of four members and twenty "hearers" ("when the roads are good, and the weather fine"). In addition to providing regular religious instruction and worship services, the Mission also operated a Sabbath school which from 1850 to 1856 had grown from 2 students and 1 teacher to 100 students and 8 teachers. There was also a day school consisting, in 1857, of 98 students and 2 teachers, one male and one female. Mr. George Thompson, formerly of the Free Church School in Kintore, Aberdeenshire, had recently been appointed as a permanent teacher. Boys and girls were taught separately and were taught different subjects. The boys learned English, Latin, Greek and mathematics; the girls studied "the common branches of an English education, together with sewing; and such as desire it, the higher branches of a female education." [81]

The congregation was organized like others in the Free Church. By 1858 it had four elders, four deacons, and was represented at the annual meeting of Synod by its minister William King and by Robert Vanuran, one of its elders, and probably one of the few blacks to sit in any of Canada's church courts in this era. Other day and Sabbath schools were established in 1858 in the northern part of the settlement. Between twenty-five and thirty students were taught here by a man who had been educated in the Buxton School. In addition to the Free Church Congregation there were also Methodist and Baptist congregations in the settlement.

Money for the support of the Buxton Mission was raised mainly through congregational collections. Buxton was frequently one of the quarterly stated collections of the Synod. As well, smaller amounts were often contributed by individuals, other denominations such as the Presbyterian Church of Ireland, or by such groups as the Ladies' Anti-Slavery Society of Dundee, Scotland. The major portion of its annual disbursements was in the form of salaries. Rev. William King's stipend was paid entirely by the Synod; that of Mr. Thompson, the school teacher, was to be derived from student fees and a government grant as well as from Synod money.[82]

Besides salaries, a major financial expenditure was anticipated for the construction of new church and school buildings. By the time of the Free Church's union with the United Presbyterian Church in 1861, however, these buildings had not been constructed, though King had raised substantial amounts of money for this purpose in Britain. As with many projects dependent upon voluntary givings, the financial stability varied from year to year. The report for 1856-57 stated that the past year had "been one of great commercial distress, and both the mission and settlement have felt the pecuniary embarrassment."[83]

Though not wealthy, and always subject to the vicissitudes of individual contributions, the Free Church did enjoy financial solvency. During its seventeen-year history it was involved in numerous projects which were dependent upon the support of its community. Only one of these failed financially. The others survived, and some, like Knox College, enjoyed substantial growth. Not least of all, many congregations built new places of worship, paid their ministers adequate stipends, and contributed to the Free Church of Scotland's Foreign Mission and the French Canadian Missionary Society. The Free Church was linked financially to a transatlantic presbyterian community, and the contributions of friends in Scotland, Ireland, and England more than made up for any loss involved in refusing Clergy Reserve money. In short, like the mother church in Scotland, the Canadian Free Church exhibited the sufficiency of voluntary support in providing a church's financial necessities.

Chapter 9

AN ARDUOUS UNION

While the Free Church was experiencing such tremendous growth and was consolidating its structures and institutions, it was also busy negotiating a union with the United Presbyterians. To the casual observer, their failure to consummate this union for upwards of fifteen years seems incomprehensible. A wide gulf of ideology, tradition and history separated the two churches, however, and this made union an arduous task. As these obstacles were removed under the influence of changed Canadian circumstances, compromises of principle, and the death of its main opponents, a union was finally possible.

The differences between the Free and United Presbyterian churches were primarily the result of the historical traditions which each had inherited from its Scottish past. The ultimate origins of the United Presbyterian church may be traced to the Erskines' secession from the Established Church in 1733 over the issue of lay patronage. This original secession church fragmented into Burghers and Anti-Burghers in 1747 over the issue of the burgesses' oath in certain towns, requiring them to acknowledge "the true religion publicly preached within the realm and authorized by the laws."[1] The Erskines admitted the legitimacy of this oath and were forced out by their opponents. Under the influence of "New Licht" both Burghers and Anti-Burghers divided into New and Old Light sections, the result being four churches in 1806 where there had been only one in 1733. The Old Light branches had affinities with the Evangelical Party in the Church of Scotland and the Free Church. In 1839 a majority of the Old Light Burghers joined the Church of Scotland and in 1852 most of the Old Light Anti-Burghers joined the Free Church. The two New Light churches joined in 1820 to form a United Secession Church consisting of 280 congregations. The Relief Church joined them in 1847 and they assumed the name of the United Presbyterian Church.[2]

The United Presbyterian Church in Canada traced its lineage to three ministers—William Proudfoot, William Robertson, and Thomas

Christie—who arrived in Canada in 1843. Robertson died soon afterwards of cholera, but Proudfoot and Christie did missionary duty in the western section of Upper Canada. In 1834 they were organized as the Missionary Presbytery of Canada in connection with the United Associate Synod of the Secession Church of Scotland. They established a theological college at London, Canada West, in 1844 with Proudfoot as Principal, and in 1847, following their parent church in Scotland, changed their church's name to the United Presbyterian Church.[3] In size it was considerably smaller than the Free Church. Establishing precise figures from the census returns is problematic. The Census of 1842 listed 18,220 "Other Presbyterians" of which the largest group was undoubtedly the United Presbyterians. The formation of the Free Church confused the census takers. Because its official name was the Presbyterian Church in Canada, many of its members who cited that as their denominational affiliation were grouped with "Other Presbyterians," rather than with the Free Church, in the Census of 1851.[4] Thus the figures of 75,308 for the United Presbyterian and 69,738 for the Free Church are inaccurate. One estimate for the Free Church in 1851 suggested a figure of 90,000, which would leave the United Presbyterians with approximately 50,000 adherents.[5] On the eve of the Union of 1861 the United Presbyterian Church contained some seventy ministers distributed among nine presbyteries, while the Free Church had one hundred and fifty-eight ministers, and eight presbyteries.[6]

On most matters of doctrine, discipline and church government the differences between the two churches were slight. Both were presbyterian in government, evangelical and Calvinistic in theology and spirit. Their differences concerned the timely and contentious issue of church-state relations. The United Presbyterians were voluntaryists, denying the propriety of receiving state endowments, but also denying the Free Church's conception of national responsibility and the Headship of Christ. The Free Church, on the other hand, both in Scotland and Canada, held as its ideal a church established and supported by the state, yet free from all civil interference in her internal ecclesiastical affairs.

As the Evangelical Party, the Free Churchmen had defended this position against the voluntaries on the one side and the Erastian Moderates on the other. During the Voluntary Controversy, which began in Scotland in 1829 with Catholic Emancipation and ended with the Disruption of 1843, they had joined forces with the Original Burgher Synod and the Cameronians against the United Secession Church, the Relief Church and the Independent Churches.[7] The most prominent of the Auld Licht Burghers were the Willises of Greenock—William the father and his son Michael, later Principal of Knox College, Toronto.[8] The Auld Licht Burghers joined the Church of Scotland in 1839 and Willis joined the Free Church after the Disruption. Thus, significantly, many of the Free Church leaders who came to Canada after 1844 had already crossed swords with the

United Secessionists in Scotland. As the *Canadian Presbyter* pointed out, "many old warriors are still alive who fought with might and main in their respective ranks."[9] Michael Willis, for example, had participated in a Glasgow lecture series designed to answer the voluntaries and organized by "The Glasgow Association for Promoting the Interests of the Church of Scotland." His lecture concerned the "Specific application of the Scripture argument to the doctrine of National Responsibility—the Qualifications necessary in Christian Rulers—the duty of National Covenanting."[10] The Free Church thus brought with them from Scotland the idea of a nation in a covenant relationship to a sovereign God. This was no mere theoretical position, but one which had profound implications for the denomination's relationship to its surrounding culture and its political activities.

Immediately following the Disruption of 1844 the Free Church Synod received union overtures from both the Niagara and Missionary Presbyteries. Both bodies sent deputies to the October 1844 Synod. The committee which conferred with the Niagara Presbytery brought in a favourable report. It and the Free Church shared a common theology and discipline, and did "not question the obligation of civil government as such to honour Christ as the King of Kings, and the Governor amongst the nations." While cooperation "in all matters of common interest relative to the conversion of souls"[11] was commended, a formal union was never enacted, though some ministers and congregations did eventually join the Free Church.[12]

The Missionary Presbytery sent a deputation consisting of Professor Proudfoot, Robert Thornton, and John Jennings to the Free Church Synod of October 1844. Their appearance was regarded as "an earnest of greater union amongst sound Presbyterian Churches in the Province"[13] and resulted in the formation of union committees by both Synods. It was clear from the start what direction these negotiations would take. Given the task of debating "the practical bearings of the doctrine of the Headship of Christ"[14] they were specifically charged with formulating position papers on such questions as the meaning of Christ's Headship over the nations; and the role of the civil magistrate in punishing sabbath desecration, and in promoting education, and religion. Moreover they were to discuss how certain passages in the Confession of Faith were to be understood, and how present forms of church establishment should be viewed.[15]

Preliminary discussions on these points were held between 1845 and 1848, revealing, as the Synod of 1848 stated, "very significant differences." Two members of the Synod who were later expelled for "heresy" were displeased with the report of this committee, and called for its dissolution and the appointment of one "with instructions . . . to propose that all points regarding the power of the Civil Magistrate should be matters of mutual forbearance." They advocated a union on the basis of the great and fundamental truths of the faith.[16] This motion was defeated 26-5, revealing the first time a division within the Synod on this issue.

The Toronto *Banner* was in favour of union on "scriptural grounds," yet aspects of its reasoning would not have commended itself to the bulk of the Free Church ministers. In September 1845 the *Banner* argued that "the Secession would bring to the Free Church an accession of good and zealous ministers, with minds clear from any bias towards Establishments, or State endowments."[17] It continued to support a union, arguing that the churches were at one on all doctrinal questions except the matter of church-state relations. Yet, whatever its theoretical position, the Free Church was, in essence, a voluntaryist church—"the practical renunciation of all State support, such as the Free Church now follows, would at once unite all Presbyterians in the Province who hold the essential doctrines of the Gospel, including the spiritual independence of the Church from State control."[18]

The voluntary controversy may have ceased in Scotland with the Disruption of 1843, but it persisted in Canada. From May 1846 until May 1848, the Toronto *Banner* was a forum for the discussion of church-state relations, national responsibility to God, and the relative merits of Free and United Presbyterian positions. The debate was frequently heated, the two principal antagonists being Robert Burns of the Free Church and William Barrie of the United Presbyterians. Occasional comments were added by Andrew Ferrier, R. H. Thornton, F. A. Fyfe of the Baptists, Peter and George Brown. Dr. Burns, in his irascible way, had expressed opinions in the Synod of 1846 and at the laying of the Knox's Church cornerstone, which in Barrie's view

> voluntary Churchmen hold to be essentially opposed to civil and religious liberty; and the view which he gave of Christ's Headship, in His divine mediatorial character as such... was, in my judgment, far from being correct, and if generally embraced, the Presbyterian Eldership would become the civil rulers of the nations in virtue of their office.[19]

Burns also succeeded in insulting the United Presbyterians; even his Free Church colleague William Rintoul regarded his comments as "sadly out of place, and as *I understood them*, equally unfounded, and I grieve to say, uncharitable."[20] Burns' reference to the United Presbyterians as separated from the Free Church "by the *mare magnum* of social infidelity" was seen by Barrie as "a personal shaft... directly aimed... at our existence as a professed christian church" and as a "wicked slander against us." The idea of union was now "perfectly preposterous" and "entirely extinguished."[21] Though he cooled down somewhat after reading a full report of Burns' speech, Barrie and his colleague R. H. Thornton were both agitated by further comments by Burns. These prompted Thornton to comment that though Burns "can meet as a member of the Committee on Union, [he] *desires no Union* . . . before ever he attended any conference of the joint Committee he had schemed to thwart its progress."[22] Burns was also accused of misrepresenting and misunderstanding the United Presbyterian position, and by Dr. Ferrier as not knowing "what Voluntaryism is, and that he is fighting against some ideal theory, of his own creation."[23] In Burns' mind, a Voluntary was:

> one who in theory or practice releases all men in their associated or national capacities, from allegiance to God, and I look on this theory as practically dangerous; for if we exclude from the range of revelation, as its guide and director, the most extensively influential of all agencies hitherto known among men, we put into the hands of the infidel an instrument of mighty potency.[24]

Nations were responsible to God for their actions, national sins existed, and God punished such sin. "Inasmuch as nations as such have no place in the future world," he argued, "they are punished in the present. We hold also that nations, like individuals, are capable of moral action, in and through the ordinary organs of national expression."[25]

Burns also defended the establishment principle, distinguishing an "established church" from an "endowed church." He accordingly asserted to Peter Brown, "Do not think, Mr. Editor, that when we of the Free Church lost our livings, we lost our principles too."[26] This establishment principle assumed "that men in their social or national capacity as well as their relations to each other as individuals are bound to honour God and to promote his cause." Moreover, "nations who enjoy revelation are bound to take the word of God as their supreme standard of duty and to regulate their public transactions accordingly." He was prepared to admit that the practical application of this theory was dependent "on the state of a people as to religious differences and political rights" though this remained largely undefined. The Sabbath, did, however, provide an example of what was sought, namely that the political authorities, while not commanding any religious duties, "may and ought to legislate and secure by authority one day in seven to be kept free from the business and amusements of ordinary days."[27]

William Barrie, speaking for the United Presbyterians, argued that both Christian and heathen magistrates had the same responsibilities. Both could ascertain their duties by appealing to "natural principles," meaning that "as civil rulers, they are not the divinely appointed guardians and administrators of the ordinances and laws of revealed religion." He suggested that the crux of the difference between the two churches was "the scriptural warrant for civil rulers to add legal sanctions to the institutions of revealed religion." He linked Burns with Scotland's Covenanters and Original Seceders who regarded the civil rulers as bound by scripture to "promote true religion, and the observance of its ordinances and laws . . . in the way of civil enactments, or legal sanctions." Indeed, Barrie argued that safeguarding "revealed religion" was not the responsibility of the civil authorities, but of the church. Magistrates

> as civil rulers do not derive their authority, *as such*, from Christ as Mediator, they have no right from him to enforce the adoption of Christianity by their

subjects, or the observance of its ordinances and precepts, by civil enactments. Civil rulers, from their high station in society, have great advantages for promoting the interests of the Church, and they are bound to improve them; but they are not bound to further religion by legal sanctions.[28]

Both Burns and Barrie brought to this exchange the legacy of past disputes in Scotland. Burns regarded the civil government as ordained by God, with responsibilities to protect the honour of His name, and His Sabbath. To Burns the ideal was a strong nationally established church, working in cooperation with the State to render the nation righteous before God. The principle of national covenanting was at the heart of his position. Barrie, on the other hand, was more skeptical about the role which the civil authorities ought to play in this process of sanctifying the nation. His greatest fear was of a civil government crushing individual Christian liberty and conscience. This continuation of the Voluntary controversy did nothing to hasten union. It undoubtedly clarified the issue for some, while muddying it for others. At the level of emotions and feelings, the Burns-Barrie clash merely added personal animosities to the obstacles of principle. Yet what was probably a greater barrier to union that these newspaper skirmishes, was the act of the Free Church Synod in deposing Andrew Ferrier for his voluntarist views.

Ferrier had applied for admission in 1845 through the Presbytery of Hamilton. In October 1845 the Presbytery of Hamilton met to consider his admission and reported "that there is nothing in his views in any respect, to hinder his admission as a minister of this church."[29] He was accordingly admitted and ministered for about six years to the congregation at Caledonia. He participated in the exchange in the *Banner* in 1846-48 and was severely critical of Dr. Burns, characterizing his remarks on the occasion of the cornerstone laying of Knox's Church, Toronto, as a "groundless and unprovoked attack" on the United Presbyterian Church. He asserted that "I would now be ashamed of my ecclesiastical connection were I not persuaded that there is not a minister in it who will support Dr. Burns in his preposterous and cruelly slanderous sentiments."[30] Later that same month Ferrier again crossed swords with Burns in the pages of the *Banner*, defending voluntaryism against the latter's attacks. Interestingly enough, Ferrier asserted that he had been received into the Free Church as a known voluntary.[31]

Perhaps if Ferrier had maintained a lower profile he would have been left alone. However, his dissenting position in the Synod of 1848, as we have already seen, placed him on record as at variance with the bulk of the Free Church. At that time Ferrier dissented from Mr. Reid's motion "because he conscientiously believed several of the principles contained in the statement of the Synod's Committee to be contrary to the Word of God."[32] Consequently, the Synod set up a committee—consisting of Bayne, Robb, Esson, Rogers, Roger, and Elder—to consider Dr. Ferrier's dissent and report back to the Synod. After hearing the report of this committee, the Synod instructed the Presbytery of Hamilton "to confer further with Dr. Ferrier on the views which he has avowed in his conference with the Synod's Committee, and to ascertain how far they coincide with the Standards of the Church." Moreover, in response to an Overture from the Presbytery of Montreal, the Synod resolved that all Presbyteries were to ensure that candidates for licensure, ordination, or admission were sound on "the subject of Christ's Headship over the nations" particularly with reference to the Westminster Confession and the statements of that year's Synod. [33]

The Presbytery of Hamilton met with Dr. Ferrier in the ensuing year and reported to the Synod of 1849 "that there appears to them to be much vagueness in the views of Dr. Ferrier, in regard to many points on which the Presbytery have conferred with him, and that in some things they appear to them to be opposed to the standards of this Church." Three written statements by Dr. Ferrier were also brought before the Synod: a statement of 8 January 1849, a memorial and petition of 18 June, and a pamphlet entitled *The Tower of Babel; or Confusion in Language on points connected with the question of Civil Establishments of Religion, a fertile source of strife and division in the Christian Church*. The Synod debated the case at length. In an unusual action Michael Willis left the Moderator's chair twice during the debate to address the Synod. On the morning of 27 June Willis presented a motion, seconded by Robert Burns, to approve of the Presbytery of Hamilton's report and find that Ferrier's position, notwithstanding any statements made at his induction, was "in various particulars inconsistent with the doctrines of Christ's supremacy over nations and civil governments, as held by this Church." [34]

The matter was then left in the hands of a special committee consisting of Willis, Burns, Gale, Bayne, Robb, Harris, Rintoul and two elders. They reported to the October meeting of the Commission of Synod their inability to reach an agreement with Dr. Ferrier, but the Commission decided to stay further proceedings in light of a letter from Ferrier pledging "his desire to respect the unity of the body, by avoiding any offensive obtrusion of his peculiar views, in opposition to the principles of the Church with which he desires to walk in fellowship." The decision stood, notwithstanding an attempt the next day to take a harder stand with him. [35]

There the matter could have rested. It arose, however, on two further occasions at the Synod of 1850. A report from the Committee to examine the records of the Commission of Synod raised certain questions about its proceedings, but the Commission's report was nonetheless sustained by a vote of 23-12. Problems in Ferrier's congregation at Caledonia occasioned the Synod's second glance at his case. The congregation was apparently divided over Ferrier's views. The Presbytery of Hamilton, unable to resolve the problem, referred it to Synod, which in turn established a special commission to review and settle the matter. [36]

This commission met in Caledonia on 9 July 1850 and in Hamilton on 13 August 1850. Ferrier was present at the first meeting, but not at the second. He sent a letter to the second which only served to confirm the commission in its opinion that his views remained unchanged and "his spirit... is that of defiance of all Presbyterial order and control." The Commission found Ferrier's views to be contrary to the Word of God and the standards of the church, and accordingly expelled him.[37] This decision the Synod of 1851 agreed to without a vote, though significantly seven ministers and one elder recorded their dissent, including Esson, Rintoul, and Gordon.[38]

Soon after the close of these proceedings Ferrier published a bitter and self-righteous pamphlet with the provocative title of *Christ Wounded in the House of His Friends: A Brief Review of Some Proceedings in Different Courts, of the Presbyterian Church of Canada*. Insisting on his own consistency, Ferrier argued that his views on the Voluntary Question in 1848-50 were identical to those of 1845 when the Presbytery of Hamilton received him into the church. He accused the Free Church of not understanding and even misrepresenting the United Presbyterian position, of being sectarian and of denying him the freedom to defend their views. He insisted that his *Tower of Babel* had been condemned without being read. His most scathing remarks, however, were reserved for the Presbytery of Hamilton and the Synod's special commission. "We have been cut off from connection with the Presbyterian Church in Canada," he declared, "in a manner the most arbitrary and tyrannical, merely, it would seem in one view, to gratify the pride and spleen of a faction of our Congregation, deserving of the scorn and reprobation of the Church Courts."[39]

Indeed, he insisted that it was not his views on voluntaryism that had split the congregation, but the actions of this faction, a group which had been encouraged and supported by some members of the Presbytery of Hamilton over and against "the honest session." He went so far as to suggest that the whole matter was "a purpose, if not a plot, of the church judicatories."[40] He was also critical of the composition and conduct of the special commission, denouncing in particular its senior member, Robert Burns of Knox Church, Toronto. Ferrier charged that Burns was attentive only to the faction, while ignoring the rest of the congregation. "Instead of trying to investigate the causes of strife and division alleged to exist, Dr. Burns' object seemed to be to stir up strife and division where there were none."[41] He was also critical of certain other procedures of the commission, including their issuing of a report containing errors. Above all, in attempting to open a new church in Caledonia they were "guilty of an act of deliberate and shameful ecclesiastical robbery, of which, when in far less glaring form, their church has often been heard loudly accusing others."[42]

Though it is far from certain that Ferrier's account is accurate in its details, it is clear, however, that Burns should never have been appointed to the commission. As one of the most outspoken critics of voluntaryism, with a cantankerous personality, and as one who had already crossed swords with Ferrier on this very issue, he could scarcely have been expected to view the evidence calmly and disinterestedly.

The Ferrier case served to indicate the difficulties surrounding a proposed union. It demonstrated that his position was regarded as inconsistent with the stand of the Free Church and was deserving of censure. Once deposed, Ferrier became an obstacle to union when he joined the United Presbyterian Church. It would be an obvious test of the Free Church's consistency, to see if they could unite with a denomination which had just received into full fellowship one of their "heretics."

At the same time as the Ferrier case was being resolved, the Synod was reassessing its attitude to certain sections of the Westminster Confession of Faith which concerned the civil magistrate. One student, John Scott, had been refused licensure by the Presbytery of Hamilton because of his problems with these passages. A re-examination thus took place at both Synod and Presbytery levels throughout 1850-54. A declaratory act was finally passed, stating that the Synod did not understand the sections in the Confession "relating to the duty of the civil magistrate, as teaching or sanctioning an Erastian control of the Church by the civil magistrate, or the persecution of individuals for conscience sake."[43]

Though no direct negotiations with the United Presbyterians were held from 1850 to 1854 the Free Church Synod gave further evidence that it was clarifying its position. The Synod of 1854, in response to overtures from its own constituents and from the United Presbyterians, expressed their desire for a union on "scriptural principles." They accordingly issued an important statement, setting forth the framework for such a union. The lawfulness of state endowments could now be considered an open question, though they were insistent on maintaining their views on the role of the civil magistrates "and the responsibilities of nations to God, to be of such vital importance as to demand that they be made a matter of ecclesiastical incorporation" and "necessary to the best interests of the Church of Christ."[44] The United Presbyterians regarded this resolution as precluding any union and thus no negotiations were held in 1854.

While the church courts might find the obstacles to a union seemingly insurmountable, a growing movement in favour of union was felt at the congregational level. A joint meeting of Free and United Presbyterian Churches, held 26 March 1855 in the English Settlement, London, for example, argued that continued separation was dishonouring to God and tainted the church's testimony. Union, moreover, "would involve no dereliction of Scriptural Principle, on either side" and would bring many blessings to the church.[45] Similar meetings were held throughout the province. One asserted that the differences between the two churches were slight and unimportant, and argued that union would present "a strong barrier to the progress of Popery, Infidelity, and Irreligion."[46] Another maintained that union would strengthen greatly the Presbyterian cause in the province "by uniting small congregations of each body into larger, thereby lessening, in many instances, the difficulty of ministerial support, and affording to pastors much wider fields of usefulness." It was asserted, moreover, that in fact, many congregations were already made up of various brands of Presbyterians "who act harmoniously, and illustrate satisfactorily that the whole Presbyterian family not only may, but should dwell together in unity."[47] Another meeting chided the two Synods for "seeming backwardness ... to lay down a basis of Union," pointing to "the increasingly pressing necessities of the country, and the boldness and arrogance of our common enemy, urgently calling for a united and determined stand being made on behalf of our common faith."[48] It was also asserted by some that "in all probability, as much difference of opinion now exists in each of the Churches *separately*, as there would be *collectively*, were they united."[49]

Similar views were expressed in Rev. John Jennings' United Presbyterian congregation in Toronto. In January 1859 the Session recorded its view "that were the Union of these two Churches consummated, it is firmly believed that the differences which now pertain to each church, as a whole, will in no wise disturb the general harmony and efficiency."[50] Not all congregations were so optimistic about union. The Kirk Session of Knox Church, Hamilton, for example, declared that the fourth article of the Basis of Union "is not only ambiguous in its phraseology, but makes no provision for the *practical* recognition of Christ's supremacy as King of Nations." Accordingly, union on this basis "would not tend to promote the harmonious action of the two Synods in great questions which may hereafter occur in this land, bearing on the jurisdiction of the Civil Magistrate."[51]

Such congregational meetings tended to emphasize the points of similarity between the two churches, the common foe of Popery and unbelief, and the pragmatic argument of strengthening the Presbyterian cause. Detractors tended to stress the difference of principle and usually tried to cast their opponents in the worst possible light. One such writer asserted that:

> The *real difficulty* in the way of Union, is, that we affirm that, all nations enjoying the light of revelation are bound, in all their national actings, to recognize the supreme authority of the Word of God, and follow its teachings, whenever it affords them direction, and our U.P. brethren deny that the nations have anything more to do with the Bible than they have with the Koran, unless a majority of the people, or, at least of the rulers, are converted men.[52]

Meanwhile, the Synod and the Union Committees continued to discuss the question. The Synod of 1855 passed a mediating motion to the effect that the Free Church considered the only difference between the two churches to be that they "consider it the imperative duty of officers and magistrates in their public and representative capacity, to legislate and rule in subjection to the authority, and in accordance with the dictates of revelation, where they are known."[53] Accordingly, they rejected Robert Burns' motion which expressed alarm over errors in the United Presbyterian position.

The Union Committees met in McNab Street Free Church, Hamilton on 4 and 5 June of the ensuing year. The meeting was well attended and considerable time was spent in devotions and prayer. General agreement on all matters except the role of the civil magistrate was evident. Even on such issues as Christ's Headship over the church, liberty of conscience, and Christ's authority over all men, there appears to have been enough common ground for a union. It was then proposed that each Synod formulate a basis of union "in which the exclusive Headship of Christ over his Church, together with the freedom of conscience on the one hand, and the duty of all men to be governed in all their private and public relations, by the authority of Christ in his word, on the other, may be fully maintained."[54]

The Union Committee reported to the Synod of 1857, as a basis of union, three articles which the joint committees had approved. The first article set forth the *Headship of Christ*, asserting that "the Lord Jesus Christ is the only King and Head of his Church; that the laws by which it is to be governed are contained only in the inspired Scriptures; that Christ hath made her free from all external or secular authority in the administration of her own affairs." The second article concerned *Liberty of Conscience*. It began with the affirmation that every individual was free to study the Scriptures, come to his own conclusions, and follow those in his conduct. At the same time, however, it asserted that such liberty of conscience was not a license to "disturb the peace of society, or to set aside the lawful authority of the magistrate, or to blaspheme the name of God openly and wantonly, or to disturb the public religious worship of his neighbour." Such were abuses which the civil magistrate might act to put down "both for the glory of God and the public weal." The last article set forth the *Duties of the Civil Magistrate*. The civil magistrate was not a church officer, had no ecclesiastical or spiritual functions, and could not act as an arbiter of scripture. However,

> he has yet an important part to act in his official capacity in relation to the Kingdom of Christ; that it is his duty in his public as well as in his private capacity, to acknowledge the authority of Christ as the Supreme Governor among the nations; and that in this view, without taking cognizance of offences against morality considered as sins against God, he ought to see that, in aiming to promote the social wellbeing in subordination to the divine glory, the laws of the land in their enactment and administration are avowedly in accordance with the principles of justice and morality inculcated in the Scriptures. At the present time we think it necessary especially to declare that he is bound to acknowledge the divine authority of the Christian Sab-

bath, and to secure to all his subjects their right to enjoy the sacred rest of that day.[55]

In the eyes of John Bayne of Galt, one of the foremost defenders of Free Church distinctives, these articles indicated that the United Presbyterians had moved closer to the Free Church, and thus, if the practical aspects could be settled, a union was not far off.

The Union committees met in Knox Church, Toronto, on 20 and 21 October to work out some of the practical implications of these articles. They discussed state endowments of religion, the use of the Bible in the Common Schools, and the appointment of days of public humiliation and thanksgiving by the civil magistrate. While the Free Church maintained its establishment principle and the United Presbyterians denied the lawfulness of state endowments, a spirit of compromise was evident, and both agreed to differ on this point. It was agreed that the use of the Bible in the Common Schools was a desirable end and that the civil government had a duty to make this possible "while abstaining from the enforcement of the use of it upon any who may be opposed thereto." Finally, it was agreed that days of public humiliation and thanksgiving were proper and that the civil authorities "may with propriety nominate the day, and recommend the observance of it by all under his rule; at the same time he has no right to prescribe the religious exercises to be observed."[56]

The joint committees met again 14 and 15 April to discuss the question of Sabbath observance. The civil magistrate's responsibility, it was agreed, involves protecting "the sacred character and obligation of the Sabbath." The church, for its part, might pressure the legislature to act on the subject. Those within the church who disagreed with the majority's stance would be given "all equitable liberty," but would be obliged "in action or dissent, to respect constitutional order and the received principles of the united body." The Free Church, having a numerical majority, would thus be able to give expression to its distinctive principles. The committees decided not to discuss this issue further since the differences "are not . . . so great, nor of such a nature, as to prevent cordial cooperation . . . and should be made matters of mutual christian forbearance."[57]

By 1858 the Synod was weary of debating the role of the civil magistrate. Although a small group of ministers, notably John Bayne of Galt and Principal Michael Willis, continued to be "watchmen on the wall" for strong Free Church statements, the majority in the Synod was prepared to push on towards union, leaving some matters undefined.[58]

The Synod of 1859 considered a more comprehensive but less detailed basis of union than that of 1857. Consideration of the fourth article—"Of the Headship of Christ over the Nations and the Duty of the Civil Magistrate"—engendered considerable debate. There were particular problems over two explanatory notes which the United Presbyteries wanted appended to this fourth article. They were objected to as "liable to misconception" and a request was made for their withdrawal.[59] Further debate on these issues was cut off by a motion of R. F. Burns. He asserted that while the Free Church was committed to a union on the basis of "national responsibility to Christ" they did not want "at this advanced stage of negotiation, to burden the Basis with an enumeration of the varied practical applications of that principle."[60] The Synod, accordingly, approved the Basis of Union and sent it down to presbyteries and sessions for discussion.

The Basis of Union was sent down to presbyteries under the Barrier Act. Although all presbyteries and 88 of 95 sessions approved of it, a substantial minority in some presbyteries disapproved, as in Hamilton where 9 of 32 disapproved.[61]

The Synod of 1860 approved by a vote of 121-37 the report of its union committee and resolved to report its approval to the United Presbyterian Synod which was also meeting in Hamilton. The United Presbyterians agreed to drop the notes to article four but wanted to insert a clause into that article which would read, "it being understood that, in the application of the doctrine of this article, mutual forbearance shall be exercised."[62] A lengthy discussion ensued during which various motions were put forward and then withdrawn. Finally, the Synod approved a motion by William Reid to the effect that while still desirous of union, the Free Church could not accept this new clause "which might seem to recognize unlimited forebearance as to the application of the said doctrine." Hence, another committee, consisting of Ure (Convener), Willis, Laing, Inglis, T. Wardrope, Scott, Gregg, Ross, Kemp, McRuar, Topp, McLaren, G. P. Young, D. McKenzie, McMurrich, McLellan, Ferrier and Sherwood, was formed to meet with the United Presbyterians to see if the problem might be overcome.[63]

By late summer 1860 the Union negotiations were almost complete. The union committee had already met after the Synod of June 1860 and had given final approval to the basis of union. Accordingly, the Moderator called a special meeting of Synod for 2-4 October in Toronto to finally consider the basis of union and to make "any necessary arrangement with a view to the consummation of the Union." This time the basis appeared with a preamble stating that as far as the practical outworkings of the fourth article was concerned, "unanimity is not required in the united body" and any cases that arose because of it would be settled by the courts of the church.[64] Some of those present at this meeting had difficulty understanding the preamble and wanted the committees to rephrase it. A motion was carried to appoint a deputation to the United Presbyterian Church (then in session in Toronto) to discuss the preamble. The United Presbyterians sent a delegation to the Free Church and a conference, held outside of the Synod, altered the wording of the preamble. A further conference between representatives of the two churches recommended that the new church be called the Canada Presbyterian church and that the union be formalized in Knox Church, Toronto, on 20 December 1860. Neither of these proposals commended themselves to the Free Church. The name Presbyterian Church in Canada was preferred, though the other name would be adopted if insisted upon. As well, the Free Church wanted the union to be consummated at the regular meeting of Synod which was scheduled for Montreal in June 1861.

Even at this stage, there were notable dissents from some Free Church ministers. Dr. Willis did not want to be committed to a union at the next Synod meeting and Mr. Smellie, the protégé of the now deceased Dr. John Bayne questioned the whole matter of union—particularly in light of significant opposition to it from within the Free Church.[65] Furthermore, in the opinion of ministers such as L. McPherson and D. Fraser, the Free Church had relinquished its principles and had "seriously endangered the doctrinal purity of the church, as well as compromised its own consistency in the eyes of the world." Moreover, in their view, the Synod had agreed to union without consulting the members and adherents of the church and in doing so "the Synod has virtually assumed the right and power of legislating within the domain of conscience, and has set aside, without the knowledge or consent of those whose interest it is, one of the most precious and sacred rights with which Christ has invested each and all of the members of His Church."[66]

With the union agreed to, the Free Church established various committees to deal with its logistics: the arrangement of presbyteries, Home Missions, theological education, and property. Interestingly enough, the Presbytery of Montreal ordained one Daniel Paterson, a licentiate of the United Presbyterian Church on 24 October 1860. Paterson had recently arrived in Canada from Scotland. In anticipation of the forthcoming union, he applied to the Free Church's Presbytery of Montreal for admission. Dr. Taylor and the Rev. Mr. McKie of the United Presbyterian Church participated. The editor of the *Record* commented that "this act may be regarded as of historical importance, being the first fruits of the union of the two churches."[67]

The final meeting of the Free Church Synod opened 4 June 1861 in the Côté Street Free Church, Montreal. The retiring moderator, W. B. Clark of Chalmers' Church, Quebec City, preached the opening sermon and the Synod was constituted. The attendance was large—128 ministers of 158 and 74 of 113 elders. William Gregg of Cooke's Church, Toronto, was elected Moderator. The forthcoming union eclipsed all discussion of regular business. An act concerning congregational property was discussed as was the possibility of a general union of all Presbyterians in the Province.

Even at this late date some members of Synod wanted to reconsider the Preamble to the Basis of Union. Although objections were raised that this was out of order and incompetent, the Moderator ruled that it was in order. However, S. C. Fraser and A. McLean challenged the Moderator's ruling and by a vote of 77-56 the Moderator's ruling was struck down. There was to be no more discussion at this point in time.

Yet clearly not all in the Free Church were happy. Five ministers from the Presbytery of London sent a letter to the Moderator, dissenting from the basis of union and charging that the preamble was open to an interpretation "that would operate to the practical abnegation of Christ's headship over the nations, and the duty of the civil magistrate, as laid down in the fourth article."[68] As well, five other ministers dissented from the union and gave in detailed reasons for doing so—all of which were, in turn, answered by committees of Synod.

While the Free Church Synod was meeting in Côté Street Church, the United Presbyterians convened in Dr. Taylor's Lagauchetière Street Church. There it was decided that the various United Presbyterian congregations could retain their names and "shall not be held, though coming in consequence of this union under the inspection of the united Church, as in any way changing its ecclesiastical connexion, or impairing any civil rights which it now possesses and enjoys."[69]

For the past several years, the Free Church *Record* had been a warm proponent of union, though always insisting that it be on sound principles. It could point to unions in Australia and Nova Scotia as examples of what was desired in Canada. As the day of the union approached, the editor wrote joyfully that "the consummation of the Union will be the most important event that has yet taken place in the history of our common Presbyterianism in Canada; it will form an epoch in the annals of our church."[70] Certainly not all would have agreed with the editor that "we had advanced to our present position, without giving up or compromising any of the great principles which it has been the glory of the Church hitherto to maintain," though they would have agreed with his call for increased zeal, spirituality, and devotedness "that we may find ourselves, through the influence of the Spirit of God, raised to a higher measure of spiritual life and power."[71]

The first Synod of the Canada Presbyterian Church opened 6 June 1861 in the Wesleyan Church, St. James Street, Montreal. Dr. Thornton and Rev. William Gregg as Moderators of the United Presbyterian and Free Churches, respectively, presided and signed the articles of union. Dr. W. Taylor of Montreal was elected Moderator of the new church and W. Reid and W. Fraser, the clerks of the former Synods, were elected clerks of the new Synod. After the formalities were over, the new church met in the Côté Street Church 7-13 June to conduct its regular business.[72]

It was a long and difficult road which led to the Union of 1861. In the eyes of some it was a union born of compromise;[73] to others, it represented the triumph of essential principles over and against those of a secondary nature. Whereas some in the Free Church regarded the basis of union as compromising their cherished principles, others insisted that the Union had left those very principles intact. Clearly, the basis of union could be read from either a Free Church or a United Presbyterian perspective. It remained to be seen whether a Free Church or a United Presbyterian emphasis would be worked out in the day-to-day life of the church. Nonetheless, it was equally clear that the new church was strong, committed to Evangelicalism and historic Calvinism, and would be a force to be reckoned with in Canadian society.

Chapter 10

CONCLUSION

The emergence of the Free Church must be understood as a form of religious revival. The secession, born of a Scottish conflict and transferred to a colonial setting, inspired a crusading spirit which was congenial to mid-nineteenth-century Canadian society. There were, to be sure, indigenous Canadian factors like the dispute over the Temporalities Bill which added fuel to the conflict. Yet had there been no split in the Church of Scotland, there would have been none in the Canadian Synod. Discord and secession disrupt the formal structures of churches and if pushed too far will dissolve a church into a series of quarrelling communities. Yet they are reflective of an active conscience in the community. The Disruption of 1844, although productive of discord, gave to those who left a renewed sense of mission, a unifying set of principles, and a greater determination to transform society. For Free Churchmen the secession left behind many of the less zealous ministers in the Kirk Synod and put the Canadian church in touch with an international evangelical movement.

At the time of the Disruption in Scotland, both the Church of Scotland and the Free Church of Scotland attempted to secure the support of Canadian Presbyterians. This, however, was hardly a contest of equals. The more aggressive, better organized Free Church of Scotland took the initiative and held the stronger position, right from the beginning. Deputies from the Free Church arrived first. At the same time Free Church supporters in Canada enjoyed the support of the considerable journalistic talents of Peter and George Brown of the Toronto *Banner*. By the time that Church of Scotland deputies arrived, the Disruption in Canada had already occurred and a Canadian Free Church was firmly established. Moreover, the Kirk supporters in Canada did little to counteract Free Church influence and failed to capture the imagination of the Presbyterian community.

The Free Church had no need to create new and unfamiliar ecclesiastical structures. There was little in the old ones to hinder their plans, or that could not be enlivened by an infusion of enthusiasm and new personnel. The familiar presbyterial organization of local congregations, attached through regional presbyteries and under the final authority of a provincial synod, was retained. This ability to avoid unnecessary change in organization eliminated a potential source of conflict.

Although there were strong ties between the Canadian and Scottish Free Churches, it was clear that the Canadians could not rely exclusively upon British ministers to fill its pulpits. It was essential to ensure a steady, reliable supply of new ministers for an expanding church. Knox College was thus organized as the denomination's seminary. By 1859, fifty ministers in the Synod had been wholly or partly trained at Knox.

By 1861, at the end of the first phase of its history, the Free Church had enjoyed a considerable measure of success. It had surpassed in numbers both the Kirk Synod and the United Presbyterians. This is not surprising as the Free Churchmen were enthusiastic and well-organized missionaries whose view was not obstructed by a Scottish exclusiveness. The Kirk Synod might take refuge in an appeal to tradition and hope to maintain its position by passive resistance. This might satisfy more worldly Presbyterians like John A. Macdonald, who would not be moved by enthusiasm, or those who instinctively opposed zeal in any form. Yet this enthusiasm brought the Free Church into missionary work, attracting to it those outside the Presbyterian community.

Having separated from the Old Kirk, it was understandable that the Free Church would attempt to seek accord with other Presbyterians in the province. Union negotiations were thus begun and held intermittently during the next seventeen years with the United Presbyterians. Although sharing a common theology and organization, the Free Church and the United Presbyterian Church were nonetheless separated by the gulf of tradition, history, and different views on the relation between the state and the church. Indeed, some Canadian Free Church ministers had debated this latter point with United Presbyterians in Scotland. In Canada this debate continued.

The most serious difference between the Free Church and the United Presbyterians was their position on church-state relations. The United Presbyterians did not see the state as an agent of religion in society and rejected church establishment in any form as an open door to worldly influence in the church. They argued that Christian and non-Christian magistrates had the same responsibilities and both should govern in accordance with natural law. From the Free Church point of view, a Christian, whether a magistrate or a private citizen, had an obligation to secure the passage of legislation and the pursuit of policies based on Christian principles. In practice, the United Presbyterians were inclined to support the same policies and candidates as the Free Church, but did not pursue these policies with the same intensity, and consequently did not exercise the same influence.

The Free Church Synod deposed Dr. Andrew Ferrier, minister at Caledonia, for his voluntaryism, undoubtedly adding to the obstacles in the way of union. Yet such matters were a legacy of the Scottish past, had little relevance to conditions in Canada, and did not excite much interest among Canadian congregations. It remained for a new generation of Canadian-trained ministers, who had little involvement in old country disputes, to decide to put aside these differences.

The Free Church belief in the importance of political action committed them to activities to combat slavery, intemperance, popery, and sabbath-breaking. As it was not in theory opposed to state support, the Free Church in 1844-45 applied for a continuation of its government grants, but was refused. By 1848 the Synod decided to abandon all claims to state support, apparently under the impact of Peel's grant to Maynooth College in Ireland, and the influence of Peter and George Brown, declaring that the state could no longer distinguish between true and false religion. Most issues placed the Free Church in the camp of the Reformers. At the same time, however, it is apparent that not all members of the Free Church were political reformers, and that the church was not exclusively made up of the followers of George Brown.

In matters of finance, the Free Church, for the most part, had to rely on its own community for support. It did receive some money from friends in Scotland, Ireland, and England, but could also count upon the support of such wealthy members as Isaac Buchanan and John Redpath. In the organization of its financial affairs it tried to adopt some Scottish Free Church practices. An attempt was thus made to institute a common Sustentation Fund out of which all ministers' stipends would be paid. However, because of lay suspicions of ordained office-holders managing congregational money, the idea never gained wide acceptance and had to be abandoned. Local congregations thus made their own arrangements for paying the minister's stipend. Pew rents, subscriptions, and collections were the usual means of raising this money. The most ambitious project financially was the establishment of Knox College. Though suffering from financial insecurity, the college had by 1856 moved into new quarters at Elmsley Villa, and by 1858 had been incorporated by an Act of the Provincial Parliament. The church as a whole experienced the financial vicissitudes of one dependent upon voluntary support, but was in turn a good example of the sufficiency of such support.

There were in the Free Church three offices to which men could be ordained: minister, elder, and deacon. Each of these required the same standards of piety and the same theological affirmations. The educational requirements, however, were different, as the ministers underwent a rigorous six-year programme of arts and theological study. With the elders, ministers were responsible for spiritual guidance and discipline in the local congregation. They also sat and deliberated together in the church courts. Deacons were to be entrusted with congregational finances, but because of reluctance to concentrate power in this office, finances were usually in the hands of managers and trustees. The church readily received ministers from the Free Church of Scotland and the Presbyterian Church of Ireland.

Those trained by the Church of Scotland would not be admitted without examination, nor would those from the New and Old School Presbyterian Churches in the United States: the former because its theology was sometimes questioned, the latter because it tolerated slavery.

Truth as they saw it was more important to Free Churchmen than organic unity. This in part explains why union negotiations with the United Presbyterians were so difficult and protracted. A concern for maintaining orthodoxy of belief and conduct led to the deposition of both Andrew Ferrier and Robert Peden, and explains the church's emphasis on discipline. Coupled with this theological orthodoxy was an ecclesiastical conservatism which manifested itself in resisting changes in form of worship— particularly the introduction of instrumental music in church services. Maintaining such orthodoxy created tensions but did not fragment the church. Those who were disciplined may have had sympathizers, but had not attracted disciples who might demonstrate their sympathy by leaving. Those in the Synod with forceful personalities, like Dr. Robert Burns, often irritated and alienated their colleagues, although they undoubtedly attracted people to the church. Clearly the Free Church was made up of busy men and not chronic schismatics.

The Free Church's theological outlook was both Calvinistic, affirming the doctrine of election, and evangelical, calling men and women to repentance and faith of Christ. They saw no inconsistency in holding both positions. They also maintained the doctrines of the substitutionary atonement of Christ and justification by faith alone. These ideas can be perceived in the sermons of Michael Willis, Mark Young Stark and George Paxton Young. Though Young has been charged with deviating from this orthodoxy, it appears that, at least during the Free Church years, he maintained his evangelical Calvinism.

The Free Church exercised an influence in Canadian society which was far beyond its numbers. There were very few concerned with Canadian politics who were not aware of the weight of its influence. It was only one voice, but often the loudest in a chorus of evangelical Protestants decrying popery, intemperance, and Sabbath-breaking. Though its critics might dismiss the Free Church as bigoted, obscurantist, and self-righteous, a more sympathetic assessment might see it as tough-minded, informed, and uncompromising. Its clear views, fervent zeal, and transcendent message, though inviting ridicule, were arguably its greatest strengths.

Though the links between the Free Church and the Reform Party are not as firm as once supposed, yet George Brown still remains a symbol of the Free Church and its influence: often feared, but not distrusted; exercising a moral influence in society, but enjoying only a transitory role in the exercise of power. In short, the Free Church may never have enjoyed great popularity, but, popular or not, it was an active and powerful force within society.

TABLES

TABLE 1
Synod of the Presbyterian Church of Canada in Connection with the Church of Scotland[a]

Year	Location	Moderator	Clerk(s)	Synod Roll			Attendance Record			
				Congregations	Ministers	Elders	Ministers	%	Elders	%
1831	Kingston	J. McKenzie	R. McGill		19		15		7	
1832	Kingston	A. Mathieson	R. McGill				12		2	
1833	York	J. Machar	R. McGill	25	25	13	18	72	2	15
1834	Montreal (adjourned)	A. Connel	J. Mackenzie				7		2	
1834	Montreal	A. Connel	J. Mackenzie "pro tempora"		41	11	17	41	4	36
1835	Williamstown	J. Cruickshank	R. McGill	46	43	26	29	67	8	31
1836	Kingston	W. Rintoul	A. Gale	50	49	21	26	53	4	19
1837	Toronto	A. Gale	W. Rintoul	56	52	30	28			
1838	Montreal	J. Cook		57	54	28	24	44	9	32
1839	Kingston	R. McGill	A. Gale	58	55	32	20	36	7	22

Table 1 133

Year	Place									
1840	Toronto	H. Urquhart		83 (includes United Synod)	77	34	34	57	10	29
1841	Kingston	J. George	A. Gale	92	82	42	36	44	13	31
1842	Montreal	H. Esson	A. Gale	86	84[b]	33	36	43	5	15
1843	Toronto	J. Clugston	W. Rintoul / A. Bell	88	86[c]	57	42	49	17	30
1844	Kingston	M. Y. Stark / J. Cook	W. Rintoul / A. Bell	91	91[b]	69	67	74	40	58
1844	Kingston	J. Cook	A. Bell	67	63[b]	44	32	51	10	23

[a] *A&P PCC in Connex CofS*, 1831-44.

[b] Includes 2 Queen's Professors 1842-44.

[c] Includes 2 Queen's Professors 1842-44, and 2 ministers who then left Synod.

TABLE 2
Free Church in Canada, 1844-1861 [a]

Year	Location	Moderator	Clerk(s)	Synod Roll			Attendance Record			
				Congregations	Ministers	Elders	Ministers	%	Elders	%
1844 (July)	Kingston	M. Y. Stark	W. Rintoul	23	23					
1844 (Oct.)	Toronto	M. Y. Stark	W. Rintoul	53	32	31	23	72	15	48
1845	Cobourg	Robt. Burns	W. Rintoul	40	33	31	20	61	10	32
1846	Hamilton	John Bayne	W. Rintoul	53	47	36	35	74	26	72
1847	Kingston	John M. Roger	W. Rintoul	86	54	39	27	50	13	49
1848	Toronto	Don. McKenzie	W. Rintoul	92	58	46	39	67	20	43
1849	Toronto	Michael Willis	W. Rintoul	106	61	46	44	72	22	40
1850	Toronto	Wm. Reid	W. Rintoul	111	65	52	43	66	24	46
1851	Kingston	Robt. Boyd	Wm. Reid John Burns	105	73	57	46	63	30	53
1852	Kingston	Thomas Wightman	Wm. Reid John Burns	115	81	57	50	62	26	46

Table 2 135

1853	Hamilton	Alex Gale	Wm. Reid	124	89	69	66	74	47	68
1854	Toronto	Henry Gordon	Wm. Reid	107	92	72	71	77	39	54
1855	Montreal	Thomas Lowry	Wm. Reid	105	104	71	63	61	30	42
1856	London	George Cheyne	Wm. Reid	121	110	102	78	71	51	50
1857	Kingston	George Smellie	Wm. Reid	129	124	80	87	70	45	56
1858	Hamilton	J. Wardrope	Wm. Reid	139	131	92	106	81	66	72
1859	Toronto	G. P. Young	Wm. Reid	153	143	105	108	76	56	53
1860 (June)	Hamilton	W. B. Clark	Wm. Reid	168	151	106	111	74	68	64
1860 (Oct.)	Toronto	W. B. Clark	Wm. Reid	168	150	108	52	35	22	20
1861	Montreal	Wm. Gregg	Wm. Reid	158	158	128	113	72	74	58

[a] Source: *Minutes of Synod*, 1844-61.

APPENDICES

APPENDIX I

The Original "Protest" of 1844

WHEREAS the Church, as the divinely constituted Depositary and Guardian of Revealed Truth, is specially bound to lift up her testimony for those particular truths of revelation which are at any time endangered or overborne by the antagonist powers of this world.

And whereas those great and fundamental truths which respect the supremacy of Christ in his Church,—the spiritual independence of her rules,—their exclusive responsibility to her Great Head,—the rights and privileges of his people, and the proper relation which should subsist between the Church and the State are at the present day endangered, and have actually been overborne in the Established Church of Scotland through recent encroachments of the State upon her spiritual province, and submitted to by her.

And whereas, in righteous testimony against these encroachments, great numbers of office-bearers and members of said Church have solemnly and deliberately come out from her, and are now favourably constituted into the Free Protesting Church of Scotland—a Church which has, during the last twelve months, enjoyed many unequivocal tokens of the approbation of the Great Head.

And whereas, this Synod of the Presbyterian Church of Canada in connexion with the Church of Scotland apart from all considerations of a general kind, which should have led them to testify against the defections and corruptions of the said Established Church, were especially bound to do so, because of their connection with the said Church, and because also of repeated testimonies solemnly and deliberately lifted up by the Synod in former years in behalf of the contendings of those who have been compelled to secede.

And whereas the due and proper testimony against the defections and corruptions of the Established Church of Scotland was a termination of the peculiarly close and untenable connexion in which this Synod stood to her.

And whereas it has been in an orderly and constitutional way proposed to this Synod, having been made the subject of petitions and overtures by congregations and Presbyteries,—and whilst it has been advocated by many of the members, that this Synod should terminate its connexion with said Church, and alter its designation accordingly.

Source: *Banner*, 12 July 1844.

And whereas this Synod has, by the vote of a majority of its members, come to the decision that it shall not terminate said connexion, nor take other such action as was required,

Therefore we, the undersigned Ministers and Elders, members of the Synod of the Presbyterian Church of Canada, in connexion with the Church of Scotland, do in our own name, as well as in the name of all who may adhere to us, hereby dissent and protest against said decision for the following reasons:

1. That in our conscientious conviction this Synod thereby giving their virtual sanction to the procedure of the Established Church of Scotland, in the great questions at issue between that Church and the Free Protesting Church of Scotland, and lending the weight of their influence as a Church to the support of principles which are incompatible with the purity and the liberty of any Church by which they are allowed, and which are fitted at the same time to do grievous injury to the cause of the Redeemer throughout the world.

2. That in a cause relating to any Church, in which they have many and obvious views for feeling a very deep and special interest,—a cause, too, in which the honour of Christ's crown and the interests of His kingdom are intimately concerned, they have refused to discharge the obvious duty of lifting up a full and unambiguous testimony for the truth, and thereby strengthening the hands of those who are witnessing for Christ and suffering for his sake.

3. That after solemnly pledging themselves in various forms, and at different times, to maintain the great principles for which the Free Protesting Church is now contending, and which the Established Church of Scotland has practically repudiated,—and after, especially, the import and the sincerity of such pledges had been brought into question by the actings of various ministers, and even of one of the inferior Church Courts—they have virtually receded from these solemn pledges, and destroyed the weight of every expression of their opinions in favour of the aforesaid principles embodied in their records.

4. That by leaving an open door for the admission of ministers and elders from the Established Church of Scotland, holding unsound views on the great principles aforesaid, they have most seriously endangered the purity of the Church, and brought even her independence into peril, through the probable introduction of office bearers prepared to submit to the same encroachments of the civil power, by which the Church of Scotland has been enslaved.

5. That they have rendered the relation in which they stand towards the Established Church of Scotland so doubtful and equivocal, that even their declaration of spiritual independence is necessarily deprived of all significance and weight,—that the terms on which their endowments are held have been, in effect, declared to be such as are incompatible with the proper regulation of their intercourse with other churches, and even with free action in many other matters of great importance; and that, moreover, they have cast away the opportunity of placing this Church on a base on which she might have gathered around her all the sound-hearted Presbyterianism of the Province.

6. That they have given additional weight to the practical argument against establishments furnished by the present position of the Established Church of Scotland, strengthened the hands of those, who, in this province, are denying the lawfulness and expediency of all national endowments for religious purposes, and rejected the opportunity which God, in his providence, had afforded them of proving to the world that entire freedom of action, and a jealous determination to guard against the encroachments of the civil power, were perfectly compatible with the enjoyment of the countenance and support of the state.

7. That in a matter in which the consciences of many of their brethren were aggrieved, and for refusing relief, in regard to which no moral necessity could be pleaded on their part, such relief has nevertheless been refused.

Wherefore, for all these and other reasons which might be stated, we dissent from the decision to which this venerable court yesterday came,—and while feeling painfully the solemnity of our position and deeply distressed in the view of the possible results, that by continuing the peculiar connexion which has hitherto subsisted between them and the Established Church of Scotland, we solemnly protest to this venerable court, conscientious belief, that, in respect of the premises, sin, in matters fundamental, has been done by this court; and that, while at the same time we continue to adhere to the Confession of Faith, and other standards of this Church, we can yet no longer with a clear conscience, hold office in the Presbyterian Church of Canada, in connexion with the Church of Scotland.

And further, we protest that the guilt of schism lies not on us, but on those who have acted in a way which compels us to depart.

And further also, we protest on behalf of ourselves and those of the people of this Church who may now, or hereafter adhere to us, that we hold ourselves entitled to all the property and emoluments of whatsoever kind, of which we are now in possession.

APPENDIX II

Formula to be Signed by Ministers, Elders, Deacons, and Probationers

I, _____, do hereby declare that I do sincerely own and believe the whole Doctrine contained in the Westminster Confession of Faith, as approved by the Church of Scotland, in the year one thousand six hundred and forty-seven, to be the truths of God, and I do own the purity of worship presently authorised and practised in this Church, and also the Presbyterian Government and Discipline thereof: which Doctrine, Worship, and Church Government I am persuaded are founded upon the Word of God and agreeable thereto; and I promise that, through the grace of God, I shall firmly and constantly adhere to the same, and to the utmost of my power, shall in my station assert, maintain, and defend the said Doctrine, Worship, Discipline, and Government of this Church by Sessions, Presbyteries, and Synods; that I shall, in my practice conform myself to the said Worship, and submit to the said Discipline and Government, and never to endeavour, directly or indirectly, the prejudice or subversion of the same; and I promise that I shall follow no divisive course from the present order in the Church; renouncing all doctrines, tenets, and opinions whatsoever contrary to or inconsistent with the said Doctrine, Worship, Discipline or Government of this Church.

Questions to be put to a Minister at his Ordination

1. Do you believe the Scriptures of the Old and New Testament to be the Word of God, and the only rule of faith and manners?
2. Do you sincerely own and believe the whole doctrine contained in the Confession of Faith, approved by the General Assembly of the Church of Scotland, in the year 1647, to be founded upon the Word of God; and do you acknowledge the same as the confession of your faith; and will you firmly and constantly adhere thereto, and to the utmost of your power assert, maintain and defend the same, and the purity of worship as presently practised in this Church?

Source: Kemp, *Digest*, 11-13.

3. Do you disown all Popish, Arian, Socinian, Arminian, Erastian, and other doctrines, tenets, and opinions whatsoever, contrary to or inconsistent with the foresaid Confession of Faith?

4. Believing, as you declare, that the Lord Jesus, as King and Head of the Church, hath therein appointed a government in the hand of Church officers distinct from the civil magistrate, are you resolved to maintain, and that at all hazards, that in the administration of spiritual things, the Church is bound to act ministerially under Christ her Head, as responsible in such administration to him alone; while, in all things secular and civil, her officers and members are subject to the laws and rules that govern civil society?

5. Are your persuaded that the Presbyterian Government and Discipline of this Church are founded upon the Word of God, and agreeable thereto, and do you promise to submit to the said Government and Discipline, and to concur with the same, and never to endeavour, directly or indirectly, the prejudice or subversion thereof, but to the utmost of your power, in your station, to maintain, support, and defend the said Discipline and Presbyterian Government by Sessions, Presbyteries, and Synods, during all the days of your life?

6. Are you persuaded that the pastoral relation can be legitimately founded only on the free choice and consent of the people?

7. Do you promise to submit yourself willingly and humbly, in the spirit of meekness, unto the admonitions of the brethren of this Presbytery, and to be subject to them and all other Presbyteries and the superior judicatory of this Church, where God in his providence shall cast your lot; and that according to your power you will maintain the unity and peace of this Church against error and schism, notwithstanding of whatever trouble or persecution may arise, and that you shall follow no divisive courses from the present Doctrine, Worship, Discipline, and Government of this Church?

8. Are not zeal for the honour of God, love to Jesus Christ, and desire of saving souls, your great motives and chief inducements to enter into the function of the holy ministry, and not worldly designs and interests?

9. Have you used any undue methods, either by yourself or others, in procuring this call?

10. Do you engage, in the strength and grace of Jesus Christ our Lord and Master, to rule well your own family, to live a holy and circumspect life, and faithfully, diligently, and cheerfully to discharge all the parts of the ministerial work, to the edification of the body of Christ?

11. Do you accept of and close with the call to be pastor of this Church, and promise through grace to perform all the duties of a faithful minister of the gospel among this people?

Questions to be put to a Probationer

1, 2, 3, 4, 5, and 6, the same as the foregoing.

7. Do you promise that you will subject yourself to the several judicatories of this Church, and are you willing to subscribe to these things?

Questions to be put to an Elder

1, 2, 3, 4, 5, and 6, the same as the foregoing.

7. Do you accept of the office of an Elder of this Church, and promise through grace, faithfully, diligently, and cheerfully, to discharge the duties thereof?

Questions to be put to a Deacon

1, 2, 3, 4, 5, and 6, the same as the foregoing.

7. Do you accept of the office of a Deacon of this Church, and promise through grace, faithfully, diligently, and cheerfully, to discharge the duties thereof?

The Synod ordained that the aforesaid Formulae and Questions, shall be used by Presbyteries at the licensing of Probationers, and the ordination and admission of Ministers, and by Sessions at the ordination and admission of Elders and Deacons.

APPENDIX III

Basis of Union between the Presbyterian Church of Canada, and the United Presbyterian Church in Canada

The Presbyterian Church of Canada and the United Presbyterian Church in Canada, believing that it would be for the glory of God, and for the advancement of the cause of Christ in the land, that they should be united, and form one Church, do hereby agree to unite on the following Basis, to be subscribed by the Moderators of the respective Synods in their name and behalf; declaring, at the same time, that no inference from the fourth article of said Basis is held to be legitimate, which asserts that the Civil Magistrate has the right to prescribe the faith of the Church, or to interfere with the freedom of her ecclesiastical action; further, that unanimity of sentiment is not required in regard to the practical applications of the principle embodied in the said fourth article, and that whatever the differences of sentiment may arise on these subjects, all action in reference thereto shall be regulated by, and be subject to, the recognised principles of Presbyterian Church order.

I. OF HOLY SCRIPTURE.—That the Scriptures of the Old and New Testaments, being the inspired Word of God, are the supreme and infallible rule of faith and life.

II. OF THE SUBORDINATE STANDARDS.—That the Westminster Confession of Faith, with the Larger and Shorter Catechisms, are received by this Church as her Subordinate Standards.

But whereas certain sections of the said Confession of Faith, which treat of the power or duty of the Civil Magistrate, have been objected to, as teaching principles adverse both to the right of private judgment in religious matters, and to the prerogative which Christ has vested in his Church, it is to be understood:

Source: *Minutes of the Synod of the Canada Presbyterian Church* (June 1861), 12-14.

1. That no interpretation or reception of these sections is held by this Church, which would interfere witth the fullest forebearance as to any difference of opinion which may prevail on the question of the endowment of the Church by the State.

2. That no interpretation or reception of these sections is required by this Church, which would accord to the State any authority to violate the liberty of conscience and right of private judgment which are asserted in chap. XX, sec. 2, of the Confession; and in accordance with the statements of which, this Church holds that every person ought to be at full liberty to search the Scriptures for himself, and to follow out what he conscientiously believes to be the teaching of Scripture, without let or hindrance; provided that no one is to be allowed under the pretext of following the dictates of conscience, to interfere with the peace and good order of society.

3. That no interpretation or reception of these sections is required by this Church, which would admit of any interference on the part of the State with the spiritual independence of the Church, as set forth in Chap. XXX of the Confession.

III. OF THE HEADSHIP OF CHRIST OVER THE CHURCH.—That the Lord Jesus Christ is the only King and Head of His Church; and He has made her free from all external or secular authority, in the administration of her affairs, and that she is bound to assert and defend this liberty to the utmost, and ought not to enter into such engagements with any party as would be prejudicial thereto.

IV. OF THE HEADSHIP OF CHRIST OVER THE NATIONS AND THE DUTY OF THE CIVIL MAGISTRATE.—That the Lord Jesus Christ, as Mediator, is invested with universal sovereignty, and is therefore King of Nations, and that all men, in every capacity and relation, are bound to obey His will as revealed in His Word; and particularly, that the Civil Magistrate (including under that term all who are in any way concerned in the Legislative or Administrative action of the State) is bound to regulate his official procedure, as well as his personal conduct, by the revealed will of Christ.

V. OF CHURCH GOVERNMENT.—That the system of polity established in the Westminster Form of Presbyterian Church Government, in so far as it declares a plurality of Elders for each congregation, the official equality of Presbyters, without any officers in the Church superior to the said Presbyters, and the unity of the Church, in a due subordination of a smaller part to a larger, and of a larger to the whole, is the Government of this Church, and is, in the features of it herein set forth, believed by this Church to be founded on and agreeable to the Word of God.

VI. OF WORSHIP.—That the ordinances of worship shall be administered in this Church, as they have heretofore been, by the respective Bodies of which it is composed, in a general accordance with the directions contained in the Westminster Directory of Worship.

NOTES

Preface

1 See Stewart J. Brown, *Thomas Chalmers and the Godly Commonwealth in Scotland* (Oxford: Oxford UP, 1982), 335; William Ferguson, *Scotland: 1689 to the Present* (Edinburgh: Oliver & Boyd, 1978, 1968), 312.

2 Ferguson, *Scotland: 1689 to the Present*, 313. See Gordon Donaldson's comment that "The Disruption split the country and the people as nothing had done since the seventeenth century" (*The Scots Overseas* [London: R. Hale, 1966], 19).

3 Quoted in J. H. S. Burleigh, *A Church History of Scotland* (London: Oxford UP, 1960), 351-52.

4 Quoted in J. M. S. Careless, *Brown of the Globe*, vol. 1 (Toronto: Macmillan, 1959), 21.

5 See Ferguson, *Scotland: 1689 to the Present*, 313; Emmet E. Eklund, "The Scottish Free Church and Its Relations to Nineteenth-Century Swedish and Swedish-American Lutheranism," *Church History*, 51, no. 4 (December 1982), 405-18; Alexander Barkley, "The Impact of Calvinism on Australasia," in W. S. Reid, ed., *John Calvin: His Influence in the Western World* (Grand Rapids, Mich.: Zondervan, 1982).

6 Donald Creighton, *John A. Macdonald*, vol. 1: *The Young Politician* (Toronto: Macmillan, 1956), 159.

Chapter 1

1 David S. MacMillan, "Scottish Enterprise and Influences in Canada, 1620-1900," in R. A. Cage, ed., *The Scots Abroad: Labour, Capital Enterprise, 1750-1914* (London: Croom Helm, 1985).

2 See R. Buchanan, *The Ten Years' Conflict*, vol. 1 (Glasgow, 1852), 23-117.

3 *Record*, August 1844. Stark as Moderator signed the Pastoral Address but John Bayne of Galt wrote it. *Stark Papers*, U.C.A. Box 1, Stark to his mother, 11 December 1844. On Stark see William Reid, *Memoir of Mark Young Stark* (Toronto, 1871); Allan L. Farris, "Mark Young Stark: Pioneer Missionary Statesman," in John S. Moir, ed., *The Tide of Time: Historical Essays by the Late Allan L. Farris* (Toronto: Knox College, 1978); A. L. Farris, "Mark Young Stark," *D.C.B.*, vol. 9, 721-42.

4 See W. S. Reid, "Presbyter," "Presbyterianism," "Presbytery" in J. D. Douglas, ed., *The New International Dictionary of the Christian Church*, rev. ed. (Grand Rapids, Mich.: Zondervan, 1978), 799ff.

5 Hew Scott, *Fasti Ecclesiae Scoticanae* [*F.E.S.*], 7 vols., rev. ed. (Edinburgh, 1914-28).

6 Stewart J. Brown, *Thomas Chalmers and the Godly Commonwealth in Scotland* (Oxford: Oxford UP, 1982), 44.

7 Richard B. Sher, *Church and University in the Scottish Enlightenment* (Princeton: Princeton UP, 1985), 124.

8 See Anand C. Chitnis, *The Scottish Enlightenment: A Social History* (London: Croom Helm, 1976), 49-51 for his analysis of representation in the Assembly and such comments as "Young lawyers used the Assembly as a theatre in which they could display their eloquence and exercise their talents."

9 See Brown, *Chalmers*, 44; Richard W. Vaudry, "The Constitutional Party in the Church of Scotland, 1834-43," *Scottish Historical Review*, 62, 1, no. 173 (April 1983), 35-46.

10 W. Stanford Reid, ed., *John Calvin: His Influence in the Western World* (Grand Rapids, Mich.: Zondervan, 1982), 43.

11 W. S. Reid, "Calvinism," in Douglas, ed., *Dictionary*, 180.

12 *Westminster Confession of Faith*, Chapter 3, Par. 6.

13 Brown, *Chalmers*, xv-xvi.

14 Kenneth Scott Latourette, *A History of Christianity*, vol. 2: *A.D. 1500-A.D. 1975* (New York: Harper & Row, 1975), 1019.

15 Ian Bradley, *The Call to Seriousness: The Evangelical Impact on the Victorians* (New York: Macmillan, 1976), 17-18.

16 Kathleen Heasman, *Evangelicals in Action: An Appraisal of Their Social Work in the Victorian Era* (London: G. Bles, 1962), 16-17. Donald M. Lewis, *Lighten Their Darkness: The Evangelical Mission to Working-Class London, 1828-1860* (New York: Greenwood Press, 1986), 9ff.

17 See Roger Anstey, *The Atlantic Slave Trade and British Abolition* (Atlantic Highlands, N.J.: Humanities Press, 1975); Bradley, *Call to Seriousness*, Heasman, *Evangelicals in Action*.

18 David Hempton, *Methodism and Politics in British Society, 1750-1850* (Stanford, Calif.: Stanford UP, 1984), 31.

19 Brown, *Chalmers*, 346.

20 Michael Willis, *Pulpit Discourses, Expository and Practical, and College Addresses, & c.* (London, 1873), 18.

21 Brown, *Chalmers*, 48.

22 Cf. ibid., 44ff.; Sher, *Church and University*; Ian D. L. Clark, "The Leslie Controversy, 1805," *Records of the Scottish Church History Society*, 14 (1963), 179-97 and his "From Protest to Reaction: The Moderate Regime in the Church of Scotland, 1752-1805," in N. T. Phillipson and R. Mitchison, eds., *Scotland in the Age of Improvement* (Edinburgh: At the University Press, 1970).

23 See Clark, "The Leslie Controversy" and "From Protest to Reaction." For my own criticisms of Clark see R. W. Vaudry, "The Problem of Church-State Relations in the Disruption of the Church of Scotland, 1843," unpublished M.A. thesis, University of Guelph, 1979, 18-21.

24 Ferguson, *Scotland: 1689 to the Present*, 121.

25 Ibid., 227. For criticisms of Ferguson, see Sher, *Church and University*.

26 See A. H. B. Balfour, *An Historical Account of the Rise and Development of Presbyterianism in Scotland* (Cambridge: Cambridge UP, 1911), 122; John MacInnes, *The Evangelical Movement in the Highlands of Scotland, 1688-1800* (Aberdeen: UP, 1951); Andrew Landale Drummond and James Bulloch, *The Scottish Church 1688-1843: The Age of the Moderates* (Edinburgh: Saint Andrew Press, 1973), 19.

27 See Sydney and Olive Checkland, *Industry and Ethos: Scotland 1832-1914* (London: Edward Arnold, 1984), 68-69.

28 W. Stanford Reid, "The Scottish Disruption and Reunion, 1843-1929," *Christendom*, 8 (Summer 1943), 320.

29 Ferguson, *Scotland: 1689 to the Present*, 228-30.

30 Alec R. Vidler, *The Church in an Age of Revolution: 1789 to the Present Day* (Harmondsworth: Penguin, 1971), 57.

31 Brown, *Chalmers*, 4-13, 16-21, 50-57.

32 Quoted in Drummond and Bulloch, *The Scottish Church 1688-1843*, 162.

33 Brown, *Chalmers*, 142. See R. A. Cage and E. O. A. Checkland, "Thomas Chalmers and Urban Poverty: The St. John's Parish Experiment in Glasgow, 1819-1837," *The Philosophical Journal*, 13 (Spring 1976), 37-56 *passim*.

34 G. D. Henderson, *The Claims of the Church of Scotland* (London: Hodder and Stoughton, 1951), 53.

35 G. I. T. Machin, "The Disruption and British Politics, 1834-43," *Scottish Historical Review*, 51 (April 1972), 22; Ferguson, *Scotland: 1689 to the Present*, 307.

36 From the Edinburgh Voluntary Church Association, quoted in A. B. Montgomery, "The Voluntary Controversy in the Church of Scotland, 1829-1843," unpublished Ph.D. dissertation, Faculty of Divinity, New College, University of Edinburgh, 1953, 40-43. Used by permission.

37 *Lectures on the Church Establishment Controversy, and Subjects Connected with It* (Glasgow, 1835), 5.

38 Buchanan, *The Ten Years' Conflict*, 239-41.

39 *Acts of the General Assembly of the Church of Scotland 1638-1842* (Edinburgh, 1843), 1037-38.

40 The literature on the Ten Years' Conflict and Disruption is enormous. Two of the best older accounts are Hugh Watt, *Thomas Chalmers and the Disruption* (Edinburgh: Thomas Nelson, 1943) and G. D. Henderson, *Heritage: A Study of the Disruption* (Edinburgh: Oliver & Boyd, 1943). An excellent recent discussion by a legal scholar will be found in Francis Lyall, *Of Presbyters and Kings: Church and State in the Law of Scotland* (Aberdeen: Aberdeen UP, 1980). See also the works by Brown, Machin, and Vaudry cited above.

41 Lyall, *Church and State in the Law of Scotland*, 27-28.

42 For a detailed examination of one aspect of these negotiations see Richard W. Vaudry, "Sir George Sinclair and the Disruption of the Church of Scotland, 1843," unpublished paper read to the Canadian Association of Scottish Studies, May 1978; cf. Machin, "Disruption and British Politics."

43 Lyall, *Church and State in the Law of Scotland*, 30, 37.

44 On this see Richard W. Vaudry, "'For Christ's Kingdom and Crown': The Evangelical Party in the Church of Scotland and the Problem of Church-State Relations, 1829-1843," *The Canadian Society of Presbyterian History Papers* (1981), 21-41.

45 Watt, *Chalmers and the Disruption*, 207-16; Lyall, *Church and State in the Law of Scotland*, 46-47.

46 Vaudry, "Problem of Church-State Relations," Chapter 3.

47 Quoted in Watt, *Chalmers and the Disruption*, 297-98.

48 Drummond and Bulloch, *The Scottish Church 1688-1843*, 247-48; Watt, *Chalmers and the Disruption*, 298.

49 See Eklund, "The Scottish Free Church," 405-18, Barkley, "The Impact of Calvinism on Australasia," 327.

Chapter 2

1 For a good overview of the history of presbyterians in Canada, see John S. Moir, *Enduring Witness: A History of the Presbyterian Church in Canada* (Toronto: Presbyterian Publications, 1974).

2 R. F. Burns, *The Life and Times of Rev. Robert Burns, D.D.* (Toronto, 1872), 153-54. For its divisive effects in the Maritimes see Moir, *Enduring Witness*, 63, 77.

3 Ian S. Rennie, "The Presbyterian Church in Canada," in Douglas, ed., *Dictionary*, 799-800. W. S. Reid, "John Cook and the Kirk in Canada," in N. G. Smith, ed., *Enkindled by the Word* (Toronto: Presbyterian Publications, 1966), 20; Moir, *Enduring Witness*, 82.

4 Dr. Henderson to R. F. Burns, Glasgow, 28 September 1971, quoted in *Life of Robert Burns*, 165, 172; H. J. Bridgman, "Robert Burns," in *D.C.B.*, vol. 9, 105.

5 Moir, *Enduring Witness*, 81-82.

6 *Acts and Proceedings of the Synod of the Presbyterian Church of Canada in Connexion with the Church of Scotland* (hereafter *A&P PCC in Connex. C of S*), 1831.

7 Ibid., 1833.

8 Ibid., 1835.

9 Ibid., 1836.

10 Ibid., 1838.

11 James Croil, *Life of the Rev. Alexander Mathieson, D.D.* (Montreal, 11870), 15-47, 68-77; *F.E.S.* 7, 645-46; *Macmillan Dictionary of Canadian Biography* (Toronto: Macmillan of Canada, 1978); W. J. Rattray, *The Scot in British North America*, vol. 3 (Toronto: Maclean and Co., n.d.), 850-53.

12 *A&P PCC in Connex. C of S*, 1840.

13 Croil, *Life of Mathieson*, 85, 165.

14 Ibid., 163.

15 *A&P PCC in Connex. C of S*, 1832-40, *passim*. Cf. Appendix III.

16 Moir, *Enduring Witness*, 97-99.

17 Peter Brown, in 1845, referred to Glengarry as "long steeped in the frigid lethargy of a formal moderatism" (*Banner*, 21 November 1845).

18 *A&P PCC in Connex. C of S*, 1841.

19 Ibid., 1843.

20 Ibid. Rennie characterized these resolutions as "temporalizing" in the face of possible loss of church property, clergy reserve funds, and Queen's ("The Free Church and the Relations of Church and State," unpublished M.A. thesis, University of Toronto, 1954, 40-42).

21 *A&P PCC in Connex. C of S*, 1843. There is a copy of Welsh's letter in the Queen's University Archives, *Church of Scotland Synod Papers*, Box 4, File 35.

22 *Banner*, 22 December 1843.

23 R. Campbell, *A History of the Scotch Presbyterian Church, St. Gabriel Street, Montreal* (Montreal: Drysdale, 1887), 458-59.

24 On Brown and the *Banner* see R. W. Vaudry, "Peter Brown, the Toronto *Banner* and the Evangelical Mind in Victorian Canada," *Ontario History*, 77, no. 1 (March 1985), 3-18; and J. M. S. Careless, *Brown of the Globe*, 1, 1-65.

According to Ian Rennie, the invitation to the Browns came from Rev. William Rintoul on behalf of 45 clergy and laymen, including McGill, Rintoul, George, Gale, Bell and Barclay. Most of the clergy, he suggested, were Free Church sympathizers ("The Free Church and the Relations of Church and State," 51, cf. *Globe*, 16 December 1861). W. L. Morton (*Kingdom of Canada* [Toronto: McClelland and Stewart, 1972], 292) has confused the details of the establishment of the *Banner*.

25 *Banner*, 18 August 1843.

26 H. J. Bridgman, "Isaac Buchanan and Religion," unpublished M.A. thesis, Queen's University, 1969; Rennie, "Free Church and Relations of Church and State," 65-66.

27 George Lewis, *Impressions of America and the American Church: From the Journal of the Rev. George Lewis, One of the Deputation of the Free Church of Scotland to the United States* (Edinburgh, 1845), 347-48.

28 *Banner*, 22 September 1843.

29 Ibid., 13 October 1843.

30 Ibid., 20 October 1843.

31 Ibid., 27 October and 24 November 1843.

32 Ibid., 3 November and 24 November 1843.

33 Moir recognizes the importance of the Temporalities Bill (*Enduring Witness*, 103).

34 Rennie, "Free Church and Relations of Church and State," 52-56.

35 *Banner*, 3 November 1843; cf. 10 November 1843. On 21 November at a meeting of the *Banner*'s supporters, the clergy tried unsuccessfully to censure the paper for its editorial policy (Rennie, "Free Church and Relations of Church and State," 56).

36 *Banner*, 17 November 1843.

37 Ibid., 10 November 1843. For Oliver Mowat's comments on the Temporalities Bill, see Oliver to John Mowat, 7 November 1843, in Peter Neary, ed., "Neither Radical nor Tory

nor Whig: Letters by Oliver Mowat to John Mowat 1843-1846," *Ontario History*, 71 (June 1979), 98.

38 *Banner*, 15 December 1843.

39 Ibid., 17 November 1843.

40 Ibid.

41 Ibid., 27 October 1843; 24 November 1843; 8 December 1843.

42 *F.E.S.*, vol. 7, 378-79.

43 See Hilda Neatby, *Queen's University*, vol. 1: 1841-1914 (Montreal: McGill-Queen's UP, 1978), 42-50.

44 *Banner*, 19 January 1844.

45 Careless, *Brown of the Globe*, 1, 17.

46 *Banner*, 19 January 1844.

47 Quoted in ibid., 2 February 1844.

48 Ibid., 26 January 1844.

49 Ibid.

50 Ibid., 23 February 1844.

51 Ibid., 15 March 1844.

52 Ibid., 15 November 1844.

53 Ibid., 8 March 1844.

54 Liddell was apparently an "old friend" of Rev. George Lewis, one of the Free Church deputies, and was an advocate of the total abolition of patronage in Scotland (Lewis, *Impressions of the American Church*, 350; *Banner*, 26 September 1845; 1 March 1844).

55 Ibid., 8 March 1844; 29 March 1844.

56 Ibid., 2 February 1844.

57 Ibid., 1 March 1844; 8 March 1844; 15 March 1844.

58 Rennie, "Free Church and Relations of Church and State," 64-65.

59 Lewis, *Impressions of the American Church*, 363.

60 Reid, *Memoir of Mark Young Stark*; A. L. Farris, "Mark Young Stark,"*D.C.B.*, vol. 9, 741-42.

61 *Stark Papers*, U.C.A. Box 1, Envelope 9. Stark to his mother, 11 February 1844.

62 Ibid. Stark to Mrs. Young, 11 March 1844.

63 Rev. D. Fraser, *A Narrative of the Rise and Progress of the Free Church, Côté Street, Montreal; Read to the Congregation at their Annual Meeting on the 25th April 1855* (Montreal, 1855), 2. W. H. Atherton (*Montreal Under British Rule, 1760-1914*, vol. 2 [Montreal: S. J. Clarke, 1914], 277), gives the date as 10 January, as does Campbell (*St. Gabriel Street Church* [Montreal, 1887], 512).

64 The date of his resignation was apparently 30 January 1844. Campbell, *St. Gabriel Street Church*, 390. On John Redpath see G. Tulchinsky in *D.C.B.*, vol. 9, 654-55, and Rev. D. H. MacVicar, *A Sermon, Preached in the Canada Presbyterian Church, Côté Street, Montreal, on Sabbath, March 14, 1869, on the occasion of the death of John Redpath, Esq.* (Montreal, 1869).

65 Campbell, *St. Gabriel Street Church*, 388-91.

66 Linda Price, *Introduction to the Social History of Scots in Quebec (1780-1840)* (Ottawa: National Museum of Man, 1981), 31.

67 See R. W. Vaudry, "The Free Church in Canada, 1844-1861," unpublished Ph.D. thesis, McGill University, 1984, Appendices IV-VI; the details of the disputes in St. Gabriel Street are recounted in Campbell, *St. Gabriel Street Church*, 461-509.

68 John A. Johnston, "Presbyterian Disruption in British North America," unpublished B.D. thesis, The Presbyterian College, Montreal, 1953, 64.

69 *Banner*, 29 March 1844.

70 Ibid., 9 March 1844.

71 Burns, *Life and Times of Rev. Robert Burns, D.D.*, 175.

72 John MacLeod, *Scottish Theology: In Relation to Church History Since the Reformation* (Edinburgh: The Banner of Truth Trust, 1974, 1943), 269-70.

73 Robert Rainy and James Mackenzie, *Life of William Cunningham D.D. Principal and Professor of Theology and Church History, New College, Edinburgh* (London, 1871), 203.

74 George Shepperson, ed., "Thomas Chalmers, The Free Church of Scotland, and the South," *Journal of Southern History*, Notes and Documents, 17 (1951), 518.

75 Rainy and Mackenzie, *Life of Cunningham*, 204, 205, 209-10. On Charles Hodge, see R. H. Nichols in *Dictionary of American Biography* (New York: Scribner's, 1977), vol. 5, 98-99; A. A. Hodge, *The Life of Charles Hodge* (New York, 1880).

76 Rainy and Mackenzie, *Life of Cunningham*, 208.

77 See Shepperson, "Chalmers, Free Church and South," 519, and his "The Free Church and American Slavery," *Scottish Historical Review*, 30, no. 110 (October 1951).

78 Shepperson, "Chalmers, Free Church and South," 519; see Lewis, *Impressions of the American Church*, *passim*.

79 *Banner*, 26 January 1844.

80 A. M. Machar, *Memorials of the Life and Ministry of the Rev. John Machar, D.D.* (Toronto, 1873), 83. On 15 April 1844, Dr. Burns wrote to William Morris requesting help in organizing a meeting at which Burns would speak concerning the Free Church of Scotland. Burns intimated that £400 and £300 had been collected at Hamilton and Toronto respectively and that in both locations "the general feeling . . . is in favour of an independent Presbyterian Church in Canada, holding Free Principles and recognizing the Free Church of Scotland as the *real* Church of Scotland with which they may be in communion" (Q.U.A., *William Morris Papers*, Burns to Morris, 15 April 1844).

81 John S. Moir, "Confrontation at Queen's: A Prelude to the Disruption in Canada," *Presbyterian History: A Newsletter of the Committee on History, The Presbyterian Church in Canada*, 15, no. 1 (May 1971).

82 Quoted in Burns, *Life and Times of Rev. Robert Burns, D.D.*, 186.

83 *Banner*, 10 May 1844.

84 *A Letter Addressed to the Ministers and Elders of the Synod of Canada, on the present duty of the Presbyterian Church, by the Rev. Robert Burns, D.D., With a Letter on the Same Subject by the Rev. W. Cunningham, D.D., and the Reply of the Convenor of the Colonial Committee of the Free Church of Scotland, to the Moderator of the Synod of Canada* (Montreal, 1844), 3.

85 Ibid., *passim*.

86 Henry Esson, *An Appeal to the Ministers and Members of the Presbyterian Church, Under the Jurisdiction of the Synod of Canada, On the Question of Adherence to the Church of Scotland As By Law Established* (Montreal, 1844), 20-21.

87 Ibid., 26.

88 Ibid., 35.

89 Rennie, "Free Church and Relations of Church and State," 75. John Bayne wrote a lengthy pamphlet in defense of the Disruption of 1844, but this was not published until 1846 (*Was the Recent Disruption of the Synod of Canada, in Connection with the Church of Scotland, Called For? An Address to the Presbyterians of Canada who still support the Synod in Connection with the Church of Scotland*, [Galt, 1846]).

90 Machar, *Memorials of John Machar*, 84.

91 *Banner*, 17 May 1844.

92 Burns, *Life and Times of Rev. Robert Burns*, 202.

93 *Banner*, 5 July 1844.

94 Ibid., 17 May 1844.

95 Ibid., 17 May 1844.

96 Ibid., 28 June 1844.

97 Ibid., 17 May 1844.

98 Ibid., 28 June 1844.

99 Machar, *Memorial of John Machar*, 83.

100 *Stark Papers*, U.C.A. Box 1, Envelope 9, Stark to his mother, 21 May 1844.

101 *A&P PCC in Connex. C of S*, July 1844.

102 Q.U.A. "Diary of William Bell," vol. 14, 107-109. Quoted in John S. Moir, ed., *The Cross in Canada* (Toronto: Ryerson Press, 1966), 142.

103 *A&P PCC in Connex. C of S*, July 1844; N. G. Smith, "Disruption of the Presbyterian Church in Canada," 178-79.

104 *Stark Papers*, U.C.A. Box 1, Envelope 9, Stark to his wife, 10 July 1844.

105 Ibid., Stark to his mother, 11 December 1844.

106 Ibid., 23 July 1844.

107 Q.U.A., "Diary of William Bell," vol. 14, 107-109, quoted in Moir, ed., *Cross in Canada*, 142.

108 *A&P PCC in Connex C of S*, July 1844.

109 Quoted in the *Banner*, 12 July 1844. This protest had apparently been drafted at a meeting of the Free Church party held the day after the vote. J. A. Johnston, "Presbyterian Disruption in British North America," 106.

Chapter 3

1 See Appendix I for text.

2 Moir, *Enduring Witness*, 106.

3 *Ecclesiastical and Missionary Record* (hereafter *Record*), September 1844.

4 *Canadian Presbyter*, 1 (January 1857), 2.

5 *Minutes of Synod*, October 1844.

6 Q.U.A., *Church of Scotland Synod Papers*, Box 4. Cook to Ironside, *c*. August 1844.

7 *A&P PCC in Connex. C of S*, September 1844.

8 *Record*, October 1844.

9 *A&P PCC in Connex. C of S*, September 1844.

10 *Record*, January 1845.

11 W. S. Reid, "John Cook and the Kirk in Canada," *Called in Witness*, vol. 1 (Toronto: Presbyterian Publications, 1975, 1980), 28.

12 *Minutes of Synod*, January 1845.

13 *Record*, May 1859, 100.

14 Cf. J. A. Johnston, "Presbyterian Disruption in British North America," 127-28.

15 Q.U.A., *Church of Scotland Synod Papers*, Box 4, *Letter of Sympathy To the Moderator and Other Members of the Presbyterian Church of Canada in Connection with the Established Church of Scotland* by Thomas Clark (1844).

16 Donald MacLeod, *Memoir of Norman MacLeod, D.D.* (London: Daldy, Isbister, 1877), 155-68.

17 Q.U.A., *Church of Scotland Synod Papers*, Box 4, *Draft of an Answer to the Dissent and Protest of Certain Ministers and Elders who have Seceded from the Synod of Canada in Connexion with the Church of Scotland. By the Committee Appointed by the Synod for that Purpose* (Kingston, 1844).

18 Peter Neary, ed., "Neither Radical nor Tory nor Whig," 116.

19 Ibid., 110.

20 The figures are from John S. Moir, *Church and State in Canada West* (Toronto: University of Toronto Press, 1968), 185.

21 Reid, "John Cook and the Kirk in Canada," 26-27.

22 *Presbyterian*, 1852, 99. Quoted in J. A. Johnston, "Factors in the Formation of the Presbyterian Church in Canada 1875," unpublished Ph.D. thesis, McGill University, 1955, 126. For a comparison of the Free and Kirk Synods, see the same, 69-72.

23 *Record*, April 1855, 84.

24 Ibid., October 1844.

25 Kemp, *Digest*, 144.

26 *Record*, July 1850, 129-30.

27 Ibid., December 1844, 40; January 1845, 47.

28 Ibid., September 1845.

29 Ibid., December 1845.

30 Ibid., November 1847, 3-4.

31 Ibid., January 1848.

32 See John Johnston on D. H. MacVicar in W. S. Reid, ed., *Called in Witness*, 2.

33 *Record*, November 1845.

34 Ibid., August 1844, 6.

35 Ibid., January 1851, 46. Cf. *Canadian Presbyter* (July 1858), 208.

36 *Record*, December 1853, 21-22; Moir, *Enduring Witness*, 1498; *Canada Directory for 1857-58*; *Banner*, 15 May 1846, 8 May 1846, 19 February 1842; *Record*, January 1859, 35; September 1858, 125.

37 Moir, *Enduring Witness*, 150.

38 *Record*, May 1854, 103-104; Moir, *Enduring Witness*, 149-50. On Duff, see J. D. Douglas, "Alexander Duff," in *The New International Dictionary of the Christian Church* (Grand Rapids, Mich.: Zondervan, 1974), 315. On the India Mission, see *Record*, November 1856, 9; June 1857, 121; August 1857, 154-55; November 1857, 7-8; December 1857, 14-25.

39 Ibid., June 1845.

40 Ibid., November 1854, 7.

41 Ibid., August 1858, 109.

42 On these "awakenings" see J. Edwin Orr, *The Second Evangelical Awakening*, popular abridged edition (London: Marshall, Morgan and Scott, 1964); Timothy L. Smith, *Revivalism and Social Reform: American Protestantism on the Eve of the Civil War* (Gloucester, Mass.: Peter Smith, 1976).

43 *Minutes of Synod*, 1859, 48.

44 Ibid., 1860, 47-49.

45 *Record*, August 1849, 145.

46 Ibid., November 1854, 3.

47 Ibid., October 1854, 178; *Minutes of Synod*, 1856, 11-13; H. J. Bridgman, "Three Scots Presbyterians in Upper Canada: A Study in Emigration, Nationalism and Religion," unpublished Ph.D. thesis, Queen's University, 1978, 298-302; Peter Neary, ed., "Letters by Oliver Mowat to John Mowat 1843-1846," Oliver to John Mowat, 20 November 1845, 122; P.A.C., *Isaac Buchanan Papers*, vol. 63, #49985, George Paxton Young to Buchanan, 7 December 1855.

48 Bridgman, "Three Scots Presbyterians in Upper Canada," 292; *Record*, December 1853, 21; David R. Nicholson, "Michael Willis: Missionary Statesman, Social Activist, Christian Educator and Reformed Theologian," M.Th. thesis, Knox College, University of Toronto, 95-103. P.C.A., *McCollum Papers*, Box 4, Envelope 5, Thomas Wightman to Mark Young Stark, 28 May 1856.

Chapter 4

1 Stewart J. Brown, *Thomas Chalmers and the Godly Commonwealth in Scotland* (Oxford: (Oxford: Oxford UP, 1982), 44, 218.

2 Vaudry, "Free Church in Canada," Appendix VII, 398.

3 *Minutes of Synod*, October 1844, 28-29.

4 *Pace* Goldwyn French, "The Evangelical Creed in Canada," in W. L. Morton, ed., *The*

Shield of Achilles: Aspects of Canada in the Victorian Age (Toronto: McClelland and Stewart, 1968), 25.

5 Michael Willis, *Pulpit Discourses Expository and Practical and College Addresses & c* (London, 1873), 18.

6 *Sermons by the late Rev. Mark Young Stark, A.M. Formerly Minister of Knox's Church, Dundas, with Memoir, By the Rev. William Reid, A.M.* (Toronto, 1871), 175.

7 Willis, *Pulpit Discourses*, 27.

8 Ian C. Bradley, *The Call to Seriousness: The Evangelical Impact on the Victorians* (New York: Macmillan, 1976), 22.

9 *Banner*, 1 December 1843.

10 *Record*, December 1843, 142.

11 Ibid., January 1846, 146.

12 Ibid.

13 P.C.A., *McCollum Papers*, Box 3, Envelope 5, 1-2.

14 *Minutes of Synod*, 1857, 50-51.

15 Ibid., 1858, 47.

16 *Record*, January 1849, 33.

17 Ibid.

18 *Minutes of Synod*, 1857, 51.

19 Lefferts A. Loetscher, *Facing the Enlightenment and Pietism: Archibald Alexander and the Founding of Princeton Theological Seminary* (Westport, Conn.: Greenwood Press, 1983), 179. Loetscher's examination of Alexander's thought has helped to clarify my own thinking about Burns.

20 *Record*, May 1855, 106; *Minutes of Synod*, 1857, 51.

21 *Record*, December 1848, 18.

22 D. C. Masters, *Protestant Church Colleges in Canada* (Toronto: University of Toronto Press, 1966), 45-46.

23 Leslie Armour and Elizabeth Trott, *The Faces of Reason: An Essay on Philosophy and Culture in English Canada 1850-1950* (Waterloo: Wilfrid Laurier UP, 1981), 85ff., especially 86-89.

24 John A. Irving, "The Development of Philosophy in Central Canada from 1800-1900," *Canadian Historical Review*, 31, no. 3 (September 1850), 259-60.

25 Masters, *Protestant Church Colleges*, 45-46.

26 P.A.C., *Buchanan Papers*, Young to Buchanan, 13 September 1860, vol. 63 #49999; cf. vol. 49 #39818. Young's comments to Buchanan on the occasion of the visit of the Prince of Wales to Knox College are suggestive of some tension between Young and Principal Willis.

27 Masters, *Protestant Church Colleges*, 45-46.

28 Ibid.

29 J. G. C. Norman, "H. F. W. Gesenius" in *New International Dictionary of the Christian Church*, 410.

30 Vaudry, "Free Church in Canada," 307-12.

31 *Record*, November 1854, 10-11.

32 George Paxton Young, *Miscellaneous Discourses and Expositions of Scripture* (Edinburgh, 1854), 94-95. Young's emphasis.

33 Irving, "Development of Philosophy," 263.

34 *Record*, May 1855, 106.

35 Ibid., February 1856, 64-65.

36 Daniel F. Rice, "Natural Theology and the Scottish Philosophy in the Thought of Thomas Chalmers," *Scottish Journal of Theology*, 24, no. 1 (February 1971), 23-46.

37 *Minutes of Synod*, 1858, 46.

38 Hodge, *The Life of Charles Hodge*, 354.

39 *Record*, January 1851, 39. A. A. Hodge's *Outlines of Theology* (n.p., n.d.), was commended to readers of the *Record* (November 1860, 1). *Minutes of Synod*, 1858, 46; *Record*, November 1856, 6-7.

40 *F.E.S.*, 7, 648; Kemp, *Digest*, 46-49.

41 *Record*, December 1848. Peden's book was published in Montreal by J. C. Beckett. By contrast, the Montreal *Witness* recommended the book "generally, to the attention of the public" suggesting that "From the earnest and at the same time, interesting manner in which it is written . . . it is likely to make a definite and lasting impression upon the minds of readers" (Montreal *Witness*, 13 December 1847, 394).

42 *Record*, Feburary 1849.

43 Ibid., March 1849, 74-75.

44 Ibid., 75.

45 Ibid., 76.

46 Cf. Louis Berkhof, *Systematic Theology*, 4th rev. ed. (Grand Rapids, Mich.: Wm. B. Eerdmans, 1977, 1938), 392-99; and his *The History of Christian Doctrines* (Edinburgh: The Banner of Truth Trust, 1975, 1937), 165-98.

47 Macleod, *Scottish Theology*, 242-51.

48 Rennie, "Free Church and Relations of Church and State," 213.

49 *Record*, February 1850, 59.

50 Kemp, *Digest*, 46.

51 Ibid., 47-48.

52 Ibid., 48.

53 *Minutes of Synod*, 1852, 18.

54 Macleod, *Scottish Theology*, 242.

55 Anstey, *The Atlantic Slave Trade*, 177.

56 Carl Berger, *Science, God, and Nature in Victorian Canada* (Toronto: University of Toronto Press, 1983), 32.

57 Mark Young Stark, *A Lecture on Hugh Miller Delivered Before the Y.M.C.A. at Dundas, Cobourg, Montreal* (Dundas, 1859), P.C.A., *Stark Papers*, AR5/H8M5., 41.

58 Davis A. Young, *Christianity and the Age of the Earth* (Grand Rapids, Mich.: Zondervan, 1982), 49.

59 *Record*, June 1848, 118.

60 Young, *Christianity and the Age of the Earth*, 55.

61 Ibid., 57-58.

62 Stark, *A Lecture on Hugh Miller*, 36-38.

63 *Record*, February 1860, 50.

Chapter 5

1 *Minutes of Synod*, 1850, 13, 20-21. For Mark Young Stark's political quietism, see U.C.A., *Stark Papers*, Box 1, File 9. Stark to his mother, 4 November 1844.

2 *Record*, December 1856, 22-23. The *Canadian Presbyter* wanted to see Presbyterians on both sides of political question; "it should thus be rendered impossible for any selfish politician to calculate on having the influence of the Presbyterian Church at his back" (2 [January 1858], 12).

3 *Record*, June 1857, 118; *Minutes of Synod*, 1857, 50; 1859, 38.

4 P. B. Waite, *The Life and Times of Confederation: 1864-1867* (Toronto: University of Toronto Press, 1963), 126.

5 Creighton, *John A. Macdonald*, 98.

6 Ibid., 159; see Rennie, "Free Church and Relations of Church and State," 39, 128; A. M. M. Evans, "The Scot as Politician," in W. S. Reid, ed., *The Scottish Tradition in*

Canada (Toronto: McClelland and Stewart, 1976); Morton, "Victorian Canada," in his *Shield of Achilles*, 314.

7 W. L. Mathieson, *Church and Reform in Scotland 1797-1843* (Edinburgh: James Maclehose and Sons, 1916), 329-30.

8 Evans, "Scot as Politician," 287; Rennie, "Free Church and Relations of Church and State," 123-24; *Record*, February 1851, 57; *Banner*, 26 November 1847.

9 Buchanan, for example, had in 1843 first supported Baldwin, but then switched to Metcalfe, thinking that the Free Church would need to be on the government's good side (Bridgman, "Isaac Buchanan and Religion," 174-80). Cameron was part of the Conservative coalition in 1836.

10 Quoted in John S. Moir, *The Church in the British Era* (Toronto: McGraw-Hill Ryerson, 1972), 61.

11 On this see J. S. Moir, " 'Loyalty and Respectability:' The Campaign for Co-Establishment of the Church of Scotland in Canada," *Scottish Tradition*, 9-10 (1979-1980), 64-83; Moir, *Church in the British Era*, 114ff.

12 Ibid., 125.

13 See above, Chapter One and my " 'For Christ's Kingdom and Crown:' The Evangelical Party in the Church of Scotland and the Problem of Church State Religions, 1829-1843," *The Canadian Society of Presbyterian History Papers*, 1981, 21-41.

14 Quoted in William Hanna, *Memoirs of the Life and Writings of Thomas Chalmers*, vol. 4 (Edinburgh and London, 1851), 348.

15 Kemp, *Digest*, 412.

16 Rennie, "Free Church and Relations of Church and State," 99-101.

17 Kemp, *Digest*, 412.

18 Rennie, "Free Church and Relations of Church and State," 96; cf. U.C.A., *Smart Papers*, "Biography of William Smart, 1811-1849," 111-17.

19 Rennie, "Free Church and Relations of Church and State," 89, 96, 114-15; *Record*, April 1847.,

20 Ibid., April 1848, 89.

21 Ibid., June 1848, 119.

22 Kemp, *Digest*, 413.

23 Rennie, "Free Church and Relations of Church and State," 143-45.

24 See Vaudry, "Peter Brown, the Toronto *Banner* and the Evangelical Mind in Victorian Canada," 3-18.

25 *Record*, June 1848, 119.

26 Kemp, *Digest*, 414.

27 *Minutes of Synod*, 1848; cf. Moir, *Enduring Witness*, 119-21. Moir regards this action as a victory for voluntaryism and especially attributable to the influence of the *Banner* and the *Globe*: "The laity of the Free Church had frustrated the desire of its clergy to obtain financial independence" (Moir, *Church and State in Canada West*, 49).

28 Kemp, *Digest*, 416-18; *Minutes of Synod*, 1850.

29 Rennie, "Free Church and Relations of Church and State," 153-69; cf. Moir, *Church and State in Canada West*, 54.

30 Rennie, "Free Church and Relations of Church and State," 169-71.

31 *Record*, July 1851.

32 Ibid., June 1853, 125.

33 Ibid., June 1850, 123; cf. Moir, *Enduring Witness*, 113.

34 Bridgman, "Isaac Buchanan and Religion," 100-104.

35 P.A.C., *Isaac Buchanan Papers*. G. P. Young to Buchanan, 8 July 1854, #49976.

36 P.A.C., *George Brown Papers*. G. P. Young to Gordon Brown, n.d. c-1601, 19-20.

37 *Record*, November 1854.

38 Ibid., January 1846.

39 *Minutes of Synod*, 1848.

40 *Banner*, 10 December 1847.
41 Ibid., 7 April 1848.
42 Moir, *Enduring Witness*, 116-19.
43 *Record*, May 1849.
44 Ibid., June 1849, 121.
45 Moir, *Enduring Witness*, 116-19.
46 Moir, *Church in the British Era*, 184.
47 Moir, *Church and State in Canada West*, 119.
48 *Record*, May 1860, 102.
49 *Minutes of Synod*, June 1860, 33.
50 Nicholson, "Michael Willis," 112-15.
51 *Record*, June 1849, 121.
52 Quoted in Rennie, "Free Church and Relations of Church and State," 219.
53 *Record*, June 1853, 115.
54 Cf. P.A.C., *Buchanan Papers*. Adam Fergusson of Woodhill to Buchanan, 14 February 1854, to get that "desecrating whistle" of a train stopped on the Sabbath (vol. 25, #21699-21702).
55 *Record*, June 1853, 115-16.
56 Ibid., September 1851, 170.
57 J. R. Burnet, "The Urban Community and Changing Moral Standards," in M. Horn and R. Sabourin, eds., *Studies in Canadian Social History* (Toronto: McClelland and Stewart, 1974), 303, 307, 324.
58 *Record*, August 1852, 148.
59 Burnet, "Changing Moral Standards," 307. Cf. *Record*, August 1852, 148. The United Presbyterian Church also used George Brown as a vehicle for presenting their Sabbath petitions. P.A.C., *Brown Papers*, William Stoughton to George Brown, 6 April 1856, MG 24 B40, vol. 2, 261.
60 *Record*, July 1853, 130. In January 1858 the *Record* called upon its readers to elect M.P.s who were sound on the Sabbath question. "It will be generally found," it declared, "that the man who is sound on this point, may be trusted on the other great moral questions, who are more or less connected with it" (*Record*, January 1858, 25).
61 Ibid., June 1850, 118-19; August 1954, 146.
62 This is Bradley's term. Ian C. Bradley, *The Call to Seriousness: The Evangelical Impact on the Victorians* (New York: Macmillan, 1976), 103-106.
63 *Minutes of Synod*, 1847, 24.
64 *Record*, May 1851, 106.
65 Ibid., June 1852, 122.
66 Ibid., September 1848, 163-64.
67 Ibid., November 1849, 7.
68 *Minutes of Synod*, 1852.
69 *Record*, April 1853, 92.
70 *Minutes of Synod*, 1853.
71 Ibid., 1854, 22.
72 *Banner*, 25 October 1847; cf. W. H. Elgee, *The Social Teaching of the Canadian Churches, Protestant, The Early Period, Before 1850* (Toronto: Ryerson Press, 1964), 154. For Isaac Buchanan's inconsistencies in the matter of alcohol, see Bridgman, "Isaac Buchanan and Religion," 192-95.
73 Jan Noel, "God's Scots: Montreal Merchants of the Millennium," unpublished paper presented to C.H.A., Guelph, 1984, 7.
74 See Bridgman, "The Scots Presbyterians in Upper Canada," 274-74; F. L. Barron, "The American Origins of the Temperance Movement in Ontario, 1828-1850," *Canadian Review of American Studies*, 11, no. 2 (Fall 1980), 131-50.
75 *Record*, December 1849, 19.

76 Ibid., July 1848, 135.

77 *Record*, August 1850, 156.

78 Ibid., July 1853, 134.

79 Lovell's *Canada Directory for 1857-58*, 453-54.

80 *Record*, July 1851, 129.

81 *Banner*, 16 May 1845.

82 R. K. Webb, *Modern England* (New York: Dodd, Mead and Co., 1974), 301.

83 *Record*, August 1851, 150-51.

84 *Minutes of Synod*, 1851, 27.

85 Moir, *Enduring Witness*, 121.

86 *Record*, April 1855, 87.

87 Ibid.

88 *Minutes of Synod*, 1853, 28-29. In February 1858 the *Record* argued that "old party lines" were largely vanishing and the new liberal lines were drawn "not so much between conservative and liberal, as between that policy that would carry out thorough Protestant principles; and the policy that would yield to the influence of Popery, even at the sacrifice of our Educational system, and of the Protestantism of the country" (40).

89 J. M. S. Careless, *The Union of the Canadas 1841-1857* (Toronto: McClelland and Stewart, 1967, 1977), 198.

90 *Record*, May 1856, 109.

91 *Canadian Presbyter*, 2 (October 1858), 291.

92 *Record*, January 1854, 37.

93 Ibid., April 1851, 91.

94 On the "Double Shuffle," see Creighton, *John A. Macdonald*, 269; Careless, *Brown of the Globe*, vol. 1, 277ff.; W. L. Morton, *The Critical Years: The Union of British North America, 1857-1873* (Toronto: McClelland and Stewart, 1968), 18-19.

95 *Record*, September 1858, 125.

96 *Canadian Presbyter*, 2 (September 1858), 257-59.

97 *Record*, September 1857, 161; cf. *Minutes of Synod 1858*, 25-26; P.C.A., *Minutes of the Kirk Session of Prescott, Canada West*, 28 September 1854, 63-64. Members of the Church were also called upon to exhibit a concern for the poor, use their money wisely, and shun extravagant living (*Record*, November 1857, 2; January 1858, 25-26).

Chapter 6

1 Kemp, *Digest*, 111-12.

2 Ibid., 354-55.

3 Ibid., 348-49.

4 *Record*, October 1845.

5 *Banner*, 12 December 1845.

6 *Minutes of Synod*, 1844.

7 *Banner*, 16 April 1847.

8 *Record*, May 1851, 106-107; *Minutes of Synod*, 1856; C. P. Mulvany, *Toronto Past and Present Until 1882* (Toronto, 1884), 94; Moir, *Enduring Witness*, 116.

9 *Record*, October 1845.

10 Moir, *Enduring Witness*, 116. According to a report in the *Record* of May 1851, six former Queen's students began in November 1844, six more arrived in December and two came in March 1845. See also *Banner*, 16 April 1847.

11 *Record*, May 1848; Moir, *Enduring Witness*, 116; *Minutes of Synod*, 1860, 54; and 1861, 22.

12 *Record*, May 1859, 100.

13 *Minutes of Synod*, 1847.

14 Masters, *Protestant Church Colleges*, 45.

15 On the issue of church/state relations cf. Alexander Turner, *The Scottish Secession of 1843* (Edinburgh and Glasgow, 1859), 316-17, 328-29. Cf. D. R. Nicholson, "Dr. Michael Willis," *Presbyterian History*, 17, no. 1 (June 1973), 2 as well as his "Michael Willis: Missionary Statesman, Social Activist, Christian Educator and Reformed Theologian," unpublished M.Th. thesis, Knox College, University of Toronto.

16 *Record*, January 1848; Nicholson, "Michael Willis," *Presbyterian History*, 2.

17 Nicholson, "Michael Willis," *Presbyterian History*, 3.

18 G. Smellie, *Memoir of the Rev. John Bayne, D.D.* (Toronto, 1871), 29.

19 On Young, see above, Chapter 4, and the works by Armour and Trott, McKillop, Masters, and Irving.

20 Burns' appointment to Knox College seems to have been a way of extricating him from his problems at Knox Church, Toronto. *Minutes of Synod*, 1856, 11-13.

21 *Minutes of Synod*, 1855, Appendix, 26-27; 1857, 15-16.

22 Ibid., 1856.

23 Ibid., 1857.

24 Ibid., 1855, 12.

25 *Record*, October 1846.

26 Ibid., December 1846.

27 Ibid., July 1847.

28 Ibid., December 1846, 240.

29 J. H. MacVicar, *Life of Principal MacVicar* (Toronto, 1904), 19.

30 *Record*, December 1846, 240; July 1847.

31 U.C.A., *Minutes of Knox College Committee and Professor's Court*, 12-14 September 1849. P.C.A., *Toronto Academy–Accounts and Subscriptions Box* (Manuscript Minutes of Management Committee, 10 August 1849). Cf. Rennie, "Free Church and Relations of Church and State," 187-90. He seems to regard the break with the Synod as more distinct than does this author.

32 P.C.A., *Toronto Academy–Accounts and Subscriptions Box*, Manuscript Minutes of Management Committee, 25 June and 22 July 1852 and Printed Circular and Manuscript Notes attached to it, 6 August 1852.

33 *Record*, May 1847. On this Burns/Esson clash see Vaudry, "Theology and Education in Early Victorian Canada: Knox College, Toronto, 1844-61," *Studies in Religion/Sciences Religieuses*, 16, no. 4 (Fall 1987), 431-47.

34 P.C.A., *McCollum Papers*, Box 3, File 5. "Knox's College Preparatory Department" (printed circular from Dr. Robert Burns).

35 See also U.C.A., *Minutes of Knox College Committee and Professor's Court*; Armour and Trott, *The Faces of Reason*, 44; Henry Esson, "Critique on Dr. Burns' letter on Knox's College," June 1848 and Henry Esson, "Statement Relative to the Educational System of Knox's College, Toronto; with suggestions for its Extension and Improvement" (Toronto, 1848).

36 Masters, *Protestant Church Colleges*, 42-43.

37 Minutes of Synod, 1855, Appendix, 26-27.

38 Canadian Presbyter, 1 (December 1857), 321-26; 2 (July 1858), 196.

39 *Record*, June 1845, 41-42.

40 Ibid., May 1847.

41 *Minutes of Synod*, 1859, 30.

42 See ibid., 1860, 23 for the intricacies surrounding these trials.

43 *Banner*, 21 April 1848. Knox College also had a "Metaphysical and Ethical Society," D. H. MacVicar, President (*Record*, December 1858, 21).

44 Ibid., December 1848.

45 Kemp, *Digest*, 459.

46 See Appendix II for text of Formula and Ordination Questions.

47 Kemp, *Digest*, 461.

48 *Minutes of Synod*, 1858, 19.

49 Ibid., 1860, 62-69.

Chapter 7

1 *Record*, June 1847.

2 *Minutes of Synod*, October 1844, 16.

3 Kemp, *Digest*, 457.

4 Ibid., 458.

5 *Canadian Presbyter*, 1 (June 1857), 172.

6 Kemp, *Digest*, 41-42, 458; *Minutes of Synod*, 1847, 16, 40; 1859, 11-12; 1860, 20.

7 Ibid., October 1844, 16-17. See also *Record*, March 1853, 69-71.

8 *Canadian Presbyter*, 1 (June 1857), 174.

9 *Record*, May 1853, 100-101.

10 *Minutes of Synod*, October 1844.

11 *Record* (Supplement), January 1856, 117. The Book of Discipline in the form in which it
was published in the *Record* was never given final approval nor published in a final form.
A. F. Kemp of Montreal, however, did prepare a digest of Free Church laws and
procedures which was published (*Digest*, 423).

12 P.C.A., *Minutes of Kirk Session–Prescott*, 30 January 1845, and 29 July 1846.

13 For the case in Osgoode of the attempts to remove a minister and the Presbytery's attempt
to reconcile parties in the church, see *Record*, September 1855, 170-71; October 1855, 187.

14 See Chapter 5, "Transforming the Nation."

15 Kemp, *Digest*, 57-58; *Minutes of Synod*, 1850, 23.

16 Kemp, *Digest*, 61.

17 Ibid., 71.

18 See Chapter 8, "Financing the Enterprise," for the debate concerning the Sustentation
Scheme. Cf. Moir, *Enduring Witness*, 108-109; Rennie, "Free Church and Relations of
Church and State," 128-29.

19 *Minutes of Synod*, October 1844, 17. Cf. *Record*, March 1849, 71-72. Rev. George
Smellie in this article argued in favour of the Diaconate but asserted that it was an inferior
office to that of the elder. Moreover, elders and deacons could meet together to discuss
financial matters "with equal powers to deliberate, vote and conclude on all cases coming
before them." It is not clear if elders and deacons did meet together as a Deacons' Court.
Cf. Kemp, *Digest*, 44, 458.

20 Ibid., 77.

21 *Minutes of Synod*, 1856, 24-25.

22 Ibid., 1857, 33.

23 Kemp, *Digest*, 458.

24 *Minutes of Synod*, 1860, 62-69.

25 Ibid., 45-46.

26 Ibid.

27 *Record*, March 1846.

28 Andrew Drummond and James Bulloch, *The Church in Victorian Scotland* (Edinburgh:
Saint Andrew Press, 1975), chap. 7, "Changing Worship," 178-214; Moir, *Enduring
Witness*, 123-24.

29 *The Directory for the Publick Worship of God: Agreed Upon By The Assembly of Divines
at Westminster, With the Assistance of Commissioners From the Church of Scotland* etc.
in *The Subordinate Standards and Other Authoritative Documents of the Free Church of
Scotland* (Edinburgh, 1955), 138ff.

30 Ibid., 138-39. G. D. Henderson, *The Claims of the Church of Scotland* (London: Hodder and Stoughton, 1851), 61-63; Frederick H. Rennie, "Spiritual Worship with a Carnal Instrument: The Organ as aid or obstacle to the 'purity of worship' in Canadian Presbyterianism, 1850-1875," unpublished M.Th. thesis, Knox College, Toronto, 1969, 52-54.

31 *Canadian Presbyter*, 2 (February 1858), 35.

32 *Record*, June 1860, 122; Rennie, "Organ Controversy," 54-56.

33 Rennie, "Organ Controversy," 54-57.

34 *Canadian Presbyter*, 1 (March 1857), 70.

35 Drummond and Bulloch, *Church in Victorian Scotland*, 183.

36 *Record*, January 1853, 42.

37 Ibid., February 1854, 61.

38 This was published in Scotland in 1851 and contained hymns by Isaac Watts, John Newton, John Wesley and John Keble. Drummond and Bulloch, *Church in Victorian Scotland*, 183-84.

39 *Canadian Presbyter*, 1 (November 1857), 297. See also ibid., 2 (May 1858), 147; and (December 1858), 375.

40 Kemp, *Digest*, 63. Johnston comments that the Brockville congregation has a "varied background" and "traits inherited from the United Presbyterian Church, U.S.A." ("Factors in the Formation of the Presbyterian Church in Canada, 1875," 388).

41 Ibid., 64-66.

42 *Banner*, 30 April 1847.

43 *Canadian Presbyter*, 1 (July 1857), 166.

44 Johnston, "Factors in the Formation of the Presbyterian Church in Canada, 1875," 389.

45 *Record*, January 1851, 35.

46 Smellie, *Life of Bayne*, 31-32.

47 Lovell's *Canada Directory for 1857-1858*, 442.

48 *Minutes of Synod*, 1848.

49 *Record*, May 1851, 103.

50 Ibid., April 1855, 83-84.

51 *Manuscript Census Returns, 1861*—Compton County, Canada East—Reels c 1276-1277.

52 *Manuscript Census Returns for 1861*—Town of Guelph, Reels c 1083; M. Katz, *The People of Hamilton, Canada West* (Cambridge: Harvard UP, 1975), 343-48.

53 *Manuscript Census Returns, 1861*, Reels c 1042-1043.

Chapter 8

1 *Record*, November 1844.

2 Ibid., December 1845, 25.

3 *Banner*, 23 October 1846. See also U.C.A., *Stark Papers*, Stark to his mother, 10 October 1846.

4 P.A.C., *Buchanan Papers*, Rev. George Cheyne to Buchanan 6 March and 1 July 1845, vol. 21, #16879; John Burns to Rev. Alexander Gale, 18 June 1845, #14894. Douglas McCalla, *The Upper Canada Trade 1834-1872: A Study of the Buchanans' Business* (Toronto: University of Toronto Press, 1979), 53.

5 P.A.C., *Buchanan Papers*, vol. 54, #43298-300.

6 Ibid., Rev. William Rintoul to Buchanan, 7 April 1845, vol. 52, #41907-10.

7 Ibid., vol. 39, #32243-49. Buchanan's donations were not limited to the Free Church. He gave money to the Church of the Ascension in Hamilton, St. Andrew's Church Montreal, and the Church of England in Eastwood. *Buchanan Papers*, vol. 27, #23179-80; vol. 76, #22331; vol. 26, #22454.

8 Brown, *Thomas Chalmers and the Godly Commonwealth*, 340.

9 Ibid., 341.

10 *Minutes of Synod*, July 1844.

11 *Record*, September 1844. In August 1844 Buchanan wrote to Willian Morris that the Sustentation Board was to be one-third clerical and two-thirds lay—though "even under this arrangement they may all be members of the Synod! Vile ecclesiastics!!" He intimated that he would not serve as chairman of the board unless the only clergy present were the Clerks of the Synod. Q.U.A., *William Morris Papers*, Buchanan to Morris, 17 August 1844.

12 *Minutes of Synod*, 1844, 21.

13 Ibid., October 1844, 20-21. Buchanan to *Banner*, 27 January 1845. Reprinted in *Record*, February 1845, 51-52. For Mark Young Stark's comments on the Sustentation Fund, see U.C.A., *Stark Papers*, Buchanan to Morris, 17 August 1844.

14 *Record*, December 1844, 34-35.

15 Ibid.

16 *Banner*, 18 April 1845.

17 Ibid., 21 March 1845.

18 Cf. ibid., 31 January 1845; 7 January 1845. On clergy/laity tension in the Free Church see Rennie, "Free Church and Relations of Church to State," 130ff.

19 *Record*, April 1850, 85.

20 P.A.C., *Buchanan Papers*, John McMurrich to Buchanan, 28 January 1845, vol. 46, #36984. Buchanan had apparently sent a letter to Dr. Robert Burns concerning the Sustentation Fund. McMurrich was critical of this, arguing that "in all probability it may be the means of preventing him from coming to Canada." As for Knox Church Toronto's opposition to the plan, McMurrich pointed out that "It was not as you seem to think dragged through the mud by Banner Brown," it was a unanimous decision.

21 *Banner*, 21 February 1845.

22 Buchanan to *Banner*, 27 January 1845. Reprinted in *Record*, February 1845, 51-52. It is sometimes difficult to know what Buchanan's own views were. He clearly wanted congregational control of temporalities. He wanted the Deacons' Court "clearly declared to be a congregational court in contradistinction to a church or spiritual court," and argued that "the views of the clergy as to the Deacons' Court would assuredly precipitate another disruption" (P.A.C., *Buchanan Papers*, vol. 26, #22692; vol. 116, #75621). See also Bridgman, "Isaac Buchanan and Religion," 51-55 re: Sustentation Fund.

23 *Record*, February 1845, 52.

24 Ibid., April 1845, 65.

25 Ibid., July 1845, 97.

26 Ibid., September 1845, 114-16.

27 *Minutes of Synod*, 1849.

28 Ibid., 1847.

29 Ibid., 1850.

30 By 1852 it seems that only the Presbytery of Cobourg had one (ibid., 1855). The Presbytery of London resolved to adopt the former Sustentation Plan (*Record*, February 1850, 59).

31 *Minutes of Synod*, 1855.

32 Ibid., 1858, 31. Amounts are given as recorded in the documents—usually in £ Halifax, sometimes in decimal/dollar currency. £1 Halifax equaled 4 dollars in 1862 (Brian Young and John A. Dickinson, *A Short History of Quebec: A Socio-Economic Perspective* [Toronto: Copp Clark Pitman, 1988], 9).

33 Ibid., 1857.

34 Ibid., 1855, 29; 1859, 64.

35 Ibid., 1848.

36 *Record*, May 1851, 106-107; *Minutes of Synod*, 1856. Mulvany, *Toronto Past and Present Until 1882*, 94.

37 *Minutes of Synod*, 1844, 26-27; cf. Kemp, *Digest*, 201.
38 Ibid., 1845. 42-43.
39 Ibid., 1848.
40 Ibid., 1846, 74.
41 Ibid., 1848, 29-30; 1849, 25-26.
42 Ibid., 1858, 52-53.
43 *Record*, April 1845.
44 Ibid., November 1847, 2-3.
45 Ibid., September 1854, 165; December 1845, 25.
46 Ibid., December 1854, 23.
47 Masters, *Protestant Church Colleges*, 44.
48 *Minutes of Synod*, 1857, 13.
49 Ibid., 44.
50 Ibid., 1858, 43-44; 1859, 31, 43; *Record*, October 1861, 183-84.
51 *Minutes of Synod*, 1852, 9-10.
52 P.A.C., *Buchanan Papers*, vol. 55, #44222-24, Spreull to Buchanan, 22 July 1854.
53 Ibid., vol. 118, #76345-46, 22 October 1855; vol. 118, #76347-50.
54 Ibid., vol. 55, #44250, Stark to Buchanan, 30 October 1855.
55 *Minutes of Synod*, 1856, 16.
56 Kemp, *Digest*, 218.
57 *Minutes of Synod*, 1857, 21-25.
58 22 Victoria, chap. 69; J. G. Hodgins, ed., *Documentary History of Education in Upper Canada*, vol. 13 (1856-58) (Toronto, 1897), 247-48; Kemp, *Digest*, 226-29.
59 Ibid., 228.
60 Ibid., 228-29.
61 *Canadian Presbyter*, 2 (June 1858), 180-83; (July 1858), 194-95.
62 Kemp, *Digest*, 230.
63 *Minutes of Synod*, 1860, 26.
64 Ibid., 26-27.
65 Ibid., 1851, 12; 1852, 14-16.
66 Vaudry, "Free Church in Canada, 1844-1861," 238.
67 *Minutes of Synod*, 1860, 51.
68 Ibid., 1861, 16; Kemp, *Digest*, 407.
69 *Minutes of Synod*, 1855, 21.
70 Ibid., 1856, 20-21.
71 Ibid., 27-29.
72 Ibid., 1857, 14.
73 Ibid., 1858, 18-19.
74 Kemp, *Digest*, 144-48.
75 Ibid., 148-50, 156.
76 *Minutes of Synod*, 1852, 22; Kemp, *Digest*, 157.
77 *Record*, August 1849, 146-47.
78 Ibid., February 1859, 61; *Minutes of Synod*, 1857, 37-38.
79 *Record*, January 1857, 34.
80 Robin Winks, *The Blacks in Canada: A History* (Montreal: McGill-Queen's UP, 1971), 209ff.
81 *Minutes of Synod*, 1857, 40-42.
82 Mr. Thompson was supposed to receive a total salary of $500 *p.a.* of which $300 would be provided by the Synod and the rest derived from student fees and a government grant. The fees and grant, however, proved inadequate so the Synod had to provide $100 more for the two past years. It was expected that henceforth the fees would increase to the necessary level (ibid., 1859, 53-54).
83 Ibid., 1857, 40; cf. *Record*, November 1856, 8.

Chapter 9

1 Burleigh, *Church History of Scotland*, 323.

2 Macleod, *Scottish Theology*, chap. 8; Burleigh, *Church History of Scotland*, 324, 427.

3 N. G. Smith, Allan L. Farris, H. Keith Markell, *A Short History of The Presbyterian Church in Canada* (Toronto: Presbyterian Publications, n.d.), 40, 47.

4 Moir, *Church and State in Canada West*, 185.

5 *Record*, November 1860, 11.

6 *Minutes of the United Presbyterian Church*, 1861, 449-52.

7 Vaudry, "Problem of Church-State Relations"; Montgomery, "Voluntary Controversy," 2.

8 Macleod, *Scottish Theology*, 238; Nicholson, "Michael Willis."

9 *Canadian Presbyter*, October 1857, 257.

10 *Lectures on the Church Establishment Controversy, and Subjects Related to it* (Glasgow, 1835).

11 Kemp, *Digest*, 274.

12 Ibid., 275; Moir, *Enduring Witness*, 106-107.

13 Kemp, *Digest*, 280. According to Ian Rennie the United Presbyterians were negotiating as a means of self-defence ("Free Church and Relations of Church and State," 207).

14 Kemp, *Digest*, 280-81.

15 *Record*, April 1846; *Banner*, 27 November 1846.

16 *Minutes of Synod*, 1848, 21.

17 *Banner*, 19 September 18, 1845.

18 Ibid., 29 May 1846; 11 June 1847.

19 Ibid., 19 June 1846.

20 Ibid., 24 September 1847.

21 Ibid., 8 October 1847.

22 Ibid., 12, 17 and 26 November 1847.

23 Ibid., 29 October 1847.

24 Ibid., 5 November 1847.

25 Ibid., 19 November 1847.

26 Ibid., 26 November 1847.

27 Ibid., 21 January 1848.

28 Ibid., 11 February 1848.

29 Ibid., October 1845.

30 Ibid., 5 October 1847.

31 Ibid., 29 October 1847.

32 *Minutes of Synod*, 1848, 22.

33 Ibid., 22, 32.

34 Ibid., 20.

35 *Record*, November 1849, 2-3.

36 Kemp, *Digest*, 54.

37 *Record*, September 1850, 162.

38 Kemp, *Digest*, 54-55; cf. Rennie, "Free Church and Relations of Church and State," 163-65. Ferrier was not enthusiastic about the Union. He wrote against it, dissented from the Basis of Union and only entered the new Church after having satisfied his conscience by his dissent. J. A. Johnston, "Factors in the Formation of the Presbyterian Church in Canada, 1875," 52-53.

39 Andrew Ferrier, *Christ Wounded in the House of His Friends: A Brief Review of Some Proceedings in Different Courts, of the Presbyterian Church of Canada* (Hamilton, 1850), 12.

40 Ibid., 12.

41 Ibid., 17.

42 Ibid., 22, 23, 28.

43 Kemp, *Digest*, 17; cf. *Canadian Presbyter*, December 1857, 326-32.

44 *Minutes of Synod*, 1854, 11-12.

45 *Record*, May 1855, 98.

46 Ibid., June 1855, 117.

47 Ibid., August 1855, 146.

48 Ibid., March 1856, 65.

49 Ibid., 76.

50 P.C.A., *Jennings Papers*, "Session Minute Book of the United Secession Congregations of the City of Toronto, 1838-1875" (Manuscript), entry for 31 January 1859.

51 P.C.A., *Knox Presbyterian Church, Hamilton*, "Facts 1-9" (manuscript notes from secession minutes), entry for 14 November 1859. Cf. P.C.A., *Minutes of Kirk Session of Prescott*, Canada West, entry for 10 October 1860.

52 *Record*, June 1855, 118-19.

53 *Minutes of Synod*, 1855.

54 Ibid., 1856, 43.

55 Ibid., 1857, 26-27.

56 *Record*, November 1857, 5.

57 Ibid., May 1858, 83.

58 *Minutes of Synod*, 1858, 15-16. Cf. ibid., 1859, 19-20; Smellie, *John Bayne*, 27-28. Dr. Willis was in Scotland at the time and thus could not participate in the debate (Nicholson, "Michael Willis," 118-24).

59 *Minutes of Synod*, 1859, 24.

60 Ibid., 25.

61 Ibid., 8; *Record*, 1859, 14.

62 *Minutes of Synod*, 1860, 16.

63 Ibid., 19-20.

64 Ibid., October 1860, 6. According to Johnston the Basis of Union, 1859, of Victoria, Australia, was used in the Canadian discussions ("Factors in the Formation of the Presbyterian Church in Canada, 1875," 149).

65 *Minutes of Synod*, October 1860, 10.

66 Ibid., 13. Apparently Lachlan Macpherson refused to enter the Canada Presbyterian Church (Johnston, "Factors in the Formation of the Presbyterian Church in Canada, 1875," 57).

67 *Record*, November 1860, 6-7.

68 *Minutes of Synod*, 1861.

69 *Record*, July 1861, 135.

70 Ibid., May 1861, 99-100.

71 Ibid., June 1861, 115.

72 Ibid., July 1861.

73 Ian Rennie sees it this way ("Free Church and Relations of Church and State," 226-27).

BIBLIOGRAPHY

1. Primary Sources

I. Manuscript

A. Private Papers

Presbyterian Church in Canada Archives
(Knox College, University of Toronto)

William Bell Papers (AR5/N4M4)
Diary of William Bell, Volume 13
Robert Boyd Papers (AR5/C5L4)
Elizabeth Esson Papers (AR5/E8L4)
Henry Esson Papers (AR5/E8L5)
Andrew Ferrier Papers (AR5/P7R4)
John Jennings Papers (AR5.1/J)
William King Papers (AR5/Kin)
W. J. H. Laurie Papers
H. S. McCollum Papers (AR5.2/McCollum)
Robert J. McDowall Papers (AR5.1)
William Proudfoot Papers, Boxes 2-3 (Correspondence) AR5.1/P6W5P3)
Mark Young Stark Papers (AR5.1/5)
George Paxton Young Papers (AR5/G4Y6)

N. B. These holdings are currently (1989) being re-catalogued; catalogue numbers
       may change.

Public Archives of Canada
(Ottawa, Ontario)

Isaac Buchanan Papers (MG 24/ D/16)
George Brown Papers (MG 24/B/40)

Public Archives of Ontario
(Toronto, Ontario)

William Lyon Mackenzie Papers, Correspondence. Volume 2, 1844-1861 (MS 516)
   (Microfilm, Reels 12, 13)

Queen's University Archives
(Kingston, Ontario)

William Morris Papers (2139), Boxes 2, 3

United Church of Canada Archives
(Emmanuel College, University of Toronto)

Robert Burns Papers (PP/B87)
Charles Chiniquy Papers (PP/C4L)
William Smart Papers (PP/S5A)
Mark Young Stark Papers (PP/STA/81)

B. Church Records

Presbyterian Church in Canada Archives

Knox College: Accounts & Subscriptions. 1846-1856, 8 vols. (AR6.1/Knox College)
Knox Presbyterian Church, Hamilton: "Facts 1-9" (Manuscript Notes from Session
    Minutes) (AR5/06/F3K5)
Minutes of the Kirk Session of the Presbyterian Church of Prescott, 4 September
    1840-1 June 1894 (AR4/06/S4M5)
Toronto Academy: Accounts & Subscription Box/Minutes of Management Com-
    mittee
Presbytery Book of the Montreal Presbytery, in connection with the Presbyterian
    Church of Canada, 3 July 1844-25 May, 1853
Minutes of the Presbytery of Montreal in Connexion with the Presbyterian Church
    of Canada (Free Church), 10 June 1853-1859
Presbytery of Hamilton: Minutes, 27 April 1854 to his Resignation, 12 January
    1858, Mark Y. Stark, Clerk. James Middlemiss, Clerk to 16 March 1859
    (Vol. 1)
Free Church: Presbytery of Hamilton. Minutes from 12 April 1859 to 29 November
    1859. Also note to 10 April 1861, which were written in full in Volume 3.
    James Middlemiss, Clerk (Vol. 2)

Queen's University Archives

Presbyterian Church in Canada: Synod Papers Box 3—1839-1842; Box
    4—1843-1845. (2263)

United Church of Canada Archives

Presbyterian Church of Canada: Minutes of Synod (Manuscript), 2 vols. 1844-
    1861 // Commission of Synod Minutes vol. 1, 1844-1861 // Dissents—Synod
    of 1848 // Clerk's Letterbook 1855-1859 (PC/FCC/S)
Presbyterian Church of Canada (Free): Synod Knox College Committee, Minutes
    1848-1851
Presbyterian Church of Canada (Free): Synod Sustentation Fund—Minutes
    1844-1849; Correspondence 1846-1847; Accounts 1845-1848 // Home Mis-
    sion Committees' Minutes 1847-1853. (PC/FCC/S.SF/HMC)

II. Printed

A. Church Records

Acts of the General Assembly of the Church of Scotland 1638-1842. Edinburgh,
    1843.

The Acts and Proceedings of the Synod of the Presbyterian Church of Canada in Connection with the Church of Scotland, 1831-1844.

The Minutes of the Synod of the Presbyterian Church of Canada, 1844-1861.

Kemp, Alex F. *Digest of the Minutes of the Presbyterian Church of Canada, with a Historical Introduction and an Appendix of Forms and Procedures.* Montreal: John Lovell, 1861.

Free Church of Scotland. Report of the Colonial and Continental Committee. May 1857.

Free Church of Scotland. Report of Colonial and Continental Committee. May 1859.

Minutes of the Twenty-Seventh Session of the Synod of the United Presbyterian Church in Canada, Held in Montreal, June 4th, 5th, and 6th, 1861. Montreal, 1861.

The Minutes of the Synod of the Canadian Presbyterian Church, 1861, 1864.

The Subordinate Standards and Other Authoritative Documents of the Free Church of Scotland Published by Authority of the General Assembly. Edinburgh: Offices of the Free Church of Scotland, 1955.

B. Private Papers

Careless, J. M. S., ed. "The Diary of Peter Brown," *Ontario History*, 42 (July 1950), 113-51.

Doughty, Arthur, ed. *The Elgin-Grey Papers, 1846-1852.* 4 vols. Ottawa, 1937.

Hanna, William, ed. *A Selection from the Correspondence of the Late Thomas Chalmers.* Edinburgh and London, 1853.

Johnson, J. K. and C. B. Stelmark, eds. *Letters of Sir John A. Macdonald, 1836-1861.* 2 vols. Ottawa, 1969.

Neary, Peter, ed. " 'Neither Radical nor Tory nor Whig': Letters by Oliver Mowat to John Mowat 1843-1846," *Ontario History*, 71 (June 1979), 84-131.

Parker, Charles Stuart, ed. *Sir Robert Peel from his Private Papers.* Vol. 3. London, 1899.

Sanderson, Charles R., ed. *Arthur Papers.* 3 vols. Toronto, 1957.

Shepperson, George, ed. "Thomas Chalmers, The Free Church of Scotland, and the South," Notes and Documents, *Journal of Southern History*, 17 (1951), 517-37.

C. Memoirs, Sermons, Pamphlets, Treatises

A Letter Addressed to the Ministers and Elders of the Synod of Canada, on the present duty of the Presbyterian Church, by the Rev. Robert Burns, D.D., With a Letter on the Same Subject by the Rev. W. Cunningham, D.D., and the Reply of the Convenor of the Colonial Committee of the Free Church of Scotland, to the Moderator of the Synod of Canada. Montreal: J. C. Becket, 1844.

Autobiography of the Rev. William Arnot, and Memoir by his Daughter Mrs. A. Fleming. 2nd ed. London: James Nisbet, 1877.

Bayne, John. *Was the Recent Disruption of the Synod of Canada, in Connection with the Church of Scotlands, Called For? An Address to the Presbyterians of Canada who still support the Synod in connection with the Church of Scotland.* Galt, 1846.

Libertas (Peter Brown). *The Fame and Glory of England Vindicated, Being an Answer to "The Glory and Shame of England."* New York and London, 1842.

Bryce, James. *Ten Years of the Church of Scotland from 1833-1843 with historical retrospect from 1560.* 2 vols. Edinburgh and London, 1850.

Buchanan, Robert. *The Ten Years' Conflict: being the history of the Disruption of the Church of Scotland.* 2 vols. Glasgow, 1852.

Burns, R. F. *The Life and Times of Rev. Robert Burns, D.D.* Toronto, 1871.

Candlish, Robert S. *Narrative Relating to Certain Recent Negotiations for the settlement of the Scottish Church Question.* Edinburgh, n.d.

Croil, James. *Life of the Rev. Alexander Mathieson, D.D.* Montreal, 1870.

Draft of an Answer to the Dissent and Protest of Certain Ministers and Elders Who Have Seceded from the Synod of Canada in Connexion With The Church of Scotland. By the Committee Appointed by the Synod for that Purpose. Kingston: Printed at the Chronicle and Gazette Office, 1844.

Esson, Henry. *An Appeal to the Ministers and Members of the Presbyterian Church, Under the Jurisdiction of the Synod of Canada, On the Question of Adherence to the Church of Scotland As By Law Established.* Montreal: Printed by J. C. Becket, 1844.

————. "Critique on Dr. Burns' letter on Knox's College." June, 1848.

————. "Statement Relative to the Educational System of Knox's College, Toronto; with Suggestions for its Extension and Improvement." Toronto: J. Cleland, 1848.

Ferrier, Andrew. *Christ Wounded in the House of His Friends: A Brief Review of Some Proceedings in Different Courts of the Presbyterian Church of Canada.* Hamilton, 1850.

Fraser, D. *A Narrative of the Rise and Progress of the Free Church, Côté Street, Montreal, Read to the Congregation at their Annual Meeting on the 15th April, 1855.* Montreal: J. C. Becket, 1855.

Hanna, William. *Memoirs of the Life and Writings of Thomas Chalmers.* Vols. 3-4. Edinburgh and London, 1851.

Hodge, A. A. *The Life of Charles Hodge.* New York, 1880.

Lectures on the Church Establishment Controversy, and subjects connected with it. Glasgow, 1835.

Letter of Sympathy, &c. To the Moderator and other Members of the Presbyterian Church of Canada in Connection with the Established Church of Scotland by Thomas Clark (1844) printed along with *An Act Declaring the Spiritual Independence of the Synod of the Presbyterian Church of Canada in Connection with the Church of Canada* (1844).

Lewis, George. *Impressions of America and the American Churches: from the Journal of the Rev. George Lewis, one of the deputation of the Free Church of Scotland to the United States.* Edinburgh, 1845.

Machar, A. M. *Memorials of the Life and Ministry of the Rev. John Machar, D.D.* Toronto, 1873.

MacLeod, Donald. *Memoir of Norman MacLeod, D.D.* London: Daldy, Isbister, 1877.

MacVicar, D. H. *A Sermon, Preached in the Canada Presbyterian Church, Côté Street, Montreal, On Sabbath, March 14th, 1869, on the occasion of the death of John Redpath, Esq.* Terrace Bank. Printed by Request. Montreal: John Lovell, 1869.

MacVicar, John H. *Life and Work of Donald Harvey MacVicar.* Toronto, 1904.

Memorial Submitted to the Right Hon. Sir Robert Peel, Bart., First Lord of the

Treasury, and the Other Members of Her Majesty's Government; adopted by A Meeting of Ministers of the Church of Scotland, Assembled at Edinburgh, on the 17th-24th November, 1842. Edinburgh and London, n.d.

Proceedings of the General Assembly's Non-Intrusion Committees; in relation to A Settlement of the Church Question, on the footing of the Liberum Arbitrium (Extracted from their Minutes). Edinburgh, 1842.

Rainy, Robert, and James Mackenzie. *Life of William Cunningham, D.D. Principal and Professor of Theology and Church History, New College, Edinburgh.* London, 1871.

Sermons by the Late Rev. Mark Y. Stark, A.M., Formerly Minister of Knox's Church, Dundas, With Memoir, By the Rev. William Reid, A.M. Toronto, 1871.

Robertson, Charles. *Report of the Auchterarder Case, The Earl of Kinnoul, and the Rev. R. Young, Against the Presbytery of Auchterarder.* 2 vols. Edinburgh and London, 1838.

Smellie, G. *Memoir of the Rev. John Bayne D.D., of Galt; with Dr. Bayne's Essay on Man's Responsibility for his belief.* Toronto, 1871.

Stark, Mark Young. *A Lecture on Hugh Miller Delivered Before the Y.M.C.A. at Dundas, Cobourg, Montreal.* Dundas, 1859.

The State of the Case for the Church of Scotland, in Her Negotiation with the Government and the Legislature, on the subject of The Law Against the Intrusion of Ministers. Edinburgh, 1839.

The Earl of Aberdeen's Correspondence with the Rev. Dr. Chalmers. Edinburgh, 1840.

Turner, Alexander. *The Scottish Secession of 1843: being an examination of the principles and narrative of the contest, which led to that remarkable event.* Edinburgh and Glasgow, 1859.

Willis, Michael. *Collectanea Graeca et Latina: Selections from the Greek and Latin Fathers; with notes, Biographical and Illustrative.* Toronto, 1865.

————. *Pulpit Discourses, Expository and Practical, and College Addresses, &c..* London, 1873.

Young, George Paxton. *Miscellaneous Discourses and Expositions and Scripture.* Edinburgh and Hamilton, 1854.

D. Newspapers and Periodicals

Blackwood's Edinburgh Magazine, April 1840, vol. 47
Canadian Presbyter, 1857-1858 (Montreal)
Montreal Gazette, May 1845
Montreal Transcript and Commercial Advertiser, 1843-1844
Montreal Witness, 1844-1845
The Ecclesiastical and Missionary Record for the Presbyterian Church of Canada, 1844-1861
Toronto *Banner*, 1843-1848
Toronto *Globe*, 1849-1860 (selected dates)

E. Government Publications: Miscellaneous

Canada Directory for 1857-58. Montreal: John Lovell, n.d.
Censuses of Canada 1665-1871. Statistics of Canada. Vol. 4: Ottawa, 1876.
Firth, Edith G., ed. *The Town of York, 1815-1834: A Further Collection of Documents of Early Toronto.* Toronto, 1966.

Hodgins, J. G., ed. *Documentary History of Education in Upper Canada*. Vols. 5-17 (1843-1861). Toronto, 1897.

Manuscript Census Returns—1861, Reels c 1276-77; c 1083; c 1042-43.

2. Secondary Sources

I. Books and Monographs

Anstey, Roger. *The Atlantic Slave Trade and British Abolition 1760-1810*. Highlands, N.J.: Humanities Press, 1975.

Armour, Leslie, and Elizabeth Trott. *The Faces of Reason: An Essay on Philosophy and Culture in English Canada 1850-1950*. Waterloo: Wilfrid Laurier University Press, 1981.

Atherton, W. H. *Montreal Under British Rule 1760-1914*. Vol. 2. Montreal: S. J. Clarke Publishing Co., 1914.

Balfour, A. H. B. *An Historical Account of the Rise and Development of Presbyterianism in Scotland*. Cambridge: At the University Press, 1911.

Berger, Carl. *Science, God and Nature in Victorian Canada*. Toronto: University of Toronto Press, 1983.

Berkhof, Louis. *Systematic Theology*. 4th ed., rev. Grand Rapids, Mich.: Wm. B. Eerdmans, 1977, 1938.

————— . *The History of Christian Doctrines*. Edinburgh: The Banner of Truth Trust, 1975, 1937.

Best, Geoffrey. *Mid-Victorian Britain, 1851-1875*. St. Albans: Panther Books, 1973, 1971.

Bradley, Ian C. *The Call to Seriousness: The Evangelical Impact on the Victorians*. New York: Macmillan, 1976.

Brown, Craig, ed. *Upper Canadian Politics in the 1850s*. Toronto: University of Toronto Press, 1967.

Brown, Stewart J. *Thomas Chalmers and the Godly Commonwealth in Scotland*. Oxford: Oxford University Press, 1982.

Bumsted, J. M., ed. *Canadian History Before Confederation: Essays and Interpretations*. 2nd ed. Georgetown, Ontario: Irwin-Dorsey, 1979.

Burleigh, J. H. S. *A Church History of Scotland*. London: Oxford University Press, 1960.

Cage, R. A., ed. *The Scots Abroad: Labour, Capital and Enterprise, 1750-1914*. London: Croom Helm, 1985.

Campbell, Robert. *A History of the Scotch Presbyterian Church, St. Gabriel Street, Montreal*. Montreal: Drysdale, 1887.

Careless, J. M. S. *Brown of the Globe*. Vol. 1: *The Voice of Upper Canada 1818-1859*. Toronto: Macmillan, 1959.

————— . *Colonists and Canadians 1760-1867*. Toronto: Macmillan, 1971.

————— . *The Union of the Canadas: The Growth of Canadian Institutions 1841-1857*. Toronto: McClelland and Stewart, 1977, 1967.

Checkland, Sydney and Olive. *Industry and Ethos: Scotland 1832-1814*. London: Edward Arnold, 1984.

Cheyne, A. C. *The Transforming of the Kirk*. Edinburgh: Saint Andrew Press, 1983.

Chitnis, Anand C. *The Scottish Enlightenment: A Social History*. London: Croom Helm, 1976.

Cooper, John Irwin. *Montreal: A Brief History*. Montreal: McGill-Queen's University Press, 1969.

Cowan, Helen I. *British Immigration Before Confederation*. Canadian Historical Association Booklet No. 22. Ottawa, 1968.

Craig, Gerald M. *Upper Canada: The Formative Years 1784-1841*. Toronto: McClelland and Stewart, 1977, 1963.

Creighton, Donald. *John A. Macdonald*. Vol. 1: *The Young Politician*. Toronto: Macmillan, 1956.

Donaldson, Gordon. *The Scots Overseas*. London: R. Hale, 1966.

Drummond, Andrew Landale, and James Bulloch. *The Scottish Church 1688-1843: The Age of the Moderates*. Edinburgh: Saint Andrew Press, 1973.

_____ . *The Church in Victorian Scotland, 1843-1875*. Edinburgh: Saint Andrew Press, 1975.

Easterbrook, W. T. and Hugh G. J. Aitken. *Canadian Economic History*. Toronto: Macmillan, 1963.

Elgee, W. H. *The Social Teaching of the Canadian Churches, Protestant, The Early Period, Before 1850*. Toronto: Ryerson Press, 1964.

Ferguson, William. *Scotland: 1689 to the Present*. Edinburgh: Oliver & Boyd, 1978, 1968.

Firth, Edith G., ed. *Profiles of a Province: Studies in the History of Ontario*. Toronto: Ontario Historical Society, 1967.

Gash, Norman. *Aristocracy and People: Britain, 1815-1865*. Cambridge, Mass.: Harvard University Press, 1979.

Grant, John Webster, ed. *The Churches and the Canadian Experience*. Toronto: Ryerson Press, 1963.

Gregg, William. *History of the Presbyterian Church in the Dominion of Canada from the Earliest Times to 1834*. Toronto, 1884.

_____ . *A Short History of the Presbyterian Church in the Dominion of Canada: From Earliest to the Present Time*. Toronto, 1892.

Handy, R. T. *A History of the Churches in the United States and Canada*. New York: Oxford University Press, 1976.

Harris, R. Cole, and John Warkentin. *Canada Before Confederation: A Study in Historical Geography*. New York: Oxford University Press, 1974.

Harrison, J. F. C. *Early Victorian Britain, 1832-1851*. London: Collins/Fontana, 1979, 1971.

Heasman, Kathleen. *Evangelicals in Action: An Appraisal of Their Social Work in the Victorian Era*. London: G. Bles, 1962.

Hempton, David. *Methodism and Politics in British Society 1750-1850*. Stanford, Calif.: Stanford University Press, 1984.

Henderson, G. D. *Heritage: A Study of the Disruption*. 2nd ed. rev. Edinburgh: Oliver & Boyd, 1943.

_____ . *The Claims of the Church of Scotland*. London: Hodder and Stoughton, 1951.

Henderson, J. L. H. *John Strachan, 1778-1867*. Toronto: University of Toronto Press, 1969.

Horn, M. and Sabourin, R., eds. *Studies in Canadian Social History*. Toronto: McClelland and Stewart, 1974.

Jamieson, Annie Straith. *William King: Friend and Champion of Slaves*. Toronto: Missions of Evangelism, 1925.

Johnson, Leo A. *History of the County of Ontario 1615-1875*. Whitby: The Corporation of the County of Ontario, 1973.

————— . *History of Guelph, 1827-1927*. Guelph: Guelph Historical Society, 1977.

Johnston, J. K., ed. *Historical Essays on Upper Canada*. Toronto: McClelland and Stewart, 1975.

Katz, M. B. *The People of Hamilton, Canada West: Family and Class in a Mid-Nineteenth Century City*. Cambridge: Harvard University Press, 1975.

Kerr, D. G. G. *A Historical Atlas of Canada*. 2nd ed. Don Mills: Thomas Nelson, 1966.

Kerr, Hugh T. *Sons of the Prophets: Leaders in Protestantism From Princeton Seminary*. Princeton: Princeton University Press, 1963.

Latourette, Kenneth Scott. *A History of Christianity*. Vol. 2: *A.D. 1500-A.D. 1975*. New York: Harper & Row, 1975.

Lewis, Donald M. *Lighten Their Darkness: The Evangelical Mission to Working-Class London, 1828-1860*. Westport, Conn.: Greenwood Press, 1986.

Lewis, John. *George Brown*. Toronto: Morang, 1907.

Lighthall, George R. *A Short History of the American Presbyterian Church of Montreal 1823-1923*. Montreal, 1923.

Loetscher, Lefferts A. *Facing the Enlightenment and Pietism: Archibald Alexander and the Founding of Princeton Theological Seminary*. Westport, Conn.: Greenwood Press, 1983.

Lyall, Francis. *Of Presbyters and Kings: Church and State in the Law of Scotland*. Aberdeen: Aberdeen University Press, 1980.

McCalla, Douglas. *The Upper Canada Trade 1834-1872: A Study of the Buchanans' Business*. Toronto: University of Toronto Press, 1979.

MacInnes, John. *The Evangelical Movement in the Highlands of Scotland, 1688-1800*. Aberdeen: The University Press, 1951.

Mackenzie, Alexander. *The Life and Speeches of Hon. George Brown*. Toronto: The Globe Printing Co., 1882.

McKillop, A. B. *A Disciplined Intelligence: Critical Inquiry and Canadian Thought in the Victorian Era*. Montreal: McGill-Queen's University Press, 1979.

Maclaren, A. Allan. *Religion and Social Class: The Disruption Years in Aberdeen*. London and Boston: Routledge and Kegan Paul, 1974.

Macleod, John. *Scottish Theology: In Relation to Church History Since the Reformation*. Edinburgh: The Banner of Truth Trust, 1974, 1943.

Macmillan, David S., ed. *Canadian Business History: Selected Studies, 1497-1971*. Toronto: McClelland and Stewart, 1972.

Marsden, George. *Fundamentalism and American Culture*. New York: Oxford University Press, 1980.

Mason, Stephen F. *A History of the Sciences*. New York: Collier, 1977, 1956.

Masters, D. C. *The Rise of Toronto 1850-1890*. Toronto: University of Toronto Press, 1947.

————— . *Protestant Church Colleges in Canada*. Toronto: University of Toronto Press, 1966.

Mathieson, William Law. *Church and Reform in Scotland: A History from 1797 to 1843*. Glasgow: James Maclehose and Sons, 1916.

Middleton, Jesse Edgar, and Fred Landon. *The Province of Ontario A History, 1615-1927*. 4 vols. Toronto: Dominion Publishing Co., 1927.

Moir, John S. *Church and State in Canada West: Three Studies in the Relation of Denominationalism and Nationalism, 1841-1867*. Toronto: University of Toronto Press, 1968, 1959.

————— . *The Church in the British Era*. Toronto: McGraw-Hill Ryerson, 1972.

_____ . *Enduring Witness: A History of the Presbyterian Church in Canada.* Toronto: Presbyterian Publications, 1974.

Moir, John S., ed. *The Cross in Canada.* Toronto: Ryerson Press, 1966.

_____ . *The Tide of Time: Historical Essays by the Late Allan L. Farris.* Toronto: Knox College, 1978.

Morton, W. L. *The Shield of Achilles: Aspects of Canada in the Victorian Age.* Toronto: McClelland and Stewart, 1968.

_____ . *The Critical Years: The Union of British North America, 1857-1873.* Toronto: McClelland and Stewart, 1968, 1964.

_____ . *The Kingdom of Canada: A General History from Earliest Times.* 2nd ed. Toronto: McClelland and Stewart, 1972.

Mulvany, C. Pelham. *Toronto Past and Present Until 1882.* Toronto: W. E. Caiger, 1884.

Muise, D. A., ed. *A Reader's Guide to Canadian History.* Vol. 1: *Beginnings to Confederation.* Toronto: University of Toronto Press, 1982.

Neatby, Hilda. *Queen's University.* Vol. 1: *1841-1914.* Montreal: McGill-Queen's University Press, 1978.

Orr, J. Edwin. *The Second Evangelical Awakening.* Popular Abridged Edition. London: Marshall, Morgan and Scott, 1964, 1949.

Palmer, Bryan D. *A Culture in Conflict: Skilled Workers and Industrial Capitalism in Hamilton, Ontario 1860-1914.* Montreal: McGill-Queen's University Press, 1979.

Phillipson, Nicholas T. and Rosalind Mitchison. *Scotland in the Age of Improvement, Essays in Scottish History in the Eighteenth Century.* Edinburgh: At the University Press, 1970.

Prentice, Alison. *The School Promoters: Education and Social Class in Mid-Nineteenth Century Upper Canada.* Toronto: McClelland and Stewart, 1977.

Price, Linda. *Introduction to the Social History of Scots in Quebec (1780-1840).* Ottawa: National Museum of Man, 1981.

Rattray, W. J. *The Scot in British North America.* 4 vols. Toronto: Maclear and Co., n.d.

Reid, W. S. *The Church of Scotland in Lower Canada: Its Struggle for Establishment.* Toronto: Presbyterian Publications, 1936.

_____ . *Called in Witness: Profiles of Canadian Presbyterians.* 2 vols. Toronto: Presbyterian Publications, 1975, 1980.

Reid, W. S., ed. *The Scottish Tradition in Canada.* Toronto: McClelland and Stewart, 1976.

_____ . *John Calvin: His Influence in the Western World.* Grand Rapids, Mich.: Zondervan, 1982.

Rogers, Jack B. and Donald K. McKim. *The Authority and Inspiration of the Bible: An Historical Approach.* San Francisco: Harper & Row, 1979.

Sandeen, Ernest R. *The Roots of Fundamentalism: British and American Millenarianism 1800-1930.* Chicago and London: University of Chicago Press, 1970.

Senior, Hereward. *Orangeism: The Canadian Phase.* Toronto: McGraw-Hill Ryerson, 1972.

_____ . *The Fenians and Canada.* Toronto: Macmillan, 1978.

Sher, Richard B. *Church and University in the Scottish Enlightenment.* Princeton: Princeton University Press, 1985.

Shortt, Adam, and Arthur Doughty. *Canada and Its Provinces.* Vol. 2. Toronto, 1913-1917.

Sissons, C. B. *Church and State in Canadian Education*. Toronto: Ryerson Press, 1959.

Skelton, Isabel. *A Man Austere: William Bell, Parson and Pioneer*. Toronto: Ryerson Press, 1947.

Smith, N. G., ed. *Enkindled by the Word: Essays on Presbyterianism in Canada*. Toronto: Presbyterian Publications, 1966.

Smith, N. G., Allan L. Farris, and H. Keith Markell. *A Short History of the Presbyterian Church in Canada*. Toronto: Presbyterian Publications, n.d.

Smith, Timothy L. *Revivalism and Social Reform: American Protestantism on the Eve of the Civil War*. Gloucester, Mass.: Peter Smith, 1976, 1957.

Stewart, Robert. *St. Andrew's Church (Presbyterian) Quebec: An Historical Sketch of the Church and Its Ministers*. N.p., n.d.

Tucker, G. N. *The Canadian Commerical Revolution 1845-1851*. Ed. H. G. J. Aitken. Toronto: McClelland and Stewart, 1964.

Tulchinsky, Gerald J. J., ed. *To Preserve and Defend: Essays on Kingston in the Nineteenth Century*. Montreal: McGill-Queen's University Press, 1976.

The University of Toronto and Its Colleges, 1827-1906. The University Library: Published by the Librarian, 1906.

Vidler, Alex R. *The Church in an Age of Revolution: 1789 to the Present Day*. Harmondsworth: Penguin, 1971.

Waite, P. B. *The Life and Times of Confederation: 1864-1867*. Toronto: University of Toronto Press, 1963.

Walsh, H. H. *The Christian Church in Canada*. Toronto: Ryerson Press, 1956.

Watt, Hugh. *Thomas Chalmers and the Disruption*. Edinburgh: Thomas Nelson, 1943.

Webb, R. K. *Modern England*. New York: Dodd, Mead and Co., 1974.

Winks, Robin. *The Blacks in Canada*. Montreal: McGill-Queen's University Press, 1971.

Young, Brian and John A. Dickinson. *A Short History of Quebec: A Socio-Economic Perspective*. Toronto: Copp Clark Pitman, 1988.

Young, Davis. *Christianity and the Age of the Earth*. Grand Rapids, Mich.: Zondervan, 1982.

II. Articles

Ahlstrom, Sidney. "The Scottish Philosophy and American Theology." *Church History*, 24, no. 3 (September 1955), 257-72.

Baer, Marc B. "Class and Community in Victorian Britain." *Journal of Urban History*, 5, no. 4 (August 1979), 521-29.

Barron, F. L. "The American Origins of the Temperance Movement in Ontario, 1828-1850." *Canadian Review of American Studies*, 11, no. 2 (Fall 1980), 131-50.

Cage, R. A. and E. O. A. Checkland. "Thomas Chalmers and Urban Poverty: the St. John's Parish Experiment in Glasgow, 1919-1837." *The Philosophical Journal*, 13 (Spring 1976), 37-56.

Careless, J. M. S. "Mid-Victorian Liberalism in Central Canadian Newspapers, 1850-67." *Canadian Historical Review*, 31, no. 3 (September 1950), 221-36.

Clark, Ian D. L. "The Leslie Controversy, 1805." *Records of the Scottish Church History Society*, 14 (1963), 179-97.

Clark, S. D. "Religious Organization and the Rise of the Canadian Nation, 1850-1885." *Canadian Historical Association Annual Report* (1944), 86-97.

_____ . "The Mission to the Fugitive Slaves at London." *Ontario History*, 46, no. 2 (Spring 1954), 131-39.

_____ . "The Social Structure of Montreal in the 1850s." Canadian Historical Association *Report* (1956), 63-73.

Cooper, John Irwin. "The Canada Education and Home Missionary Society." *Canadian Historical Review*, 26, no. 1 (March 1945), 42-47.

_____ . "The Early Editorial Policy of the *Montreal Witness*." Canadian Historical Association *Report* (1957), 53-62.

Eklund, Emmet E. "The Scottish Free Church and Its Relations to Nineteenth-Century Swedish and Swedish-American Lutheranism." *Church History*, 51, no. 4 (December 1982), 405-18.

Greer, Allen. "The Sunday Schools of Upper Canada." *Ontario History*, 67, no. 3 (1975), 169-84.

Gregg, William R. "The African in North America: Their Welfare After Freedom as Effected and Influenced by the Life of William King." *Toronto City World* (6 July 1924).

Hillis, Peter. "Presbyterianism and Social Class in Mid-Nineteenth Century Glasgow: A Study of Nine Churches." *Journal of Ecclesiastical History*, 32, no. 1 (January 1981), 47-64.

Irving, John A. "The Development of Philosophy in Central Canada from 1850 to 1900." *Canadian Historical Review*, 31, no. 3 (September 1850), 252-87.

Landon, Fred. "The Anti-Slavery Society of Canada." *Ontario History*, 48, no. 1 (Summer 1956), 125-31.

_____ . "When Uncle Tom's Cabin Came to Canada." *Ontario History*, 44, no. 1 (January 1952), 1-5.

Mealing, S. R. "The Concept of Social Class and the Interpretation of Canadian History." *Canadian Historical Review*, 44, no. 3 (September 1965), 201-18.

Millar, W. P. J. "The Remarkable Thaddeus Osgood: A Study of the Evangelical Spirit in the Canadas." *Histoire Sociale/Social History* (1977), 59-76.

Millman, T. R. "The Church's Ministry to Sufferers from Typhus Fever in 1847." *Canadian Journal of Theology*, 8, no. 2 (1962), 126-36.

Machin, G. I. T. "The Disruption and British Politics 1834-43." *Scottish Historical Review*, 51, no. 151 (April 1972), 20-51.

McNaught, K. "E. P. Thompson vs. Harold Logan: Writing About Labour and the Left in the 1970's." *Canadian Historical Review*, 62, no. 2 (1981), 141-68.

Moir, John S. "American Influences on Canadian Protestant Churches before Confederation." *Church History*, 36, no. 4 (December 1967), 440-55.

_____ . "Confrontation at Queen's: A Prelude to the Disruption in Canada." *Presbyterian History*, 15, no. 1 (May 1971).

_____ . "'Loyalty and Respectability': The Campaign for Co-Establishment of the Church of Scotland in Canada." *Scottish Tradition*, 9-10 (1979-1980), 64-81.

Nicholson, D. R. "Dr. Michael Willis, D. D., LL. D. Professor and First Professor of Knox College." *Presbyterian History*, 17, no. 1 (June 1973), 1-6.

Reid, W. Stanford. "The Scottish Disruption and Reunion, 1843-1929." *Christendom*, 8 (Summer 1943).

Rice, Daniel F. "Natural Theology and the Scottish Philosophy in the Thought of Thomas Chalmers." *Scottish Journal of Theology*, 24, no. 1 (February 1971), 23-46.

_____ . "An Attempt at Systematic Reconstruction in the Theology of Thomas Chalmers." *Church History*, 38, no. 2 (June 1979), 174-88.

Riesen, Richard A. " 'Higher Criticism' in the Free Church Fathers." *Records of the Scottish Church History Society*, 20, Pt. 2 (1979), 119-42.

Russell, Peter A. "Church of Scotland Clergy in Upper Canada: Culture Shock and Conservatism on the Frontier." *Ontario History*, 73, no. 2 (June 1981), 88-111.

Shepperson, George. "The Free Church and American Slavery." *Scottish Historical Review*, 30, no. 110 (October 1951), 126-43.

Smith, N. G. "By Schism Rent Asunder: A Study of the Disruption of the Presbyterian Church in Canada in 1844." *Canadian Journal of Theology*, 1 (October 1955), 175-83.

———. "Nationalism in the Canadian Churches." *Canadian Journal of Theology*, 9 (April 1963), 112-25.

———. "Religious Tensions in Pre-Confederation Politics." *Canadian Journal of Theology*, 9 (October 1963), 248-62.

Stunt, Timothy. "Geneva and British Evangelicals in the Early Nineteenth Century." *Journals of Ecclesiastical History*, 32, no. 1 (January 1981), 35-46.

Thompson, F. M. L. "Social Control in Victorian Britain." *Economic History Review*, Second Series, 34, no. 2 (May 1981), 189-208.

Vaudry, Richard W. " 'For Christ's Kingdom and Crown': The Evangelical Party in the Church of Scotland and the Problem of Church-State Relations, 1829-1843." The Canadian Society of Presbyterian History *Papers*, 1981, 21-41.

———. "The Constitutional Party in the Church of Scotland 1834-43." *Scottish Historical Review*, 62, 1: no. 173 (April 183), 35-46.

———. "Peter Brown, the Toronto *Banner* and the Evangelical Mind in Victorian Canada." *Ontario History*, 77, no. 1 (March 1985), 3-18.

———. "Theology and Education in Early Victorian Canada: Knox College, Toronto, 1844-1861." *Studies in Religion/Sciences Religieuses*, 16, no. 4 (Fall 1987), 431-47.

Walsh, H. H. "Canada and the Church: A Job for the Historians." *Queen's Quarterly*, 61, no. 1 (Spring 1954), 71-79.

———. "Research in Canadian Church History." *Canadian Historical Review*, 35, no. 3 (September 1954), 208-16.

Zerker, Sally. "George Brown and the Printers' Union." *Journal of Canadian Studies*, 10, no. 1 (February 1975), 41-48.

III. Dictionaries, Biographical Aids

Dictionary of American Biography, 2nd ed. New York: Charles Scribner's Sons, 1977.

Dictionary of Canadian Biography, 4th ed., 11 vols. Toronto: University of Toronto Press, 1966.

Dictionary of National Biography. Oxford: Oxford University Press, 1917.

Douglas, J. D., ed. *The New International Dictionary of the Christian Church*. Grand Rapids, Mich.: Zondervan, 1974. Rev. ed., 1978.

Morgan, H. J., ed. *The Canadian Men and Women of the Time: A Hand-Book of Canadian Biography*. 1st ed. Toronto: William Briggs, 1898.

Scott, Hew. *Fasti Ecclesiae Scoticanae*. New edition, 7 vols. Edinburgh, Oliver & Boyd, 1915-1928.

Wallace, W. Stewart. *The Macmillan Dictionary of Canadian Biography*. 4th ed. Toronto: Macmillan, 1978.

IV. Theses and Unpublished Studies

Bridgman, Harry John. "Isaac Buchanan and Religion, 1810-1883." M.A. Thesis, Queen's University, Kingston, 1969.

_____ . "Three Scots Presbyterians in Upper Canada. A Study on Emigration, Nationalism and Religion." Ph.D. Thesis, Queen's University, Kingston, 1978.

Johnston, John Alexander. "Presbyterian Disruption in British North America." B.D. Thesis, The Presbyterian College, Montreal, 1953.

_____ . "Factors in the Formation of the Presbyterian Church in Canada 1875." Ph.D. Thesis, McGill University, 1955.

Lucas, C. Glenn. "Presbyterianism in Carleton County to 1867." M.A. Thesis, Carleton University, Ottawa, 1973.

McDougall, Elizabeth Ann. "The Presbyterian Church in Western Lower Canada 1815-1842." Ph.D. Thesis, McGill University, 1969.

Montgomery, Alfred Baxter. "The Voluntary Controversy in the Church of Scotland: 1829-1843; with particular reference to its practical and theological roots." Ph.D. Thesis, Faculty of Divinity, New College, University of Edinburgh, 1953.

Nicholson, David R. "Michael Willis; Missionary Statesman, Social Activist, Christian Educator, and Reformed Theologian." M.Th. Thesis, Knox College, University of Toronto, n.d.

Noel, Jan. "God's Scots: Montreal Merchants of the Millennium." Unpublished paper presented to C.H.A., Guelph, 1984, 7.

Rennie, Frederick H. "Spiritual Worship with a Carnal Instrument: The Organ as aid or obstacle to the 'purity of worship' in Canadian Presbyterianism, 1850-1875." M.Th. Thesis, Knox College, University of Toronto, 1969.

Rennie, Ian S. "The Free Church and the Relations of Church and State in Canada 1844-1854." M.A. Thesis, University of Toronto, 1954.

Smith, Françoise Noël. "The Establishment of Religious Communities in the Eastern Townships of Lower Canada, 1799-1851." M.A. Thesis, McGill University, 1976.

Vaudry, Richard William. "The Problem of Church-State Relations in the Disruption of the Church of Scotland, 1843." M.A. Thesis University of Guelph, 1979.

_____ . "Sir George Sinclair and the Disruption of the Church of Scotland, 1843." Paper read to the Canadian Association of Scottish Studies, University of Western Ontario, May 1978.

INDEX

Date D